THE GOOD NEWS FOR MUSLIMS

QURANIC QUOTATIONS
FROM THE FOUR GOSPELS

The Abrahamic Family Bible Series

1/5

The Abrahamic Family Bible Series

THE GOOD NEWS FOR MUSLIMS

QURANIC QUOTATIONS
FROM THE FOUR GOSPELS

PROCLAIM
PUBLISHERS

ORLANDO, FLORIDA

© 2023 by Dr. Ahmed Joktan

The Good News for Muslims: Quranic Quotations from the Four Gospels (The
Abrahamic Family Bible Series)

ISBN: 978-1-954858-40-4 eBook
            978-1-954858-41-1 Paperback
            978-1-954858-42-8 Hard cover

Proclaim Publishers
1317 Edgewater Drive, Suite 4774, Orlando, Florida, 32804
proclaimpublishers.com

First Printing, July 2023
Manufactured in the United States of America

F

Table of Contents

Perhaps you have wondered why Islam has so many similarities to the Christian faith (even Jesus is mentioned in Islam). Or perhaps you have challenged your imam friend to read the Scripture if you read the Quran! Maybe you are like me, struggling to convey that the Bible is not corrupt to Muslim friends. This left me wondering why the scriptural, historical, and systematic evidence for the Bible is unconvincing for many Muslims.

Then it hit me: most Muslims take sole authority from the Quran. Yet the Quran is full of Biblical references and quotations. I decided to show my Muslim friend that the Quran quoted from the Bible more than 7,000 verses, some verbatim and many by the meaning. If we apply the citation standards of today, then two-thirds of the Quran is based on the Bible. Furthermore, the Quran doesn't deny that at all, as in Q 3:3, 5:48, and 10:37, among other verses you will discover in this book.

I firmly believe that the Word of God has the power to teach, correct, rebuke, train, and enlighten those who seek the Lord. If you are a Muslim background believer (M.B.B.) I pray also this would be a helpful tool to correct your prior knowledge and show you the missing gaps.

If you are a Muslim reading this, I pray that you would come to know Jesus through His words in this book and that He is the Way, the Truth, and the Life (John 14:6). I also pray if you are on your quest to find a way to join the Abrahamic family, then to find the only way that you can inherit the eternal blessing being promised to Abraham's spiritual descendants, as mentioned clearly in Galatians 3: 6-9, 29.

I know that, through Christ, all things are possible. He alone can bring these goals to pass. My deepest desire is for Christ to build his church. We know that "the gates of hell will not prevail against it" (Matthew 16:18).

Dr. Ahmed Joktan
09/11/2023

The Good News According to Matthew[a]

[a] Q. 4:163

1

[1]The book of the genealogy of Jesus Christ,[*] the son of David, the son of Abraham.

[2]Abraham became the father of Isaac. Isaac became the father of Jacob. Jacob became the father of Judah and his brothers. [3]Judah became the father of Perez and Zerah by Tamar. Perez became the father of Hezron. Hezron became the father of Ram. [4]Ram became the father of Amminadab. Amminadab became the father of Nahshon. Nahshon became the father of Salmon. [5]Salmon became the father of Boaz by Rahab. Boaz became the father of Obed by Ruth. Obed became the father of Jesse. [6]Jesse became the father of King David. David the king[†] became the father of Solomon by her who had been Uriah's wife.

[7]Solomon became the father of Rehoboam. Rehoboam became the father of Abijah. Abijah became the father of Asa. [8]Asa became the father of Jehoshaphat. Jehoshaphat became the father of Joram. Joram became the father of Uzziah. [9]Uzziah became the father of Jotham. Jotham became the father of Ahaz. Ahaz became the father of Hezekiah. [10]Hezekiah became the father of Manasseh. Manasseh became the father of Amon. Amon became the father of Josiah. [11]Josiah became the father of Jechoniah and his brothers at the time of the exile to Babylon.

[12]After the exile to Babylon, Jechoniah became the father of Shealtiel. Shealtiel became the father of Zerubbabel.

---

[*]1:1 Messiah (Hebrew) and Christ (Greek) both mean "Anointed One"
[†]1:6 NU omits "the king".

¹³Zerubbabel became the father of Abiud. Abiud became the father of Eliakim. Eliakim became the father Azor. ¹⁴Azor became the father of Zadok. Zadok of became the father of Achim. Achim became the father of Eliud. ¹⁵Eliud became the father of Eleazar. Eleazar became the father of Matthan. Matthan became the father of Jacob. ¹⁶Jacob became the father of Joseph, the husband of Mary, from whom was born^b Jesus,* who is called Christ.

ᵇ Q. 3:35

¹⁷So all the generations from Abraham to David are fourteen generations, from David to the exile to Babylon fourteen generations, and from the carrying away to Babylon to the Christ, fourteen generations.

¹⁸Now the birth of Jesus Christ was like this. After his mother, Mary,^c was engaged to Joseph, before they came together, she was found pregnant by the Holy Spirit. ¹⁹Joseph, her husband, being a righteous man, and not willing to make her a public example, intended to put^d her away secretly. ²⁰But when he thought about these things, behold,† an angel of the Lord appeared to him in a dream, saying, "Joseph, son of David, don't be afraid to take to yourself Mary as your wife, for that which is conceived in her is of the Holy Spirit. ²¹She shall give birth to a son. You shall name him Jesus,‡for it is he who shall save his people from their sins." ²²Now all this has happened that it might be fulfilled which was spoken by the Lord through the prophet, saying,

ᶜ Q. 3:42; 19:34

ᵈ Q. 33:49

²³"Behold, the virgin shall be with child, and shall give birth to a son.
They shall call his name Immanuel,"
which is, being interpreted, "God with us."§

²⁴Joseph arose from his sleep, and did as the angel of

---

* 1:16 "Jesus" means "Salvation"
† 1:20 "Behold", from "ἰδού", means look at, take notice, observe, see, or gaze at. It is often used as an interjection.
‡ "Jesus" means "Salvation".
§ 1:23 Isaiah 7:14

the Lord commanded him, and took his wife to himself; [25]and didn't know her sexually until she had given birth to her firstborn son. He named him Jesus.

2

[1]Now when Jesus was born in Bethlehem of Judea in the days of King Herod, behold, wise men[e][*] from the east came to Jerusalem, saying, [2]"Where is he who is born King of the Jews? For we saw his star in the east, and have come to worship him." [3]When King Herod heard it, he was troubled, and all Jerusalem with him. [4]Gathering together all the chief priests and scribes of the people, he asked them where the Christ would be born. [5]They said to him, "In Bethlehem of Judea, for this is written through the prophet,

[6]'You Bethlehem, land of Judah, are in no way least among the princes of Judah;

for out of you shall come a governor who shall shepherd my people, Israel.' "[†]

[7]Then Herod secretly called the wise men, and learned from them exactly what time the star appeared. [8]He sent them to Bethlehem, and said, "Go and search diligently for the young child. When you have found him, bring me word, so that I also may come and worship him." [9]They, having heard the king, went their way; and behold, the star, which they saw in the east, went before them until it came and stood over where the young child was. [10]When they saw the star, they rejoiced with exceedingly great joy. [11]They came into the house and saw the young child with Mary, his mother, and they fell down and worshiped[f] him. Opening their treasures, they offered to him gifts, gold, frankincense, and myrrh. [12]Being warned in a dream not to return to Herod, they went back to their own country another way.

[e] Q. 22:17

[f] Q. 2:21

---

[*] 2:1 The word for "wise men" (magoi) can also mean teachers, scientists, physicians, astrologers, seers, interpreters of dreams, or sorcerers.
[†] 2:6 Micah 5:2

¹³Now when they had departed, behold, an angel of the Lord appeared to Joseph in a dream, saying, "Arise and take the young child and his mother, and flee into Egypt, and stay there until I tell you, for Herod will seek the young child to destroy him."

¹⁴He arose and took the young child and his mother by night and departed into Egypt, ¹⁵and was there until the death of Herod, that it might be fulfilled which was spoken by the Lord through the prophet, saying,

"Out of Egypt I called my son."*

¹⁶Then Herod, when he saw that he was mocked by the wise men, was exceedingly angry, and sent out and killed all the male children who were in Bethlehem and in all the surrounding countryside, from two years old and under, according to the exact time which he had learned from the wise men. ¹⁷Then that which was spoken by Jeremiah the prophet was fulfilled, saying,

¹⁸"A voice was heard in Ramah, lamentation, weeping and great mourning,

Rachel weeping for her children; she wouldn't be comforted, because they are no more."†

¹⁹But when Herod was dead, behold, an angel of the Lord appeared in a dream to Joseph in Egypt, saying, ²⁰"Arise and take the young child and his mother, and go into the land of Israel, for those who sought the young child's life are dead."

²¹He arose and took the young child and his mother, and came into the land of Israel. ²²But when he heard that Archelaus was reigning over Judea in the place of his father, Herod, he was afraid to go there. Being warned in a dream, he withdrew into the region of Galilee, ²³and came and lived in a city called Nazareth; that it might be fulfilled which was spoken through the prophets that he will be called a Nazarene.

---

* 2:15 Hosea 11:1
† 2:18 Jeremiah 31:15

3

¹In those days, John the Baptizer came, preaching in the wilderness of Judea, saying, ²"Repent, for the Kingdom of Heaven is at hand!" ³For this is he who was spoken of by Isaiah the prophet, saying,

"The voice of one crying in the wilderness, make the way of the Lord ready!
Make his paths straight!"*

⁴Now John himself wore clothing made of camel's hair with a leather belt around his waist. His food was locusts and wild honey. ⁵Then people from Jerusalem, all of Judea, and all the region around the Jordan went out to him. ⁶They were baptized by him in the Jordan, confessing their sins.

⁷But when he saw many of the Pharisees and Sadducees coming for his baptism, he said to them, "You offspring of vipers, who warned you to flee from the wrath to come? ⁸Therefore produce fruit worthy of repentance! ⁹Don't think to yourselves, 'We have Abraham for our father,' for I tell you that God is able to raise^g up children to Abraham from these stones. ¹⁰Even now the ax lies at the root of the trees. Therefore, every tree that doesn't produce good fruit is cut down and cast into the fire.

¹¹"I indeed baptize you in water for repentance, but he who comes after me is mightier than I, whose sandals I am not worthy to carry. He will baptize you in the Holy Spirit.† ¹²His winnowing fork is in his hand, and he will thoroughly cleanse his threshing floor. He will gather his wheat into the barn, but the chaff he will burn up with unquenchable fire."

¹³Then Jesus came from Galilee to the Jordan‡ to John, to be baptized by him. ¹⁴But John would have hindered him, saying, "I need to be baptized by you, and you come to me?"

^g Q. 35:16

---

* 3:3 Isaiah 40:3

† 3:11 TR and NU add "and with fire"

‡ 3:13 i.e., the Jordan River

¹⁵But Jesus, answering, said to him, "Allow it now, for this is the fitting way for us to fulfill all righteousness." Then he allowed him. ¹⁶Jesus,^h when he was baptized, went up directly from the water: and behold, the heavens were opened to him. He saw the Spirit of God descending as a dove, and coming on him. ¹⁷Behold, a voiceⁱ out of the heavens said, "This is my beloved Son, with whom I am well pleased."

^h Q. 2:87, 253; 5:110; 33:7

ⁱ Q. 53:26

4

¹Then Jesus was led up by the Spirit into the wilderness to be tempted by the devil. ²When he had fasted forty days and forty nights, he was hungry^j afterward. ³The tempter came and said to him, "If you are the Son of God, command that these stones become bread." ⁴But he answered,

^j Q. 25:20

"It is written, 'Man shall not live by bread alone, but by every word that proceeds out of God's mouth.' "*

⁵Then the devil took him into the holy city. He set him on the pinnacle of the temple, ⁶and said to him, "If you are the Son of God, throw yourself down, for it is written,

'He will command his angels concerning you,' and, 'On their hands they will bear you up, so that you don't dash your foot against a stone.' "†

⁷Jesus said to him, "Again, it is written, 'You shall not test the Lord, your God.' "‡ ⁸Again, the devil took him to an exceedingly high mountain, and showed him all the kingdoms of the world and their glory. ⁹He said to him, "I will give you all of these things, if you will fall down and worship me."^k ¹⁰Then Jesus said to him, "Get behind me,§ Satan! For it is written,

^k Q. 23:97

'You shall worship the Lord your God, and you shall

---

* 4:4 Deuteronomy 8:3

† 4:6 Psalm 91:11-12

‡ 4:7 Deuteronomy 6:16

§ 4:10 TR and NU read "Go away" instead of "Get behind me"

serve him only.'"[1][*]

[11]Then the devil left him, and behold, angels[m] came and served him.

[12]Now when Jesus heard that John was delivered up, he withdrew into Galilee. [13]Leaving Nazareth, he came and lived in Capernaum, which is by the sea, in the region of Zebulun and Naphtali, [14]that it might be fulfilled which was spoken through Isaiah the prophet, saying,

> [15]"The land of Zebulun and the land of Naphtali, toward the sea, beyond the Jordan, Galilee of the Gentiles,
> [16]the people who sat in darkness saw a great light[n];
> to those who sat in the region and shadow of death,
> to them light has dawned."[†]

[17]From that time, Jesus began to preach, and to say, "Repent! For the Kingdom[o] of Heaven is at hand."

[18]Walking by the sea of Galilee, he[‡] saw two brothers: Simon, who is called Peter, and Andrew, his brother, casting a net into the sea; for they were fishermen. [19]He said to them, "Come after me, and I will make you fishers for men." [20]They immediately left their nets and followed him. [21]Going on from there, he saw two other brothers, James the son of Zebedee, and John his brother, in the boat with Zebedee their father, mending their nets. He called them. [22]They immediately left the boat and their father, and followed him.

[23]Jesus went about in all Galilee, teaching in their synagogues, preaching the Good News of the Kingdom, and healing[p] every disease and every sickness among the people. [24]The report about him went out into all Syria. They brought to him all who were sick, afflicted with various diseases and torments, possessed with demons, epileptics, and paralytics; and he healed them. [25]Great multitudes from Galilee, Decapolis, Jerusalem, Judea, and from beyond the Jordan

[1] Q. 3:79; 33:39; 46:21; 98:5

[m] Q. 43:53

[n] Q. 2:257; 4:174; 14:5; 24:35; 57:9

[o] Q. 24:42

[p] Q. 3:49

---

[*] 4:10 Deuteronomy 6:13
[†] 4:16 Isaiah 9:1-2
[‡] 4:18 TR reads "Jesus" instead of "he"

followed him.

5

¹Seeing the multitudes, he went up onto the mountain. When he had sat down, his disciples came to him. ²He opened his mouth and taught them, saying,

^q Q. 23:2; 35:15

³"Blessed^q are the poor in spirit, for theirs is the Kingdom of Heaven.

⁴Blessed are those who mourn, for they shall be comforted.

^r Q. 19:40; 23:10; 39:74

⁵Blessed^r are the gentle, for they shall inherit the earth.

⁶Blessed are those who hunger and thirst for righteousness, for they shall be filled.

^s Q. 24:56; 57:27

⁷Blessed^s are the merciful, for they shall obtain mercy.

⁸Blessed are the pure in heart, for they shall see God.

^t Q. 60:7

⁹Blessed^t are the peacemakers, for they shall be called children of God.

^u Q. 23:11

¹⁰Blessed^u are those who have been persecuted for righteousness ' sake, for theirs is the Kingdom of Heaven.

¹¹"Blessed are you when people reproach you, persecute you, and say all kinds of evil against you falsely, for my sake.

^v Q. 2:177; 3:57, 144; 64:15

¹²Rejoice, and be exceedingly glad, for great^v is your reward in heaven. For that is how they persecuted the prophets who were before you.

¹³"You are the salt of the earth, but if the salt has lost its flavor, with what will it be salted? It is then good for nothing, but to be cast out and trodden under the feet of men.

^w Q. 61:8

¹⁴You are the light^w of the world. A city located on a hill can't be hidden. ¹⁵Neither do you light a lamp and put it under a measuring basket, but on a stand; and it shines to all who are in the house. ¹⁶Even so, let your light shine before men, that they may see your good works and glorify your Father who is in heaven.

[17]"Don't think that I came to destroy the law or the prophets. I didn't come to destroy, but to fulfill.[x] [18]For most certainly, I tell you, until heaven and earth pass away,[y] not even one smallest letter[*] or one tiny pen stroke[†] shall in any way pass away from the law, until all things are accomplished. [19]Therefore, whoever shall break one of these least commandments and teach others to do so, shall be called least in the Kingdom of Heaven; but whoever shall do and teach them shall be called great in the Kingdom of Heaven. [20]For I tell you that unless your righteousness exceeds that of the scribes and Pharisees, there is no way you will enter into the Kingdom of Heaven.

[21]"You have heard that it was said to the ancient ones, 'You shall not murder;'[‡] and 'Whoever murders will be in danger of the judgment.' [22]But I tell you that everyone who is angry with his brother without a cause[§] will be in danger of the judgment.[z] Whoever says to his brother, 'Raca!'[**] will be in danger of the council. Whoever says, 'You fool!' will be in danger of the fire[a] of Gehenna.[††]

[23]"If therefore you are offering your gift at the altar, and there remember that your brother has anything against you, [24]leave your gift there before the altar, and go your way. First be reconciled to your brother, and then come and offer your gift. [25]Agree with your adversary quickly while you are with him on the way; lest perhaps the prosecutor deliver you to the judge, and the judge deliver you to the officer, and you be cast into prison. [26]Most certainly I tell you, you shall by no means get out of there

[x] Q. 2:106, 177; 3:50, 79; 61:6

[y] Q. 35:41

[z] Q. 2:225

[a] Q. 3:151

---

[*] 5:18 literally, iota

[†] 5:18 or, serif

[‡] 5:21 Exodus 20:13

[§] 5:22 NU omits "without a cause".

[**] 5:22 "Raca" is an Aramaic insult, related to the word for "empty" and conveying the idea of empty-headedness

[††] 5:22 or, Hell

10

until you have paid the last penny.[*]

27"You have heard that it was said,[†] 'You shall not commit adultery;'[‡] 28but I tell you that everyone who gazes at a woman to lust after her has committed adultery with her already in his heart. 29If your right eye causes you to stumble, pluck it out and throw it away from you. For it is more profitable for you that one of your members should perish than for your whole body to be cast into Gehenna[§]. 30If your right hand causes you to stumble, cut it off, and throw it away from you. For it is more profitable for you that one of your members should perish, than for your whole body to be cast into Gehenna[**].

31"It was also said, 'Whoever shall put away his wife, let him give her a writing of divorce,'[b][††] 32but I tell you that whoever puts away his wife, except for the cause of sexual immorality, makes her an adulteress; and whoever marries her when she is put away commits adultery.

33"Again you have heard that it was said to the ancient ones, 'You shall not make false vows, but shall perform to the Lord your vows,'[c][‡‡] 34but I tell you, don't swear at all: neither by heaven, for it is the throne of God; 35nor by the earth, for it is the footstool of his feet; nor by Jerusalem, for it is the city of the great King. 36Neither shall you swear by your head, for you can't make one hair white or black. 37But let your 'Yes' be 'Yes' and your 'No' be 'No.' Whatever is more than these is of the evil one.

38"You have heard that it was said, 'An eye for an eye, and a tooth for a tooth.'[d][§§] 39But I tell you, don't resist him who

[b] Q. 65:1

[c] Q. 2:177, 224; 3:76

[d] Q. 5:45

---

[*] 5:26 literally, kodrantes. A kodrantes was a small copper coin worth about 2 lepta (widow's mites)—not enough to buy very much of anything.
[†] 5:27 TR adds "to the ancients"
[‡] 5:27 Exodus 20:14
[§] 5:29 or, Hell
[**] 5:30 or, Hell
[††] 5:31 Deuteronomy 24:1
[‡‡] 5:33 Numbers 30:2; Deuteronomy 23:21; Ecclesiastes 5:4
[§§] 5:38 Exodus 21:24; Leviticus 24:20; Deuteronomy 19:21

is evil; but whoever strikes you on your right cheek, turn to him the other also.[e] 40If anyone sues you to take away your coat, let him have your cloak also. 41Whoever compels you to go one mile, go with him two. 42Give to him who asks you, and don't turn away him who desires to borrow[f] from you.

43"You have heard that it was said, 'You shall love your neighbor and hate your enemy.' 44But I tell you, love your enemies, bless those who curse you, do good to those who hate you, and pray for those who mistreat you and persecute you, 45that you may be children of your Father who is in heaven. For he makes his sun to rise on the evil and the good, and sends rain on the just and the unjust.[g]* 46For if you love those who love you, what reward do you have? Don't even the tax collectors do the same?

47If you only greet your friends, what more do you do than others? Don't even the tax collectors do the same? 48Therefore you shall be perfect, just as your Father in heaven is perfect.

6

1"Be careful that you don't do your charitable giving before men, to be seen by them, or else you have no reward from your Father who is in heaven."[h]† 2Therefore, when you do merciful deeds, don't sound a trumpet before yourself, as the hypocrites do in the synagogues and in the streets, that they may get glory from men. Most certainly I tell you, they have received their reward. 3But when you do merciful deeds, don't let your left hand know what your right hand does, 4so that your merciful deeds may be in secret, then your

[e] Q. 31:18

[f] Q. 93:10

[g] see footnote

[h] see footnote

---

* [g] Q. 2:22, 164; 6:6, 99; 7:57; 8:11; 10:25; 11:52; 13:17; 14:32; 15:22; 16:10, 65; 18:45; 20:53; 22:5, 63; 23:18; 24:43; 25:48; 27:60; 29:63; 30:24; 30:48; 31:10, 34; 32:27; 39:21; 41:40; 42:28; 43:11; 50:9; 71:11
† [h] Q. 2:264, 271; 3:57; 4:38; 14:31; 16:71; 35:29

12

[i] Q.
4:134;
36:11;
62:8

[j] Q.
4:142;
14:31;
72:19;
98:5;
107:5

[k] Q.
62:8

[l] Q.
27:62

[m] Q.
3:135

[n] Q.
10:86;
27:62

[o] Q.
4:58

[p] Q.
2:183

[q] Q.
62:8

Father who sees in secret will reward you openly.[i]

5"When you pray, you shall not be as the hypocrites, for they love to stand and pray in the synagogues and in the corners of the streets, that they may be seen by men.[j] Most certainly, I tell you, they have received their reward. 6But you, when you pray, enter into your inner room, and having shut your door, pray to your Father who is in secret; and your Father who sees in secret[k] will reward you openly. 7In praying, don't use vain repetitions as the Gentiles do; for they think that they will be heard for their much speaking. 8Therefore don't be like them, for your Father knows what things you need[l] before you ask him. 9Pray like this:

"'Our Father in heaven, may your name be kept holy. 10Let your Kingdom come. Let your will be done on earth as it is in heaven.

11Give us today our daily bread.

12Forgive us our debts,[m] as we also forgive our debtors.

13Bring us not into temptation, but deliver us[n] from the evil one. For yours is the Kingdom, the power, and the glory forever. Amen.'*

14"For if you forgive men their trespasses, your heavenly Father will also forgive you.[o] 15But if you don't forgive men their trespasses, neither will your Father forgive your trespasses.

16"Moreover when you fast,[p] don't be like the hypocrites, with sad faces. For they disfigure their faces that they may be seen by men to be fasting. Most certainly I tell you, they have received their reward. 17But you, when you fast, anoint your head and wash your face, 18so that you are not seen by men to be fasting, but by your Father who is in secret[q]; and your Father, who sees in secret, will reward you.

19"Don't lay up treasures for yourselves on the earth,

---

* 6:13 NU omits "For yours is the Kingdom, the power, and the glory forever. Amen."

where moth and rust consume, and where thieves break through and steal; [20]but lay up for yourselves treasures in heaven, where neither moth nor rust consume, and where thieves don't break through and steal; [21]for where your treasure is, there your heart will be also.[r]

[22]"The lamp of the body is the eye. If therefore your eye is sound, your whole body will be full of light. [23]But if your eye is evil, your whole body will be full of darkness. If therefore the light that is in you is darkness, how great is the darkness![s]

[24]"No one can serve two masters,[t] for either he will hate the one and love the other, or else he will be devoted to one and despise the other. You can't serve both God and Mammon. [25]Therefore I tell you, don't be anxious for your life: what you will eat, or what you will drink; nor yet for your body, what you will wear.[u] Isn't life more than food, and the body more than clothing? [26]See the birds[v] of the sky, that they don't sow, neither do they reap, nor gather into barns. Your heavenly Father feeds them. Aren't you of much more value than they?

[27]"Which of you by being anxious, can add one moment to his lifespan?[w]* [28]Why are you anxious about clothing? Consider the lilies of the field, how they grow. They don't toil, neither do they spin, [29]yet I tell you that even Solomon in all his glory was not dressed like one of these. [30]But if God so clothes the grass of the field, which today exists and tomorrow is thrown into the oven,[x] won't he much more clothe you, you of little faith?

[31]"Therefore don't be anxious, saying, 'What will we eat?', 'What will we drink?' or, 'With what will we be clothed?' [32]For the Gentiles seek after all these things; for your heavenly Father knows that you need all these things. [33]But seek first God's Kingdom[y] and his righteousness; and all these things will be given to you as well.

[r] Q. 16:96; 59:18; 83:14

[s] Q. 2:257

[t] Q. 2:200; 89:20

[u] Q. 29:60; 30:40; 62:11; 67:21

[v] Q. 16:79; 22:58; 67:19

[w] see footnote

[x] Q. 18:45

[y] Q. 29:17; 35:13; 57:27

---

* [w] Q. 7:34; 10:49; 16:61; 23:43; 34:30

z Q.
76:11

³⁴Therefore don't be anxious for tomorrow, for tomorrow will be anxious for itself. Each day's own evil[z] is sufficient.

7

¹"Don't judge, so that you won't be judged. ²For with whatever judgment you judge, you will be judged; and with whatever measure you measure, it will be measured to you. ³Why do you see the speck that is in your brother's eye, but don't consider the beam that is in your own eye? ⁴Or how will you tell your brother, 'Let me remove the speck from your eye,' and behold, the beam is in your own eye? ⁵You hypocrite! First remove the beam out of your own eye, and then you can see clearly to remove the speck out of your brother's eye.

⁶"Don't give that which is holy to the dogs, neither throw your pearls before the pigs,[a] lest perhaps they trample them under their feet, and turn and tear you to pieces.

a Q.
2:65;
5:61;
7:166

⁷"Ask, and it will be given you. Seek, and you will find. Knock, and it will be opened for you. ⁸For everyone who asks receives.[b] He who seeks finds. To him who knocks it will be opened. ⁹Or who is there among you who, if his son asks him for bread, will give him a stone? ¹⁰Or if he asks for a fish, who will give him a serpent? ¹¹If you then, being evil, know how to give good gifts to your children, how much more will your Father who is in heaven give good things[c] to those who ask him! ¹²Therefore, whatever you desire for men to do to you, you shall also do to them[d], for this is the law and the prophets.

b Q.
2:186

c Q.
3:8;
38:35

d Q.
33:6

¹³"Enter in by the narrow gate; for the gate is wide and the way is broad that leads to destruction, and there are many who enter in by it. ¹⁴How* narrow is the gate and the

---

* 7:14 TR reads "Because" instead of "How"

way is restricted that leads to life! There are few who find it.[e]

[15]"Beware of false prophets, who come to you in sheep's clothing, but inwardly are ravening wolves. [16]By their fruits you will know them. Do you gather grapes from thorns or figs from thistles? [17]Even so, every good tree produces good fruit, but the corrupt tree produces evil fruit.[f] [18]A good tree can't produce evil fruit, neither can a corrupt tree produce good fruit. [19]Every tree that doesn't grow good fruit is cut down and thrown into the fire. [20]Therefore by their fruits you will know them.

[21]"Not everyone who says to me, 'Lord, Lord,' will enter into the Kingdom of Heaven, but he who does the will of my Father who is in heaven.[g] [22]Many will tell me in that day, 'Lord, Lord, didn't we prophesy in your name, in your name cast out demons, and in your name do many mighty works?' [23]Then I will tell them, 'I never knew you. Depart from me, you who work iniquity.'

[24]"Everyone therefore who hears these words of mine and does them, I will liken him to a wise man who built his house on a rock. [25]The rain came down, the floods came, and the winds blew and beat on that house; and it didn't fall, for it was founded on the rock. [26]Everyone who hears these words of mine and doesn't do them will be like a foolish man who built his house on the sand. [27]The rain came down, the floods came, and the winds blew and beat on that house; and it fell—and its fall was great".[h]

[28]When Jesus had finished saying these things, the multitudes were astonished at his teaching, [29]for he taught them with authority, and not like the scribes.

8[i]*

[1]When he came down from the mountain, great

[e] Q. 3:82; 39:71; 90:11; 110:2

[f] Q. 14:24, 26

[g] Q. 3:50

[h] Q. 9:109

[i] see footnote

---

* [i] Q. 2:87; 3:49, 52; 5:110, 112; 19:30; 43:63

j Q.
5:110

multitudes followed him. ²Behold, a leperʲ came to him and worshiped him, saying, "Lord, if you want to, you can make me clean."

³Jesus stretched out his hand and touched him, saying, "I want to. Be made clean." Immediately his leprosy was cleansed. ᵏ ⁴Jesus said to him, "See that you tell nobody; but go, show yourself to the priest, and offer the gift that Moses commanded, as a testimony to them."

k Q.
3:49

⁵When he came into Capernaum, a centurion came to him, asking him for help, ⁶saying, "Lord, my servant lies in the house paralyzed, grievously tormented." ⁷Jesus said to him, "I will come and heal him."ˡ ⁸The centurion answered, "Lord, I'm not worthy for you to come under my roof. Just say the word, and my servant will be healed. ⁹For I am also a man under authority, having under myself soldiers. I tell this one, 'Go,' and he goes; and tell another, 'Come,' and he comes; and tell my servant, 'Do this,' and he does it." ¹⁰When Jesus heard it, he marveled and said to those who followed, "Most certainly I tell you, I haven't found so great a faith, not even in Israel. ¹¹I tell you that many will come from the east and the west, and will sit down with Abraham, Isaac, and Jacob in the Kingdom of Heaven, ¹²but the children of the Kingdom will be thrown out into the outer darkness.ᵐ* There will be weeping and gnashing of teeth." ¹³Jesus said to the centurion, "Go your way. Let it be done for you as you have believed."ⁿ His servant was healed in that hour.

l Q.
3:49

m see
footnote

n Q.
2:253

¹⁴When Jesus came into Peter's house, he saw his wife's mother lying sick with a fever. ¹⁵He touched her hand, and the fever left her.º So she got up and served him.† ¹⁶When evening came, they brought to him many possessed with demons. He cast out the spirits with a word, and healed all who were sick,ᵖ ¹⁷that it might be fulfilled which was spoken through Isaiah the prophet,

o Q.
2:253

p Q.
3:49

---

* ᵐ Q. 2:196; 3:11; 5:2; 8:13; 10:27; 13:6; 24:40; 40:3; 59:4
† 8:15 TR reads "them" instead of "him

saying, "He took our infirmities and bore our diseases."[*] [18]Now when Jesus saw great multitudes around him, he gave the order to depart to the other side.

[19]A scribe came and said to him, "Teacher, I will follow you wherever you go."

[20]Jesus said to him, "The foxes have holes and the birds of the sky have nests, but the Son of Man has nowhere to lay his head."[q]

[q] Q. 2:253

[21]Another of his disciples said to him, "Lord, allow me first to go and bury my father." [22]But Jesus said to him, "Follow me, and leave the dead to bury their own dead."

[23]When he got into a boat, his disciples followed him. [24]Behold, a violent storm came up on the sea, so much that the boat was covered with the waves; but he was asleep. [25]The disciples came to him and woke him up, saying, "Save us, Lord! We are dying!" [26]He said to them, "Why are you fearful, O you of little faith?" Then he got up, rebuked the wind and the sea, and there was a great calm. [27]The men marveled, saying, "What kind of man is this, that even the wind and the sea obey him?"[r]

[r] Q. 42:34

[28]When he came to the other side, into the country of the Gergesenes,[†] two people possessed by demons met him there, coming out of the tombs, exceedingly fierce, so that nobody could pass that way. [29]Behold, they cried out, saying, "What do we have to do with you, Jesus, Son of God? Have you come here to torment us before the time?" [30]Now there was a herd of many pigs feeding far away from them. [31]The demons begged him, saying, "If you cast us out, permit us to go away into the herd of pigs." [32]He said to them, "Go!" They came out and went into the herd of pigs; and behold, the whole herd of pigs rushed down the cliff into the sea and died in the water. [33]Those who fed them fled and went away into the city and told everything, including what happened to those who were possessed with demons.

[*] 8:17 Isaiah 53:4

[†] 8:28 NU reads "Gadarenes"

³⁴Behold, all the city came out to meet Jesus. When they saw him, they begged that he would depart from their borders.

9^s*

^s see footnote

¹He entered into a boat and crossed over, and came into his own city. ²Behold, they brought to him a man who was paralyzed, lying on a bed. Jesus, seeing their faith, said to the paralytic, "Son, cheer up! Your sins are forgiven you." ³Behold, some of the scribes said to themselves, "This man blasphemes." ⁴Jesus, knowing their thoughts,^t said, "Why do you think evil in your hearts? ⁵For which is easier, to say, 'Your sins are forgiven;' or to say, 'Get up, and walk?' ⁶But that you may know that the Son of Man has authority on earth to forgive sins" — (then he said to the paralytic), "Get up, and take up your mat, and go to your house." ⁷He arose and departed to his house. ⁸But when the multitudes saw it, they marveled and glorified God, who had given such authority to men.

^t Q. 7:188

⁹As Jesus passed by from there, he saw a man called Matthew sitting at the tax collection office. He said to him, "Follow me." He got up and followed him.

¹⁰As he sat in the house, behold, many tax collectors and sinners came and sat down with Jesus and his disciples. ¹¹When the Pharisees saw it, they said to his disciples, "Why does your teacher eat with tax collectors and sinners?" ¹²When Jesus heard it, he said to them, "Those who are healthy have no need for a physician, but those who are sick do. ¹³But you go and learn what this means: 'I desire mercy, and not sacrifice,'[†] for I came not to call the righteous, but sinners to repentance."[‡]

¹⁴Then John's disciples came to him, saying, "Why do we and the Pharisees fast often, but your disciples don't

---

* ^s Q. 2:87; 3:49, 52; 5:110, 112; 19:30; 43:63

[†] 9:13 Hosea 6:6

[‡] 9:13 NU omits "to repentance"

fast?" ¹⁵Jesus said to them, "Can the friends of the bridegroom mourn as long as the bridegroom is with them? But the days will come when the bridegroom will be taken away from them, and then they will fast. ¹⁶No one puts a piece of unshrunk cloth on an old garment; for the patch would tear away from the garment, and a worse hole is made. ¹⁷Neither do people put new wine into old wine skins, or else the skins would burst, and the wine be spilled, and the skins ruined. No, they put new wine into fresh wine skins, and both are preserved."

¹⁸While he told these things to them, behold, a ruler came and worshiped him, saying, "My daughter has just died, but come and lay your hand on her, and she will live." ¹⁹Jesus got up and followed him, as did his disciples. ²⁰Behold, a woman who had a discharge of blood for twelve years came behind him, and touched the fringe*† of his garment; ²¹for she said within herself, "If I just touch his garment, I will be made well." ²²But Jesus, turning around and seeing her, said, "Daughter, cheer up! Your faith has made you well." And the woman was made well from that hour. ²³When Jesus came into the ruler's house and saw the flute players and the crowd in noisy disorder, ²⁴he said to them, "Make room, because the girl isn't dead, but sleeping."ᵘ They were ridiculing him. ²⁵But when the crowd was sent out, he entered in, took her by the hand, and the girl arose.ᵛ ²⁶The report of this went out into all that land.

ᵘ Q. 2:154

ᵛ Q. 3:49

²⁷As Jesus passed by from there, two blind men followed him, calling out and saying, "Have mercy on us, son of David!" ²⁸When he had come into the house, the blind men came to him. Jesus said to them, "Do you believe that I am able to do this?" They told him, "Yes, Lord." ²⁹Then he touched their eyes, saying, "According to your faith be it done to you." ³⁰Then their eyes were opened. Jesus

* 9:20 or, tassel

strictly commanded them, saying, "See that no one knows about this." ³¹But they went out and spread abroad his fame in all that land.

³²As they went out, behold, a mute man who was demon possessed was brought to him. ³³When the demon was cast out, the mute man spoke. The multitudes marveled, saying, "Nothing like this has ever been seen in Israel!"ʷ ³⁴But the Pharisees said, "By the prince of the demons, he casts out demons."

³⁵Jesus went about all the cities and the villages, teaching in their synagogues and preaching the Good News of the Kingdom, and healing every disease and every sickness among the people.ˣ ³⁶But when he saw the multitudes, he was moved with compassion for them because they were harassed and scattered, like sheep without a shepherd. ³⁷Then he said to his disciples, "The harvest indeed is plentiful, but the laborers are few. ³⁸Pray therefore that the Lord of the harvest will send out laborers into his harvest."

10ʸ*

¹He called to himself his twelve disciples, and gave them authority over unclean spirits, to cast them out, and to heal every disease and every sickness. ²Now the names of the twelve apostles are these. The first, Simon, who is called Peter; Andrew, his brother; James the son of Zebedee; John, his brother; ³Philip; Bartholomew; Thomas; Matthew the tax collector; James the son of Alphaeus; Lebbaeus, who was also called Thaddaeus; ⁴Simon the Zealot; and Judas Iscariot, who also betrayed him.

⁵Jesus sent these twelve out and commanded them, saying, "Don't go among the Gentiles, and don't enter into any city of the Samaritans. ⁶Rather, go to the lost sheep of

w Q. 3:49; 5:110

x Q. 3:49

y see footnote

* ʸ Q. 2:87; 3:49, 52; 5:110, 112; 19:30; 43:63

the house of Israel. [7]As you go, preach, saying, 'The Kingdom of Heaven is at hand!' [8]Heal the sick, cleanse the lepers, and cast out demons. Freely you received, so freely give. [9]Don't take any gold, silver, or brass in your money belts. [10]Take no bag for your journey, neither two coats, nor sandals, nor staff: for the laborer is worthy of his food. [11]Into whatever city or village you enter, find out who in it is worthy, and stay there until you go on.[z] [12]As you enter into the household, greet it. [13]If the household is worthy, let your peace come on it, but if it isn't worthy, let your peace return to you. [14]Whoever doesn't receive you or hear your words, as you go out of that house or that city, shake the dust off your feet. [15]Most certainly I tell you, it will be more tolerable for the land of Sodom and Gomorrah[a] in the day of judgment than for that city.

[16]"Behold, I send you out as sheep among wolves. Therefore, be wise as serpents and harmless as doves. [17]But beware of men, for they will deliver you up to councils, and in their synagogues, they will scourge you. [18]Yes, and you will be brought before governors and kings for my sake, for a testimony to them and to the nations. [19]But when they deliver you up, don't be anxious how or what you will say, for it will be given you in that hour what you will say. [20]For it is not you who speak, but the Spirit of your Father who speaks in you. [21]"Brother will deliver up brother to death, and the father his child. Children will rise up against parents and cause them to be put to death.[b] [22]You will be hated by all men for my name's sake, but he who endures to the end will be saved.[c] [23]But when they persecute you in this city, flee into the next, for most certainly I tell you, you will not have gone through the cities of Israel until the Son of Man has come. [24]"A disciple is not above his teacher, nor a servant above his lord. [25]It is enough for the disciple that he be like his teacher, and the servant like his

[z] Q. 2:218

[a] Q. 18:59

[b] Q. 64:14

[c] Q. 3:146; 16:126

lord. If they have called the master of the house Beelzebul,[*] how much more those of his household!

[26]Therefore don't be afraid of them, for there is nothing covered that will not be revealed, or hidden that will not be known. [27]What I tell you in the darkness, speak in the light; and what you hear whispered in the ear, proclaim on the housetops. [28]Don't be afraid of those who kill the body, but are not able to kill the soul. Rather, fear him who is able to destroy both soul and body in Gehenna.[d][†] [29]"Aren't two sparrows sold for an assarion coin?[‡] Not one of them falls to the ground apart from your Father's will.[e] [30]But the very hairs of your head are all numbered.[f] [31]Therefore don't be afraid. You are of more value than many sparrows. [32]Everyone therefore who confesses me before men, I will also confess him before my Father who is in heaven. [33]But whoever denies me before men, I will also deny him before my Father who is in heaven.

[34]"Don't think that I came to send peace on the earth. I didn't come to send peace, but a sword. [35]For I came to set a man at odds against his father, and a daughter against her mother, and a daughter-in-law against her mother-in-law. [36]A man's foes will be those of his own household.[g][§] [37]He who loves father or mother more than me is not worthy of me; and he who loves son or daughter more than me isn't worthy of me.[h] [38]He who doesn't take his cross and follow after me isn't worthy of me. [39]He who seeks his life will lose it; and he who loses his life for my sake will find it.

[40]"He who receives you receives me, and he who receives me receives him who sent me. [41]He who receives a prophet in the name of a prophet will receive a prophet's

[d] Q. 2:150; 3:131, 141, 175

[e] Q. 6:59; 41:47; 67:19

[f] Q. 72:28

[g] Q. 64:14

[h] Q. 9:24; 58:22; 64:15

---

[*] 10:25 Literally, Lord of the Flies, or the devil

[†] 10:28 or, Hell

[‡] 10:29 An assarion is a small coin worth one tenth of a drachma or a sixteenth of a denarius. An assarion is approximately the wages of one half hour of agricultural labor

[§] 10:36 Micah 7:6

reward. He who receives a righteous man in the name of a righteous man will receive a righteous man's reward.[i] [42]Whoever gives one of these little ones just a cup of cold water to drink in the name of a disciple, most certainly I tell you, he will in no way lose his reward."

[i] Q. 3:57; 9:20; 28:84; 36:11

11[j]*

[j] see footnote

[1]When Jesus had finished directing his twelve disciples, he departed from there to teach and preach in their cities.

[2]Now when John heard in the prison the works of Christ, he sent two of his disciples [3]and said to him, "Are you he who comes, or should we look for another?" [4]Jesus answered them, "Go and tell John the things which you hear and see: [5]the blind receive their sight, the lame walk, the lepers are cleansed, the deaf hear, the dead are raised up, and the poor have good news preached to them.[k] [6]Blessed is he who finds no occasion for stumbling in me."

[k] Q. 5:110; 10:42; 43:40

[7]As these went their way, Jesus began to say to the multitudes concerning John, "What did you go out into the wilderness to see? A reed shaken by the wind? [8]But what did you go out to see? A man in soft clothing? Behold, those who wear soft clothing are in kings' houses. [9]But why did you go out? To see a prophet? Yes, I tell you, and much more than a prophet. [10]For this is he, of whom it is written,

'Behold, I send my messenger[l] before your face, who will prepare your way before you.'

[l] Q. 3:164

[11]Most certainly I tell you, among those who are born of women there has not arisen anyone greater than John the Baptizer; yet he who is least in the Kingdom of Heaven is greater than he. [12]From the days of John the Baptizer until now, the Kingdom of Heaven suffers violence, and the violent take it by force. [13]For all the prophets and the law

---

*[j] Q. 2:87; 3:49, 52; 5:110, 112; 19:30; 43:63

prophesied until John. ¹⁴If you are willing to receive it, this is Elijah,ᵐ who is to come. ¹⁵He who has ears to hear, let him hear.

ᵐ Q. 37:130

¹⁶"But to what shall I compare this generation? It is like children sitting in the marketplaces, who call to their companions

¹⁷and say, 'We played the flute for you, and you didn't dance. We mourned for you, and you didn't lament.'

¹⁸For John came neither eating nor drinking, and they say, 'He has a demon.' ¹⁹The Son of Man came eating and drinking, and they say, 'Behold, a gluttonous man and a drunkard, a friend of tax collectors and sinners!' But wisdom is justified by her children."*

²⁰Then he began to denounce the cities in which most of his mighty works had been done, because they didn't repent. ²¹"Woe to you, Chorazin! Woe to you, Bethsaida! For if the mighty works had been done in Tyre and Sidon which were done in you, they would have repented long ago in sackcloth and ashes. ²²But I tell you, it will be more tolerable for Tyre and Sidon on the day of judgment than for you. ²³You, Capernaum, who are exalted to heaven, you will go down to Hades. † For if the mighty works had been done in Sodom which were done in you, it would have remained until today. ²⁴But I tell you that it will be more tolerable for the land of Sodom on the day of judgment, than for you."

²⁵At that time, Jesus answered, "I thank you, Father, Lord of heaven and earth, that you hid these things from the wise and understanding, and revealed them to infants. ²⁶Yes, Father, for so it was well-pleasing in your sight.ⁿ ²⁷All things have been delivered to me by my Father. No one knows the Son, except the Father; neither does anyone know the Father, except the Son and he to whom the Son desires to reveal him. ²⁸"Come to me, all you who labor

ⁿ Q. 49:18

*11:19 NU reads "actions" instead of "children"
† 11:23 or, Hell

and are heavily burdened, and I will give you rest. [29]Take my yoke upon you and learn from me, for I am gentle and humble in heart; and you will find rest for your souls. [30]For my yoke is easy, and my burden is light".[o][*]

[o] see footnote

12[p]

[p] Q. 3:49; 5:110, 112; 19:30

[1]At that time, Jesus went on the Sabbath day through the grain fields. His disciples were hungry and began to pluck heads of grain and to eat. [2]But the Pharisees, when they saw it, said to him, "Behold, your disciples do what is not lawful to do on the Sabbath." [3]But he said to them, "Haven't you read what David did when he was hungry, and those who were with him: [4]how he entered into God's house and ate the show bread, which was not lawful for him to eat, nor for those who were with him, but only for the priests? [5]Or have you not read in the law that on the Sabbath day the priests in the temple profane the Sabbath[q] and are guiltless? [6]But I tell you that one greater than the temple is here. [7]But if you had known what this means, 'I desire mercy, and not sacrifice,' you wouldn't have condemned the guiltless. [8]For the Son of Man is Lord of the Sabbath."

[q] Q. 2:65

[9]He departed from there and went into their synagogue. [10]And behold, there was a man with a withered hand. They asked him, "Is it lawful to heal[r] on the Sabbath day?" so that they might accuse him. [11]He said to them, "What man is there among you who has one sheep, and if this one falls into a pit on the Sabbath day, won't he grab on to it and lift it out? [12]Of how much more value then is a man than a sheep! Therefore it is lawful to do good on the Sabbath day. [13]Then he told the man, "Stretch out your hand." He stretched it out; and it was restored whole, just like the other. [14]But the Pharisees went out and

[r] Q. 3:49

---

[*] [o] Q. 2:204, 225; 3:154, 159; 4:33; 5:101; 9:114; 11:29; 17:25; 22:59; 26:89; 33:51; 35:38; 37:84; 94:2

conspired against him, how they might destroy him.

[15]Jesus, perceiving that, withdrew from there. Great multitudes followed him; and he healed them all, [16]and commanded them that they should not make him known, [17]that it might be fulfilled which was spoken through Isaiah the prophet, saying,

> [18]"Behold, my servant whom I have chosen, my beloved in whom my soul is well pleased.
>
> I will put my Spirit on him. He will proclaim justice to the nations.
>
> [19]He will not strive, nor shout, neither will anyone hear his voice in the streets.
>
> [20]He won't break a bruised reed. He won't quench a smoking flax, until he leads justice to victory. [21]In his name, the nations will hope."[*]

[22]Then one possessed by a demon, blind and mute, was brought to him; and he healed[s] him, so that the blind and mute man both spoke and saw. [23]All the multitudes were amazed, and said, "Can this be the son of David?" [24]But when the Pharisees heard it, they said, "This man does not cast out demons except by Beelzebul, the prince of the demons." [25]Knowing their thoughts,[t] Jesus said to them, "Every kingdom divided against itself is brought to desolation, and every city or house divided against itself will not stand. [26]If Satan casts out Satan, he is divided against himself. How then will his kingdom stand? [27]If I by Beelzebul cast out demons, by whom do your children cast them out? Therefore they will be your judges. [28]But if I by the Spirit of God cast out demons, then God's Kingdom has come upon you. [29]Or how can one enter into the house of the strong man and plunder his goods, unless he first bind[u] the strong man? Then he will plunder his house. [30]"He who is not with me is against me, and he who doesn't gather with me, scatters. [31]Therefore I tell

[s] Q. 3:49

[t] Q. 7:188

[u] Q. 38:38

---

[*] 12:21 Isaiah 42:1-4

you, every sin and blasphemy will be forgiven men, but the blasphemy against the Spirit will not be forgiven men. [32]Whoever speaks a word against the Son of Man, it will be forgiven him; but whoever speaks against the Holy Spirit, it will not be forgiven him, either in this age, or in that which is to come.

[33]"Either make the tree good and its fruit good, or make the tree corrupt and its fruit corrupt; for the tree is known by its fruit. [34]You offspring of vipers, how can you, being evil, speak good things? For out of the abundance of the heart, the mouth speaks. [35]The good man out of his good treasure[*] brings out good things, and the evil man out of his evil treasure brings out evil things. [36]I tell you that every idle word that men speak, they will give account of it in the day of judgment.[v] [37]For by your words you will be justified, and by your words you will be condemned."

[38]Then certain of the scribes and Pharisees answered, "Teacher, we want to see a sign[w] from you." [39]But he answered them, "An evil and adulterous generation seeks after a sign, but no sign will be given to it but the sign of Jonah the prophet. [40]For as Jonah was three days and three nights in the belly of the huge fish, so will the Son of Man be three days and three nights in the heart of the earth. [41]The men of Nineveh will stand up in the judgment with this generation and will condemn it, for they repented at the preaching of Jonah; and behold, someone greater than Jonah is here. [42]The Queen of the South will rise up in the judgment with this generation and will condemn it, for she came from the ends of the earth to hear the wisdom of Solomon; and behold, someone greater than Solomon is here.

[43]"When an unclean spirit has gone out of a man, he passes through waterless places seeking rest, and doesn't find it. [44]Then he says, 'I will return into my house from

[v] Q. 45:26; 52:16

[w] Q. 2:118

---

[*] 12:35 TR adds "of the heart"

which I came;' and when he has come back, he finds it empty, swept, and put in order. ⁴⁵Then he goes and takes with himself seven other spirits more evil than he is, and they enter in and dwell there. The last state of that man becomes worse than the first. Even so will it be also to this evil generation."

⁴⁶While he was yet speaking to the multitudes, behold, his mother and his brothers stood outside, seeking to speak to him. ⁴⁷One said to him, "Behold, your mother and your brothers stand outside, seeking to speak to you." ⁴⁸But he answered him who spoke to him, "Who is my mother? Who are my brothers?" ⁴⁹He stretched out his hand toward his disciples, and said, "Behold, my mother and my brothers! ⁵⁰For whoever does the will of my Father who is in heaven, he is my brother, and sister, and mother."

13

¹On that day Jesus went out of the house and sat by the seaside. ²Great multitudes gathered to him, so that he entered into a boat and sat; and all the multitude stood on the beach. ³He spoke to them many things in parables, saying, "Behold, a farmer went out to sow. ⁴As he sowed, some seeds fell by the roadside, and the birds came and devoured them. ⁵Others fell on rocky ground, where they didn't have much soil, and immediately they sprang up, because they had no depth of earth. ⁶When the sun had risen, they were scorched. Because they had no root, they withered away. ⁷Others fell among thorns. The thorns grew up and choked them. ⁸Others fell on good soil and yielded fruit: some one hundred times as much,ˣ some sixty, and some thirty. ⁹He who has ears to hear, let him hear."

¹⁰The disciples came, and said to him, "Why do you speak to them in parables?"ʸ He answered them, "To you

ˣ Q. 2:261

ʸ Q. 2:26; 74:31

it is given to know the mysteries of the Kingdom of Heaven, but it is not given to them. [12]For whoever has, to him will be given, and he will have abundance,[z] but whoever doesn't have, from him will be taken away even that which he has. [13]Therefore I speak to them in parables, because seeing they don't see, and hearing, they don't hear, neither do they understand. [14]In them the prophecy of Isaiah is fulfilled, which says,

> 'By hearing you will hear, and will in no way understand; Seeing you will see, and will in no way perceive;[a*]
>
> [15]for this people's heart has grown callous, their ears are dull of hearing, and they have closed their eyes[b];
> or else perhaps they might perceive with their eyes, hear with their ears,
> understand with their heart,
> and would turn again,
> and I would heal them.'

[16]"But blessed are your eyes, for they see; and your ears, for they hear. [17]For most certainly I tell you that many prophets and righteous men desired to see the things which you see, and didn't see them; and to hear the things which you hear, and didn't hear them.

[18]"Hear, then, the parable of the farmer. [19]When anyone hears the word of the Kingdom and doesn't understand it, the evil one comes and snatches away that which has been sown in his heart. This is what was sown by the roadside. [20]What was sown on the rocky places, this is he who hears the word and immediately with joy receives it; [21]yet he has no root in himself, but endures for a while. When oppression or persecution arises because of the word, immediately he stumbles.[c] [22]What was sown among the thorns, this is he who hears the word, but the cares of this age and the deceitfulness of riches choke the

[z] Q. 14:7; 47:17

[a] see footnote

[b] Q. 7:179; 8:22

[c] Q. 22:11

---

* [a] Q. 16:108; 17:72; 18:101 24:37; 29:43

word,[d] and he becomes unfruitful.

[d] Q. 63:9

23 What was sown on the good ground, this is he who hears the word and understands it, who most certainly bears fruit and produces, some one hundred times as much,[e] some sixty, and some thirty."

[e] Q. 2:261

24 He set another parable before them, saying, "The Kingdom of Heaven is like a man who sowed good seed in his field, 25 but while people slept, his enemy came and sowed darnel weeds[*] also among the wheat, and went away. 26 But when the blade sprang up and produced grain, then the darnel weeds appeared also. 27 The servants of the householder came and said to him, 'Sir, didn't you sow good seed in your field? Where did these darnel weeds come from?' 28 "He said to them, 'An enemy has done this.' "The servants asked him, 'Do you want us to go and gather them up?' 29 "But he said, 'No, lest perhaps while you gather up the darnel weeds, you root up the wheat with them. 30 Let both grow together until the harvest, and in the harvest time I will tell the reapers, "First, gather up the darnel weeds, and bind them in bundles to burn them; but gather the wheat into my barn.' "

31 He set another parable before them, saying, "The Kingdom of Heaven is like a grain of mustard seed[f] which a man took, and sowed in his field, 32 which indeed is smaller than all seeds. But when it is grown, it is greater than the herbs and becomes a tree, so that the birds of the air come and lodge in its branches."

[f] Q. 21:47

33 He spoke another parable to them. "The Kingdom of Heaven is like yeast which a woman took and hid in three measures[†] of meal, until it was all leavened."

34 Jesus spoke all these things in parables to the multitudes; and without a parable, he didn't speak to them,

---

[*] 13:25 darnel is a weed grass (probably bearded darnel or lolium temulentum) that looks very much like wheat until it is mature, when the difference becomes very apparent

[†] 13:33 literally, three sata. Three sata is about 39 liters or a bit more than a bushel

³⁵That it might be fulfilled which was spoken through the prophet, saying,

"I will open my mouth in parables;^g
I will utter things hidden from the foundation of the world."[*]

³⁶Then Jesus sent the multitudes away, and went into the house. His disciples came to him, saying, "Explain to us the parable of the darnel weeds of the field." ³⁷He answered them, "He who sows the good seed is the Son of Man, ³⁸the field is the world, the good seeds are the children of the Kingdom, and the darnel weeds are the children of the evil one. ³⁹The enemy who sowed them is the devil. The harvest is the end of the age, and the reapers are angels.^h ⁴⁰As therefore the darnel weeds are gathered up and burned with fire; so will it be at the end of this age. ⁴¹The Son of Man will send out his angels, and they will gather out of his Kingdom all things that cause stumbling and those who do iniquity,ⁱ ⁴²and will cast them into the furnace of fire.^{j†} There will be weeping and gnashing of teeth. ⁴³Then the righteous will shine^k like the sun in the Kingdom of their Father. He who has ears to hear, let him hear.

h Q.
21:103

i Q.
77:4

j see
footnote

k Q.
10:67;
13:43

⁴⁴"Again, the Kingdom of Heaven is like treasure hidden in the field, which a man found and hid. In his joy, he goes and sells all that he has and buys that field.

⁴⁵"Again, the Kingdom of Heaven is like a man who is a merchant seeking fine pearls, ⁴⁶who having found one pearl of great price, he went and sold all that he had and bought it.

⁴⁷"Again, the Kingdom of Heaven is like a dragnet that was cast into the sea and gathered some fish of every kind, ⁴⁸which, when it was filled, fishermen drew up on the beach. They sat down and gathered the good into

---

[*] 13:35 Psalm 78:2
^{† j} Q. 2:196; 3:11; 8:13; 13:6; 40:3; 59:4

containers, but the bad they threw away. ⁴⁹So it will be in the end of the world. The angels will come and separate the wicked from among the righteous, ⁵⁰and will cast them into the furnace of fire.^l There will be weeping and gnashing of teeth."

⁵¹Jesus said to them, "Have you understood all these things?" They answered him, "Yes, Lord." He said to them, "Therefore every scribe who has been made a discile in the Kingdom of Heaven is like a man who is a householder, who brings out of his treasure new and old things."

⁵³When Jesus had finished these parables, he departed from there. ⁵⁴Coming into his own country, he taught them in their synagogue, so that they were astonished and said, "Where did this man get this wisdom and these mighty works? ⁵⁵Isn't this the carpenter's son? Isn't his mother called Mary, and his brothers James, Joseph, Simon, and Judas? ⁵⁶Aren't all of his sisters with us? Where then did this man get all of these things?"^m ⁵⁷They were offended by him. But Jesus said to them, "A prophet is not without honor, except in his own country and in his own house." ⁵⁸He didn't do many mighty works there because of their unbelief.

14^{n*}

¹At that time, Herod the tetrarch heard the report concerning Jesus, ²and said to his servants, "This is John the Baptizer. He is risen from the dead.^o That is why these powers work in him." ³For Herod had arrested John, bound him, and put him in prison for the sake of Herodias, his brother Philip's wife. ⁴For John said to him, "It is not lawful for you to have her." ⁵When he would have put him to death, he feared the multitude, because they counted him as a prophet. ⁶But when Herod's birthday came, the

---

^{* n} Q. 2:87; 3:49, 52; 5:110, 112; 19:30; 43:63

Margin notes:
^l Q. 3:11; 8:13; 40:3; 59:4
^m Q. 22:17
ⁿ see footnote
^o Q. 19:15

daughter of Herodias danced among them and pleased Herod. ⁷Therefore he promised with an oath to give her whatever she should ask. ⁸She, being prompted by her mother, said, "Give me here on a platter the head of John the Baptizer." ⁹The king was grieved, but for the sake of his oaths and of those who sat at the table with him, he commanded it to be given, ¹⁰and he sent and beheaded[p] John in the prison. ¹¹His head was brought on a platter and given to the young lady; and she brought it to her mother. ¹²His disciples came, took the body, and buried it. Then they went and told Jesus.

¹³Now when Jesus heard this, he withdrew from there in a boat to a deserted place apart. When the multitudes heard it, they followed him on foot from the cities. ¹⁴Jesus went out, and he saw a great multitude. He had compassion on them and healed their sick.[q] ¹⁵When evening had come, his disciples came to him, saying, "This place is deserted, and the hour is already late. Send the multitudes away, that they may go into the villages, and buy themselves food." ¹⁶But Jesus said to them, "They don't need to go away. You give them something to eat." ¹⁷They told him, "We only have here five loaves and two fish." ¹⁸He said, "Bring them here to me." ¹⁹He commanded the multitudes to sit down on the grass; and he took the five loaves and the two fish, and looking up to heaven, he blessed,[r] broke and gave the loaves to the disciples; and the disciples gave to the multitudes. ²⁰They all ate and were filled. They took up twelve baskets full of that which remained left over from the broken pieces. ²¹Those who ate were about five thousand men, in addition to women and children.

²²Immediately Jesus made the disciples get into the boat and go ahead of him to the other side, while he sent the multitudes away. ²³After he had sent the multitudes away, he went up into the mountain by himself to pray. When evening had come, he was there alone. ²⁴But the boat was

[p] Q. 19:15

[q] Q. 3:49; 5:112

[r] Q. 5:114

now in the middle of the sea, distressed by the waves, for the wind was contrary. ²⁵In the fourth watch of the night, Jesus came to them, walking on the sea. ²⁶When the disciples saw him walking on the sea, they were troubled, saying, "It's a ghost!" and they cried out for fear. ²⁷But immediately Jesus spoke to them, saying, "Cheer up! It is I! Don't be afraid." ²⁸Peter answered him and said, "Lord, if it is you, command me to come to you on the waters." ²⁹He said, "Come!" Peter stepped down from the boat and walked on the waters to come to Jesus. ³⁰But when he saw that the wind was strong, he was afraid, and beginning to sink, he cried out, saying, "Lord, save me!" ³¹Immediately Jesus stretched out his hand, took hold of him, and said to him, "You of little faith, why did you doubt?" ³²When they got up into the boat, the wind ceased. ³³Those who were in the boat came and worshiped him, saying, "You are truly the Son of God!"

³⁴When they had crossed over, they came to the land of Gennesaret. ³⁵When the people of that place recognized him, they sent into all that surrounding region and brought to him all who were sick; ³⁶and they begged him that they might just touch the fringe of his garment. As many as touched it were made whole.

15ˢ*

ˢ see footnote

¹Then Pharisees and scribes came to Jesus from Jerusalem, saying, ²"Why do your disciples disobey the tradition of the elders? For they don't wash their hands when they eat bread." ³He answered them, "Why do you also disobey the commandment of God because of your tradition? ⁴For God commanded, 'Honor your father and your mother,'†† and, 'He who speaks evil of father or

ᵗ Q. 2:177

---

* ˢ Q. 2:87; 3:49, 52; 5:110, 112; 19:30; 43:63
†15:4 Exodus 20:12; Deuteronomy 5:16

mother, let him be put to death.'* But you say, 'Whoever may tell his father or his mother, "Whatever help you might otherwise have gotten from me is a gift devoted to God," [6]he shall not honor his father or mother.' You have made the commandment of God void because of your tradition. [7]You hypocrites! Well did Isaiah prophesy of you, saying,

> [8]'These people draw near to me with their mouth, and honor me with their lips; but their heart is far from me.
> [9]And they worship me in vain, teaching as doctrine rules made by men.' "†

[10]He summoned the multitude, and said to them, "Hear, and understand. [11]That which enters into the mouth doesn't defile the man; but that which proceeds out of the mouth, this defiles the man." [12]Then the disciples came and said to him, "Do you know that the Pharisees were offended when they heard this saying?" [13]But he answered, "Every plant which my heavenly Father didn't plant will be uprooted.[u] [14]Leave them alone. They are blind[v] guides of the blind. If the blind guide the blind, both will fall into a pit." [15]Peter answered him, "Explain the parable to us." [16]So Jesus said, "Do you also still not understand? [17]Don't you understand that whatever goes into the mouth passes into the belly and then out of the body? [18]But the things which proceed out of the mouth come out of the heart, and they defile the man. [19]For out of the heart come evil thoughts, murders, adulteries, sexual sins, thefts, false testimony, and blasphemies.[w]‡ [20]These are the things which defile the man; but to eat with unwashed hands doesn't defile the man."

[21]Jesus went out from there and withdrew into the region of Tyre and Sidon. [22]Behold, a Canaanite woman

[u] Q. 14:26

[v] Q. 2:171; 42:48

[w] see footnote

---

* 15:4 Exodus 21:17; Leviticus 20:9

† 15:9 Isaiah 29:13

‡ [w] Q. 10:44; 12:53; 14:34; 16:61; 17:67; 22:66; 29:40; 33:72; 43:15; 80:42; 91:8; 103:2

36

came out from those borders and cried, saying, "Have mercy on me, Lord, you son of David! My daughter is severely possessed by a demon!" ²³But he answered her not a word. His disciples came and begged him, saying, "Send her away; for she cries after us." ²⁴But he answered, "I wasn't sent to anyone but the lost sheep of the house of Israel." ²⁵But she came and worshiped him, saying, "Lord, help me." ²⁶But he answered, "It is not appropriate to take the children's bread and throw it to the dogs." ²⁷But she said, "Yes, Lord, but even the dogs eat the crumbs which fall from their masters' table." ²⁸Then Jesus answered her, "Woman, great is your faith! Be it done to you even as you desire." And her daughter was healed˟ from that hour.

˟ Q. 3:49

²⁹Jesus departed from there and came near to the sea of Galilee; and he went up on the mountain and sat there. ³⁰Great multitudes came to him, having with them the lame, blind, mute, maimed, and many others, and they put them down at his feet. He healed them, ³¹so that the multitude wondered when they saw the mute speaking, the injured healed, the lame walking, and the blind seeing. And they glorified the God of Israel.

³²Jesus summoned his disciples and said, "I have compassion on the multitude, because they have continued with me now three days and have nothing to eat. I don't want to send them away fasting, or they might faint on the way." ³³The disciples said to him, "Where could we get so many loaves in a deserted place as to satisfy so great a multitude?"ʸ ³⁴Jesus said to them, "How many loaves do you have?" They said, "Seven, and a few small fish." ³⁵He commanded the multitude to sit down on the ground; ³⁶and he took the seven loaves and the fish. He gave thanksᶻ and broke them, and gave to the disciples, and the disciples to the multitudes. ³⁷They all ate and were filled. They took up seven baskets full of the broken pieces that were left over. ³⁸Those who ate were four thousand men, in addition to women and children. ³⁹Then he sent away

ʸ Q. 5:112

ᶻ Q. 5:11

the multitudes, got into the boat, and came into the borders of Magdala.

16

¹The Pharisees and Sadducees came, and testing him, asked him to show them a sign from heaven.ᵃ ²But he answered them, "When it is evening, you say, 'It will be fair weather, for the sky is red.' ³In the morning, 'It will be foul weather today, for the sky is red and threatening.' Hypocrites! You know how to discern the appearance of the sky, but you can't discern the signs of the times! ⁴An evil and adulterous generation seeks after a sign, and there will be no sign given to it, except the sign of the prophet Jonah." He left them and departed.

⁵The disciples came to the other side and had forgotten to take bread. ⁶Jesus said to them, "Take heed and beware of the yeast of the Pharisees and Sadducees." They reasoned among themselves, saying, "We brought no bread." Jesus, perceiving it, said, "Why do you reason among yourselves, you of little faith, because you have brought no bread? ⁹Don't you yet perceive or remember the five loaves for the five thousand, and how many baskets you took up, ¹⁰or the seven loaves for the four thousand, and how many baskets you took up? ¹¹How is it that you don't perceive that I didn't speak to you concerning bread? But beware of the yeast of the Pharisees and Sadducees." ¹²Then they understood that he didn't tell them to beware of the yeast of bread, but of the teaching of the Pharisees and Sadducees.

¹³Now when Jesus came into the parts of Caesarea Philippi, he asked his disciples, saying, "Who do men say that I, the Son of Man, am?" ¹⁴They said, "Some say John the Baptizer, some, Elijah, and others, Jeremiah or one of the prophets."ᵇ ¹⁵He said to them, "But who do you say that I am?" ¹⁶Simon Peter answered, "You are the Christ, the Son of the living God." ¹⁷Jesus answered him, "Blessed are you,

ᵃ Q. 13:7

ᵇ Q. 3:49

Simon Bar Jonah, for flesh and blood has not revealed this to you, but my Father who is in heaven. [18]I also tell you that you are Peter,[*] and on this rock [†] I will build my assembly, and the gates of Hades[‡] will not prevail against it. [19]I will give to you the keys of the Kingdom of Heaven,[c] and whatever you bind on earth will have been bound in heaven; and whatever you release on earth will have been released in heaven."[d] [20]Then he commanded the disciples that they should tell no one that he was Jesus the Christ.

[21]From that time, Jesus began to show his disciples that he must go to Jerusalem and suffer many things from the elders, chief priests, and scribes, and be killed, and the third day be raised up. [22]Peter took him aside and began to rebuke him, saying, "Far be it from you, Lord! This will never be done to you." [23]But he turned and said to Peter, "Get behind me, Satan! You are a stumbling block to me, for you are not setting your mind on the things of God, but on the things of men."

[24]Then Jesus said to his disciples, "If anyone desires to come after me, let him deny himself, take up his cross, and follow me. [25]For whoever desires to save his life will lose it, and whoever will lose his life for my sake will find it. [26]For what will it profit a man if he gains the whole world and forfeits his life?[e] Or what will a man give in exchange for his life? [27]For the Son of Man will come in the glory of his Father with his angels, and then he will render to everyone according to his deeds.[f] [28]Most certainly I tell you, there are some standing here who will in no way taste of death until they see the Son of Man coming in his Kingdom."

[c] Q. 39:63

[d] Q. 38:38; 42:12

[e] Q. 3:91; 10:54; 39:15

[f] Q. 3:57; 13:42; 27:90; 45:28

---

[*] 16:18 Peter's name, Petros in Greek, is the word for a specific rock or stone.

[†] 16:18 Greek, petra, a rock mass or bedrock.

[‡] 16:18 or, Hell

17[g]*

[g] see footnote

[1]After six days, Jesus took with him Peter, James, and John his brother, and brought them up into a high mountain by themselves. [2]He was changed before them. His face shone like the sun, and his garments became as white as the light. [3]Behold, Moses and Elijah appeared to them talking with him. [4]Peter answered and said to Jesus, "Lord, it is good for us to be here. If you want, let's make three tents here: one for you, one for Moses, and one for Elijah." [5]While he was still speaking, behold, a bright cloud overshadowed them. Behold, a voice came out of the cloud, saying, "This is my beloved Son, in whom I am well pleased. Listen to him." [6]When the disciples heard it, they fell on their faces, and were very afraid. [7]Jesus came and touched them and said, "Get up, and don't be afraid." [8]Lifting up their eyes, they saw no one, except Jesus alone.

[9]As they were coming down from the mountain, Jesus commanded them, saying, "Don't tell anyone what you saw, until the Son of Man has risen from the dead."[h] [10]His disciples asked him, saying, "Then why do the scribes say that Elijah must come first?" [11]Jesus answered them, "Elijah indeed comes first, and will restore all things; [12]but I tell you that Elijah has come already, and they didn't recognize him, but did to him whatever they wanted to. Even so the Son of Man will also suffer by them." [13]Then the disciples understood that he spoke to them of John the Baptizer.

[h] Q. 12:5

[14]When they came to the multitude, a man came to him, kneeling down to him and saying, [15]"Lord, have mercy on my son, for he is epileptic and suffers grievously; for he often falls into the fire, and often into the water. [16]So I brought him to your disciples, and they could not cure him." [17]Jesus answered, "Faithless and perverse generation! How long will I be with you? How long will I bear with you? Bring him here to me." [18]Jesus rebuked the demon, and it

---

* [g] Q. 2:87; 3:49, 52; 5:110, 112; 19:30; 43:63

i Q.
3:49

j Q.
13:31

went out of him, and the boy was cured[i] from that hour. [19]Then the disciples came to Jesus privately, and said, "Why weren't we able to cast it out?" [20]He said to them, "Because of your unbelief. For most certainly I tell you, if you have faith as a grain of mustard seed, you will tell this mountain, 'Move from here to there,' and it will move[j]; and nothing will be impossible for you. [21]But this kind doesn't go out except by prayer and fasting."[*]

[22]While they were staying in Galilee, Jesus said to them, "The Son of Man is about to be delivered up into the hands of men, [23]and they will kill him, and the third day he will be raised up." They were exceedingly sorry.

[24]When they had come to Capernaum, those who collected the didrachma coins[†] came to Peter, and said, "Doesn't your teacher pay the didrachma?" [25]He said, "Yes." When he came into the house, Jesus anticipated him, saying, "What do you think, Simon? From whom do the kings of the earth receive toll or tribute? From their children, or from strangers?" [26]Peter said to him, "From strangers." Jesus said to him, "Therefore the children are exempt. [27]But, lest we cause them to stumble, go to the sea, cast a hook, and take up the first fish that comes up. When you have opened its mouth, you will find a stater coin.[‡] Take that, and give it to them for me and you."

18

[1]In that hour the disciples came to Jesus, saying, "Who

---

[*] 17:21 NU omits verse 21.

[†] 17:24 A didrachma is a Greek silver coin worth 2 drachmas, about as much as 2 Roman denarii, or about 2 days' wages. It was commonly used to pay the half-shekel temple tax, because 2 drachmas were worth one half shekel of silver. A shekel is about 10 grams or about 0.35 ounces.

[‡] 17:27 A stater is a silver coin equivalent to four Attic or two Alexandrian drachmas, or a Jewish shekel: just exactly enough to cover the half-shekel temple tax for two people. A shekel is about 10 grams or about 0.35 ounces, usually in the form of a silver coin.

then is greatest in the Kingdom of Heaven?" [2]Jesus called a little child to himself, and set him in the middle of them [3]and said, "Most certainly I tell you, unless you turn and become as little children, you will in no way enter into the Kingdom of Heaven. [4]Whoever therefore humbles[k] himself as this little child is the greatest in the Kingdom of Heaven.

[5]Whoever receives one such little child in my name receives me, [6]but whoever causes one of these little ones who believe in me to stumble,[l] it would be better for him if a huge millstone were hung around his neck and that he were sunk in the depths of the sea.

[7]"Woe to the world because of occasions of stumbling! For it must be that the occasions come, but woe to that person through whom the occasion comes! [8]If your hand or your foot causes you to stumble, cut it off and cast it from you. It is better for you to enter into life maimed or crippled, rather than having two hands or two feet to be cast into the eternal fire. [9]If your eye causes you to stumble, pluck it out and cast it from you. It is better for you to enter into life with one eye, rather than having two eyes to be cast into the Gehenna[*] of fire.

[10]See that you don't despise one of these little ones, for I tell you that in heaven their angels always see the face of my Father who is in heaven. [11]For the Son of Man came to save that which was lost.[†] [12]"What do you think? If a man has one hundred sheep, and one of them goes astray, doesn't he leave the ninety- nine, go to the mountains, and seek that which has gone astray? [13]If he finds it, most certainly I tell you, he rejoices over it more than over the ninety-nine which have not gone astray. [14]Even so it is not the will of your Father who is in heaven that one of these little ones should perish.[m]

[15]"If your brother sins against you, go, show him his fault between you and him alone. If he listens to you, you

[k] Q. 11:23

[l] Q. 2:54

[m] Q. 10:4

---

[*] 18:9 or, Hell
[†] 18:11 NU omits verse 11.

have gained back your brother. [16]But if he doesn't listen, take one or two more with you, that at the mouth of two or three witnesses every word may be established.[n][*] [17]If he refuses to listen to them, tell it to the assembly. If he refuses to hear the assembly also, let him be to you as a Gentile or a tax collector. [18]Most certainly I tell you, whatever things you bind[o] on earth will have been bound in heaven, and whatever things you release on earth will have been released in heaven. [19]Again, assuredly I tell you, that if two of you will agree on earth concerning anything that they will ask, it will be done for them by my Father who is in heaven. [20]For where two or three are gathered together in my name, there I am in the middle of them."[p]

[21]Then Peter came and said to him, "Lord, how often shall my brother sin against me, and I forgive him? Until seven times?" [22]Jesus said to him, "I don't tell you until seven times, but, until seventy times seven.[q]

[23]Therefore the Kingdom of Heaven is like a certain king who wanted to settle accounts[r] with his servants. [24]When he had begun to settle, one was brought to him who owed him ten thousand talents. [25]But because he couldn't pay, his lord commanded him to be sold, with his wife, his children, and all that he had, and payment to be made. [26]The servant therefore fell down and knelt before him, saying, 'Lord, have patience with me, and I will repay you all!' [27]The lord of that servant, being moved with compassion, released him and forgave him the debt. [28]"But that servant went out and found one of his fellow servants who owed him one hundred denarii, and he grabbed him and took him by the throat, saying, 'Pay me what you owe!' [29]"So his fellow servant fell down at his feet and begged him, saying, 'Have patience with me, and I will repay you!' [30]He would not, but went and cast him into

[n] Q. 49:9

[o] Q. 38:38; 89:26

[p] Q. 58:7

[q] Q. 43:89

[r] Q. 55:31

---

[*] 18:16 Deuteronomy 19:15

prison until he should pay back that which was due. [31]So when his fellow servants saw what was done, they were exceedingly sorry, and came and told their lord all that was done. [32]Then his lord called him in and said to him, 'You wicked servant! I forgave you all that debt because you begged me. [33]Shouldn't you also have had mercy on your fellow servant, even as I had mercy on you?' [34]His lord was angry, and delivered him to the tormentors until he should pay all that was due to him. [35]So my heavenly Father will also do to you, if you don't each forgive your brother from your hearts for his misdeeds.[s]*"

[s] see footnote

19

[1]When Jesus had finished these words, he departed from Galilee and came into the borders of Judea beyond the Jordan. [2]Great multitudes followed him, and he healed[t] them there.

[3]Pharisees came to him, testing him[u] and saying, "Is it lawful for a man to divorce his wife for any reason?" He answered, "Haven't you read that he who made them from the beginning made them male and female,[†] [5]and said, 'For this cause a man shall leave his father and mother, and shall be joined to his wife; and the two shall become one flesh?'[‡] [6]So that they are no more two, but one flesh. What therefore God has joined together, don't let man tear apart." [7]They asked him, "Why then did Moses command us to give her a certificate of divorce and divorce her?" [8]He

[t] Q. 3:49

[u] Q. 43:63

---

* [s] Q. 2:7; 3:4; 4:14; 5:18; 6:15; 7:38; 8:14; 9:3; 11:4; 12:107; 13:34; 14:2; 15:50;
16:63; 17:11; 18:55; 20:61; 22:2; 24:19; 25:19; 26:135; 27:5; 29:23; 30:16; 31:6; 32:14; 33:8; 34:5, 21; 35:7; 37:9; 38:8; 39:13; 40:7; 41:16; 42:16; 43:39; 44:57; 45:8; 46:18; 48:6; 50:26; 51:37; 52:7; 57:20; 58:4; 59:3; 61:10; 64:5 65:10; 67:5; 68:33; 70:1; 71:1; 72:17; 73:13; 76:31; 78:30; 84:24; 85:10; 88:24
[†] 19:4 Genesis 1:27
[‡] 19:5 Genesis 2:24

said to them, "Moses, because of the hardness of your hearts, allowed you to divorce your wives, but from the beginning it has not been so. 9I tell you that whoever divorces[v] his wife, except for sexual immorality, and marries another, commits adultery; and he who marries her when she is divorced commits adultery."

[v] Q. 65:1

10His disciples said to him, "If this is the case of the man with his wife, it is not expedient to marry." 11But he said to them, "Not all men can receive this saying, but those to whom it is given. 12For there are eunuchs who were born that way from their mother's womb, and there are eunuchs who were made eunuchs by men; and there are eunuchs who made themselves eunuchs for the Kingdom of Heaven's sake. He who is able to receive it, let him receive it."

13Then little children were brought to him that he should lay his hands on them and pray; and the disciples rebuked them. 14But Jesus said, "Allow the little children, and don't forbid them to come to me; for the Kingdom of Heaven belongs to ones like these." 15He laid his hands on them, and departed from there.

16Behold, one came to him and said, "Good teacher, what good thing shall I do, that I may have eternal[w] life?" 17He said to him, "Why do you call me good?[*] No one is good but one, that is, God. But if you want to enter into life, keep the commandments."[x] 18He said to him, "Which ones?" Jesus said, 'You shall not murder.' 'You shall not commit adultery.' 'You shall not steal.' 'You shall not offer false testimony.' 19'Honor your father and your mother.'[†] And, 'You shall love your neighbor as yourself.' "[‡] 20The young man said to him, "All these things I have observed from my youth. What do I still lack?" 21Jesus said to him, "If you want to be

[w] Q. 22:6

[x] Q. 65:1

---

[*] 19:17 So MT and TR. NU reads "Why do you ask me about what is good?"
[†] 19:19 Exodus 20:12-16; Deuteronomy 5:16-20
[‡] 19:19 Leviticus 19:18

perfect, go, sell what you have, and give to the poor,^y and you will have treasure in heaven; and come, follow me." ²²But when the young man heard this, he went away sad, for he was one who had great possessions.

²³Jesus said to his disciples, "Most certainly I say to you, a rich man will enter into the Kingdom of Heaven with difficulty. ²⁴Again I tell you, it is easier for a camel to go through a needle's eye^z than for a rich man to enter into God's Kingdom." ²⁵When the disciples heard it, they were exceedingly astonished, saying, "Who then can be saved?" ²⁶Looking at them, Jesus said, "With men this is impossible, but with God all things are possible."^{a*} ²⁷Then Peter answered, "Behold, we have left everything and followed you. What then will we have?" ²⁸Jesus said to them, "Most certainly I tell you that you who have followed me, in the regeneration when the Son of Man will sit on the throne of his glory, you also will sit on twelve thrones,^b judging the twelve tribes of Israel. ²⁹Everyone who has left houses, or brothers, or sisters, or father, or mother, or wife, or children, or lands, for my name's sake, will receive one hundred times,^c and will inherit eternal life. ³⁰But many will be last who are first, and first who are last.

20^d

¹"For the Kingdom of Heaven is like a man who was the master of a household, who went out early in the morning to hire laborers for his vineyard. ²When he had agreed with the laborers for a denarius a day, he sent them into his vineyard. ³He went out about the third hour, and saw others standing idle in the marketplace. ⁴He said to them, 'You also go into the vineyard, and whatever is right I will

^y Q. 2:177; 3:92

^z Q. 7:40

^a see footnote

^b Q. 18:31; 28:84

^c Q. 50:35; 61:13

^d Q. 3:49; 5:110, 112; 19:30

---

^{*a} Q. 2:20. 106, 109. 148, 259, 284; 3:26; 5:17, 19; 6:17; 8:41; 11:4; 16:77; 18:45; 24:45; 29:20; 30:50; 33:27; 35:1; 41:39; 42:9; 46:33; 48:21; 57:2; 64:1; 65:12; 66:8; 67:1

46

give you.' ⁵So they went their way. Again he went out about the sixth and the ninth hour, and did likewise. ⁶About the eleventh hour he went out and found others standing idle. He said to them, 'Why do you stand here all day idle?' ⁷"They said to him, 'Because no one has hired us.' "He said to them, 'You also go into the vineyard, and you will receive whatever is right.' ⁸"When evening had come, the lord of the vineyard said to his manager, 'Call the laborers and pay them their wages, beginning from the last to the first.' ⁹"When those who were hired at about the eleventh hour came, they each received a denarius. ¹⁰When the first came, they supposed that they would receive more; and they likewise each received a denarius. ¹¹When they received it, they murmured against the master of the household, ¹²saying, 'These last have spent one hour, and you have made them equal to us who have borne the burden of the day and the scorching heat!ᵉ' ¹³"But he answered one of them, 'Friend, I am doing you no wrong. Didn't you agree with me for a denarius? ¹⁴Take that which is yours, and go your way. It is my desire to give to this last just as much as to you. ¹⁵Isn't it lawful for me to do what I want to with what I own? Or is your eye evil, because I am good?' ¹⁶So the last will be first, and the first last. For many are called, but few are chosen.'"

ᵉ Q. 113:5

¹⁷As Jesus was going up to Jerusalem, he took the twelve disciples aside, and on the way he said to them, ¹⁸"Behold, we are going up to Jerusalem, and the Son of Man will be delivered to the chief priests and scribes, and they will condemn him to death, ¹⁹and will hand him over to the Gentiles to mock, to scourge, and to crucifyᶠ* and the third day he will be raised up."

ᶠ see footnote

²⁰Then the mother of the sons of Zebedee came to him with her sons, kneeling and asking a certain thing of him. ²¹He said to her, "What do you want?" She said to him,

---

*ᶠ Q. 4:157; 6:10; 13:32; 15:11; 21:41; 36:30; 43:7

"Command that these, my two sons, may sit, one on your right hand and one on your left hand, in your Kingdom." ²²But Jesus answered, "You don't know what you are asking. Are you able to drink the cup that I am about to drink, and be baptized with the baptism that I am baptized with?" They said to him, "We are able." ²³He said to them, "You will indeed drink my cup, and be baptized with the baptism that I am baptized with; but to sit on my right hand and on my left hand is not mine to give, but it is for whom it has been prepared by my Father." ²⁴When the ten heard it, they were indignant with the two brothers. ²⁵But Jesus summoned them, and said, "You know that the rulers of the nations lord it over them, and their great ones exercise authority over them. ²⁶It shall not be so among you; but whoever desires to become great among you shall be[*] your servant. ²⁷Whoever desires to be first among you shall be your bondservant, ²⁸even as the Son of Man came not to be served, but to serve, and to give his life as a ransom for many."

²⁹As they went out from Jericho, a great multitude followed him. ³⁰Behold, two blind men sitting by the road, when they heard that Jesus was passing by, cried out, "Lord, have mercy on us, you son of David!" ³¹The multitude rebuked them, telling them that they should be quiet, but they cried out even more, "Lord, have mercy on us, you son of David!" ³²Jesus stood still and called them, and asked, "What do you want me to do for you?" ³³They told him, "Lord, that our eyes may be opened." ³⁴Jesus, being moved with compassion, touched their eyes; and immediately their eyes received their sight, and they followed him.

---

[*] 20:26 TR reads "let him be" instead of "shall be"

21^g

¹When they came near to Jerusalem and came to Bethsphage,[*] to the Mount of Olives, then Jesus sent two disciples, ²saying to them, "Go into the village that is opposite you, and immediately you will find a donkey tied, and a colt with her. Untie them and bring them to me. ³If anyone says anything to you, you shall say, 'The Lord needs them,' and immediately he will send them." ⁴All this was done that it might be fulfilled which was spoken through the prophet, saying,

⁵"Tell the daughter of Zion,

behold, your King comes to you, humble, and riding

on a donkey, on a colt, the foal of a donkey."[†]

⁶The disciples went and did just as Jesus commanded them, ⁷and brought the donkey and the colt and laid their clothes on them; and he sat on them. ⁸A very great multitude spread their clothes on the road. Others cut branches from the trees and spread them on the road. ⁹The multitudes who went in front of him, and those who followed, kept shouting, "Hosanna[‡] to the son of David! Blessed is he who comes in the name of the Lord! Hosanna in the highest!" [§] ¹⁰When he had come into Jerusalem, all the city was stirred up, saying, "Who is this?" ¹¹The multitudes said, "This is the prophet,^h Jesus, from Nazareth of Galilee."

¹²Jesus entered into the temple of God and drove out all of those who sold and bought in the temple, and overthrew the money changers' tables and the seats of those who sold the doves. ¹³He said to them, "It is written, 'My house shall be called a house of prayer,'^{**} but you have made it a den

---

[*] 21:1 TR & NU read "Bethphage" instead of "Bethsphage"

[†] 21:5 Zechariah 9:9

[‡] 21:9 "Hosanna" means "save us" or "help us, we pray".

[§] 21:9 Psalm 118:26

^{**}21:13 Isaiah 56:7

of robbers!"*

¹⁴The lame and the blind came to him in the temple, and he healedⁱ them. ¹⁵But when the chief priests and the scribes saw the wonderful things that he did, and the children who were crying in the temple and saying, "Hosanna to the son of David!" they were indignant, ¹⁶and said to him, "Do you hear what these are saying?" Jesus said to them, "Yes. Did you never read,

'Out of the mouth of children and nursing babies, you have perfected praise?' "[†]

¹⁷He left them and went out of the city to Bethany, and camped there.

¹⁸Now in the morning, as he returned to the city, he was hungry. ¹⁹Seeing a fig tree by the road, he came to it and found nothing on it but leaves. He said to it, "Let there be no fruit from you forever!" Immediately the fig tree withered away.

²⁰When the disciples saw it, they marveled, saying, "How did the fig tree immediately wither away?" ²¹Jesus answered them, "Most certainly I tell you, if you have faith and don't doubt, you will not only do what was done to the fig tree, but even if you told this mountain,^j 'Be taken up and cast into the sea,' it would be done. ²²All things, whatever you ask in prayer, believing, you will receive."

²³When he had come into the temple, the chief priests and the elders of the people came to him as he was teaching, and said, "By what authority do you do these things? Who gave you this authority?" ²⁴Jesus answered them, "I also will ask you one question, which if you tell me, I likewise will tell you by what authority I do these things. ²⁵The baptism of John, where was it from? From heaven or from men?" They reasoned with themselves, saying, "If we say, 'From heaven,' he will ask us, 'Why

i Q. 3:49

j Q. 13:31; 14:46

* 21:13 Jeremiah 7:11
† 21:16 Psalm 8:2

then did you not believe him?' [26]But if we say, 'From men,' we fear the multitude, for all hold John as a prophet." [27]They answered Jesus, and said, "We don't know." He also said to them, "Neither will I tell you by what authority I do these things.

[28]But what do you think? A man had two sons, and he came to the first, and said, 'Son, go work today in my vineyard.' [29]He answered, 'I will not,' but afterward he changed his mind, and went. [30]He came to the second, and said the same thing. He answered, 'I'm going, sir,' but he didn't go. [31]Which of the two did the will of his father?" They said to him, "The first." Jesus said to them, "Most certainly I tell you that the tax collectors and the prostitutes are entering into God's Kingdom before you. [32]For John came to you in the way of righteousness, and you didn't believe him; but the tax collectors and the prostitutes believed him. When you saw it, you didn't even repent afterward, that you might believe him.

[33]"Hear another parable. There was a man who was a master of a household who planted a vineyard, set a hedge about it, dug a wine press in it, built a tower, leased it out to farmers, and went into another country. [34]When the season for the fruit came near, he sent his servants to the farmers to receive his fruit. [35]The farmers took his servants, beat one, killed another, and stoned another. [36]Again, he sent other servants more than the first; and they treated them the same way. [37]But afterward he sent to them his son, saying, 'They will respect my son.' [38]But the farmers, when they saw the son, said among themselves, 'This is the heir. Come, let's kill him and seize his inheritance.' [39]So they took him and threw him out of the vineyard, then killed him. [40]When therefore the lord of the vineyard comes, what will he do to those farmers?"

[k] Q.
6:15

[41]They told him, "He will miserably destroy[k] those miserable men, and will lease out the vineyard to other farmers who will give him the fruit in its season."

[42]Jesus said to them, "Did you never read in the Scriptures,

'The stone which the builders rejected[l] was made the head of the corner.

This was from the Lord.

It is marvelous in our eyes'?

[43]"Therefore I tell you, God's Kingdom will be taken away from you and will be given to a nation producing its fruit.[m]* [44]He who falls on this stone will be broken to pieces, but on whomever it will fall, it will scatter him as dust."

[45]When the chief priests and the Pharisees heard his parables, they perceived that he spoke about them. [46]When they sought to seize him, they feared the multitudes, because they considered him to be a prophet.[n]

[l] Q. 23:44

[m] see footnote

[n] Q. 4:14; 22:17

22

[1]Jesus answered and spoke to them again in parables, saying, [2]"The Kingdom of Heaven is like a certain king, who made a wedding feast for his son, [3]and sent out his servants to call those who were invited to the wedding feast, but they would not come. [4]Again he sent out other servants, saying, 'Tell those who are invited, "Behold, I have prepared my dinner. My cattle and my fatlings are killed, and all things are ready. Come to the wedding feast!"' [5]But they made light of it, and went their ways, one to his own farm, another to his merchandise; [6]and the rest grabbed his servants, treated them shamefully, and killed them. [7]When the king heard that, he was angry, and sent his armies, destroyed those murderers, and burned their city. [8]"Then he said to his servants, 'The wedding is ready, but those who were invited weren't worthy. [9]Go therefore to the intersections of the highways, and as many as you may find, invite to

---

* [m] Q. 4:133; 5:54; 6:89; 9:39; 47:38; 56:61; 70:41

the wedding feast.' [10]Those servants went out into the highways and gathered together as many as they found, both bad and good. The wedding was filled with guests. [11]"But when the king came in to see the guests, he saw there a man who didn't have on wedding clothing, [12]and he said to him, 'Friend, how did you come in here not wearing wedding clothing?' He was speechless. [13]Then the king said to the servants, 'Bind him hand and foot, take him away, and throw him into the outer darkness. That is where the weeping and grinding of teeth will be.'[o]* ' [14]For many are called, but few chosen.'"[p]

[o] see footnote

[p] Q. 3:82; 17:62

[15]Then the Pharisees went and took counsel how they might entrap him in his talk. [16]They sent their disciples to him, along with the Herodians, saying, "Teacher, we know that you are honest, and teach the way of God in truth, no matter whom you teach; for you aren't partial to anyone. [17]Tell us therefore, what do you think? Is it lawful to pay taxes to Caesar, or not?" [18]But Jesus perceived their wickedness, and said, "Why do you test me, you hypocrites? [19]Show me the tax money." They brought to him a denarius. [20]He asked them, "Whose is this image and inscription?" [21]They said to him, "Caesar's." Then he said to them, "Give therefore to Caesar the things that are Caesar's, and to God the things that are God's." [22]When they heard it, they marveled, and left him and went away.

[23]On that day Sadducees (those who say that there is no resurrection) came to him. They asked him, [24]saying, "Teacher, Moses said, 'If a man dies, having no children, his brother shall marry his wife and raise up offspring[†] for his brother.' [25]Now there were with us seven brothers. The first married and died, and having no offspring left his wife to his brother. [26]In the same way, the second also, and the third, to the seventh. [27]After them all, the woman died.

---

* [o] Q. 2:196; 3:11; 8:13; 10:27; 13:6; 24:40; 40:3; 59:4
† 22:24 or, seed

²⁸In the resurrection therefore, whose wife will she be of the seven? For they all had her."

²⁹But Jesus answered them, "You are mistaken, not knowing the Scriptures, nor the power of God. ³⁰For in the resurrection they neither marry nor are given in marriage, but are like God's angels in heaven. ³¹But concerning the resurrection of the dead, haven't you read that which was spoken to you by God, saying, ³²I am the God of Abraham, and the God of Isaac, and the God of Jacob?'* God is not the God of the dead, but of the living." ³³When the multitudes heard it, they were astonished at his teaching.

³⁴But the Pharisees, when they heard that he had silenced the Sadducees, gathered themselves together. ³⁵One of them, a lawyer, asked him a question, testing him. ³⁶"Teacher, which is the greatest commandment in the law?" ³⁷Jesus said to him, "'You shall love the Lord your God with all your heart, with all your soul, and with all your mind.'† ³⁸This is the first and great commandment. ³⁹A second likewise is this, 'You shall love your neighbor as yourself.'‡ ⁴⁰The whole law and the prophets depend on these two commandments."

⁴¹Now while the Pharisees were gathered together, Jesus asked them a question, ⁴²saying, "What do you think of the Christ? Whose son is he?" They said to him, "Of David." ⁴³He said to them, "How then does David in the Spirit call him Lord, saying,

⁴⁴'The Lord said to my Lord, sit on my right hand, until I make your enemies a footstool for your feet'?§

⁴⁵"If then David calls him Lord, how is he his son?" ⁴⁶No one was able to answer him a word, neither did any man dare ask him any more questions from that day forward.

---

* 22:32 Exodus 3:6
† 22:37 Deuteronomy 6:5
‡ 22:39 Leviticus 19:18
§ 22:44 Psalm

23�q

q Q.
5:78

r Q.
26:226;
61:2

s Q.
3:64;
9:31;
33:5

t Q.
28:76

u see
footnote

v Q.
58:16

¹Then Jesus spoke to the multitudes and to his disciples, ²saying, "The scribes and the Pharisees sit on Moses' seat. ³All things therefore whatever they tell you to observe, observe and do, but don't do their works; for they say, and don't do.ʳ ⁴For they bind heavy burdens that are grievous to be borne, and lay them on men's shoulders; but they themselves will not lift a finger to help them. ⁵But they do all their works to be seen by men. They make their phylacteries broad and enlarge the fringes of their garments, ⁶and love the place of honor at feasts, the best seats in the synagogues, ⁷the salutations in the marketplaces, and to be called 'Rabbi, Rabbi by men. ⁸But you are not to be called 'Rabbi', for one is your teacher, the Christ, and all of you are brothers. ⁹Call no man on the earth your father, for one is your Father, he who is in heaven.ˢ ¹⁰Neither be called masters, for one is your master, the Christ. ¹¹But he who is greatest among you will be your servant. ¹²Whoever exalts himself will be humbled,ᵗ and whoever humbles himself will be exalted.

¹³"Woe to you, scribes and Pharisees, hypocrites!ᵘ* For you devour widows' houses, and as a pretense you make long prayers. Therefore you will receive greater condemnation. "But woe to you, scribes and Pharisees, hypocrites! Because you shut up the Kingdom of Heaven against men; for you don't enter in yourselves, neither do you allow those who are entering in to enter. ¹⁵Woe to you, scribes and Pharisees, hypocrites! For you travel around by sea and land to make one proselyte; and when he becomes one, you make him twice as much a son of Gehenna† as yourselves.

¹⁶"Woe to you,ᵛ you blind guides, who say, 'Whoever

---

* ᵘ Q. 3:99; 4:55, 160; 7:45; 8:47; 9:9; 11:19; 14:2; 16:88; 22:25; 47:1, 34; 58:16; 63:2; 107:6
† 23:15 or, Hell

swears by the temple, it is nothing; but whoever swears by the gold of the temple, he is obligated.' ¹⁷You blind fools! For which is greater, the gold or the temple that sanctifies the gold? ¹⁸And, 'Whoever swears by the altar, it is nothing; but whoever swears by the gift that is on it, he is obligated?' ¹⁹You blind fools! For which is greater, the gift, or the altar that sanctifies the gift? ²⁰He therefore who swears by the altar, swears by it and by everything on it. ²¹He who swears by the temple, swears by it and by him who has been living* in it. ²²He who swears by heaven, swears by the throne of God and by him who sits on it.

²³"Woe to you, scribes and Pharisees, hypocrites! For you tithe mint, dill, and cumin,† and have left undone the weightier matters of the law: justice, mercy, and faith. But you ought to have done these, and not to have left the other undone. ²⁴You blind guides, who strain out a gnat, and swallow a camel!

²⁵"Woe to you, scribes and Pharisees, hypocrites! For you clean the outside of the cup and of the platter, but within they are full of extortion and unrighteousness.‡ ²⁶You blind Pharisee, first clean the inside of the cup and of the platter, that its outside may become clean also.

²⁷"Woe to you, scribes and Pharisees, hypocrites! For you are like whitened tombs, which outwardly appear beautiful, but inwardly are full of dead men's bones and of all uncleanness. ²⁸Even so you also outwardly appear righteous to men, but inwardly you are full of hypocrisy and iniquity.

²⁹"Woe to you, scribes and Pharisees, hypocrites! For you build the tombs of the prophets and decorate the

---

* 23:21 NU reads "lives"

† 23:23 cumin is an aromatic seed from Cuminum cyminum, resembling caraway in flavor and appearance. It is used as a spice.

‡ 23:25 TR reads "self-indulgence" instead of "unrighteousness"

tombs of the righteous, ³⁰and say, 'If we had lived in the days of our fathers, we wouldn't have been partakers with them in the blood of the prophets.' ³¹Therefore you testify to yourselves that you are children of those who killed the prophets.^w ³²Fill up, then, the measure of your fathers. ³³You serpents, you offspring of vipers, how will you escape the judgment of Gehenna?[*] ³⁴Therefore, behold, I send to you prophets, wise men, and scribe.^x Some of them you will kill and crucify; and some of them you will scourge in your synagogues and persecute from city to city, ³⁵that on you may come all the righteous blood shed on the earth, from the blood of righteous Abel to the blood of Zachariah son of Barachiah, whom you killed between the sanctuary and the altar. ³⁶Most certainly I tell you, all these things will come upon this generation.

³⁷"Jerusalem, Jerusalem, who kills the prophets and stones those who are sent to her!^y How often I would have gathered your children together, even as a hen gathers her chicks under her wings, and you would not! ³⁸Behold, your house is left to you desolate. ³⁹For I tell you, you will not see me from now on, until you say, 'Blessed is he who comes in the name of the Lord!' "[†]

w Q.
2:177;
3:80;
57:26

y Q.
2:61;
3:21;
4:155;
5:70;
57:26

24

¹Jesus went out from the temple, and was going on his way. His disciples came to him to show him the buildings of the temple. ²But he answered them, "You see all of these things, don't you? Most certainly I tell you, there will not be left here one stone on another, that will not be thrown down."

³As he sat on the Mount of Olives, the disciples came to him privately, saying, "Tell us, when will these things be?

---

[*] 23:33 or, Hell
[†] 23:39 Psalm 118:26

What is the sign of your coming, and of the end of the age?"[z] [4]Jesus answered them, "Be careful that no one leads you astray. [5]For many will come in my name, saying, 'I am the Christ,' and will lead many astray. [6]You will hear of wars and rumors of wars. See that you aren't troubled, for all this must happen, but the end is not yet. [7]For nation will rise against nation, and kingdom against kingdom; and there will be famines, plagues, and earthquakes in various places. [8]But all these things are the beginning of birth pains.

[9]"Then they will deliver you up to oppression and will kill you. You will be hated by all of the nations for my name's sake. [10]Then many will stumble, and will deliver up one another, and will hate one another.[a] [11]Many false prophets will arise and will lead many astray.[b] [12]Because iniquity will be multiplied, the love of many will grow cold. [13]But he who endures to the end will be saved.[c] [14]This Good News of the Kingdom will be preached in the whole world for a testimony to all the nations,[d] and then the end will come.

[15]"When, therefore, you see the abomination of desolation,* which was spoken of through Daniel the prophet, standing in the holy place (let the reader understand), [16]then let those who are in Judea flee to the mountains.[e] [17]Let him who is on the housetop not go down to take out the things that are in his house. [18]Let him who is in the field not return back to get his clothes. [19]But woe to those who are with child and to nursing mothers in those days![f] [20]Pray that your flight will not be in the winter nor on a Sabbath,[g] [21]for then there will be great suffering,[h†] such as has not been from the beginning of the world until now, no, nor ever will be. [22]Unless those days had been shortened, no flesh would have been saved. But for the

[z] Q. 47:18

[a] Q. 64:14

[b] Q. 3:82

[c] Q. 16:32; 28:80

[d] Q. 12:96, 101

[e] Q. 17:5, 7

[f] Q. 22:2

[g] Q. 41:35

[h] Q. 17:7

* 24:15 Daniel 9:27; 11:31; 12:11
† 24:21 or, oppression

58

sake of the chosen ones, those days will be shortened. [23]"Then if any man tells you, 'Behold, here is the Christ!' or, 'There!' don't believe it. [24]For false christs and false prophets will arise, and they will show great signs and wonders, so as to lead astray, if possible, even the chosen ones. [25]"Behold, I have told you beforehand. [26]"If therefore they tell you, 'Behold, he is in the wilderness,' don't go out; or 'Behold, he is in the inner rooms,' don't believe it. [27]For as the lightning flashes[i] from the east, and is seen even to the west,[j] so will the coming of the Son of Man be. [28]For wherever the carcass is, that is where the vultures[*] gather together.

[29]"But immediately after the suffering[†] of those days, the sun will be darkened, the moon will not give its light, the stars will fall from the sky,[k] and the powers of the heavens will be shaken;[‡] [30]and then the sign of the Son of Man[l] will appear in the sky. Then all the tribes of the earth will mourn, and they will see the Son of Man coming on the clouds of the sky with power and great glory. [31]He will send out his angels with a great sound of a trumpet, and they will gather together his chosen ones from the four winds, from one end of the sky to the other.

[32]"Now from the fig tree learn this parable: When its branch has now become tender and produces its leaves, you know that the summer is near. [33]Even so you also, when you see all these things, know that he is near, even at the doors. [34]Most certainly I tell you, this generation will not pass away until all these things are accomplished. [35]Heaven and earth will pass away, but my words will not pass away.[m]

[36]"But no one knows of that day and hour, not even the angels of heaven, but my Father only."[n][§] [37]As the days of

[i] Q. 67:26

[j] Q. 73:9

[k] Q. 81:2

[l] Q. 43:61

[m] Q. 11:107; 35:41; 46:3

[n] see footnote

---

[*] 24:28 or, eagles

[†] 24:29 or, oppression

[‡] 24:29 Isaiah 13:10; 34:4

[§] [n] Q. 5:116; 7:187; 27:65; 33:63

Noah were, so will the coming of the Son of Man be. [38]For as in those days which were before the flood they were eating and drinking, marrying and giving in marriage, until the day that Noah entered into the ship, [39]and they didn't know until the flood came and took them all away, so will the coming of the Son of Man be.[o] [40]Then two men will be in the field: one will be taken and one will be left. [41]Two women will be grinding at the mill: one will be taken and one will be left. [42]Watch therefore, for you don't know in what hour your Lord comes. [43]But know this, that if the master of the house had known in what watch of the night the thief was coming, he would have watched, and would not have allowed his house to be broken into. [44]Therefore also be ready, for in an hour that you don't expect, the Son of Man will come.

[o] Q. 15:3

[45]"Who then is the faithful and wise servant, whom his lord has set over his household, to give them their food in due season? [46]Blessed is that servant whom his lord finds doing so when he comes. [47]Most certainly I tell you that he will set him over all that he has. [48]But if that evil servant should say in his heart, 'My lord is delaying his coming,' [49]and begins to beat his fellow servants, and eat and drink with the drunkards, [50]the lord of that servant will come in a day when he doesn't expect it and in an hour when he doesn't know it, [51]and will cut him in pieces and appoint his portion with the hypocrites.[p][*] That is where the weeping and grinding of teeth will be.

[p] see footnote

25

[1]"Then the Kingdom of Heaven will be like ten virgins who took their lamps and went out to meet the bridegroom. [2]Five of them were foolish, and five were wise. [3]Those who were foolish, when they took their lamps, took no

---

[*][p] Q. 2:196; 3:11; 8:13; 13:6; 40:3; 59:4

q Q.
57:14

r Q.
3:154

s Q.
57:13

t Q.
57:14

u Q.
18:2;
24:55;
70:35

oil with them, [4]but the wise took oil in their vessels with their lamps.[q] [5]Now while the bridegroom delayed, they all slumbered and slept.[r] [6]But at midnight there was a cry, 'Behold! The bridegroom is coming! Come out to meet him!' [7]Then all those virgins arose, and trimmed their lamps. [8]The foolish said to the wise, 'Give us some of your oil, for our lamps are going out.[s]' [9]But the wise answered, saying, 'What if there isn't enough for us and you? You go rather to those who sell, and buy for yourselves.' [10]While they went away to buy, the bridegroom came, and those who were ready went in with him to the wedding feast, and the door was shut. [11]Afterward the other virgins also came, saying, 'Lord, Lord, open to us.'[t] [12]But he answered, 'Most certainly I tell you, I don't know you.' [13]Watch therefore, for you don't know the day nor the hour in which the Son of Man is coming.

[14]"For it is like a man going into another country, who called his own servants and entrusted his goods to them. [15]To one he gave five talents,[*] to another two, to another one, to each according to his own ability. Then he went on his journey. [16]Immediately he who received the five talents went and traded with them, and made another five talents. [17]In the same way, he also who got the two gained another two. [18]But he who received the one talent went away and dug in the earth and hid his lord's money. [19]"Now after a long time the lord of those servants came, and settled accounts with them. [20]He who received the five talents came and brought another five talents, saying, 'Lord, you delivered to me five talents. Behold, I have gained another five talents in addition to them.' [21]"His lord said to him, 'Well done, good and faithful servant. You have been faithful over a few things, I will set you over many things. Enter into the joy of your lord.'[u] [22]"He also who got the two

---

[*] 25:15 A talent is about 30 kilograms or 66 pounds (usually used to weigh silver unless otherwise specified)

talents came and said, 'Lord, you delivered to me two talents. Behold, I have gained another two talents in addition to them.' ²³"His lord said to him, 'Well done, good and faithful servant. You have been faithful over a few things. I will set you over many things. Enter into the joy of your lord.' ²⁴"He also who had received the one talent came and said, 'Lord, I knew you that you are a hard man, reaping where you didn't sow, and gathering where you didn't scatter. ²⁵I was afraid, and went away and hid your talent in the earth. Behold, you have what is yours.' ²⁶"But his lord answered him, 'You wicked and slothful servant. You knew that I reap where I didn't sow, and gather where I didn't scatter. ²⁷You ought therefore to have deposited my money with the bankers, and at my coming I should have received back my own with interest. ²⁸Take away therefore the talent from him and give it to him who has the ten talents. ²⁹For to everyone who has will be given, and he will have abundance, but from him who doesn't have, even that which he has will be taken away. ³⁰Throw out the unprofitable servant into the outer darkness,ᵛ* where there will be weeping and gnashing of teeth.'

ᵛ see footnote

³¹"But when the Son of Man comes in his glory, and all the holy angels with him, then he will sit on the throne of his glory. ³²Before him allʷ the nations will be gathered, and he will separate them one from another,ˣ† as a shepherd separates the sheep from the goats. ³³He will set the sheep on his right hand, but the goats on the left. ³⁴Then the King will tell those on his right hand, 'Come, blessed of my Father, inherit the Kingdom prepared for you from the foundation of the world; ³⁵for I was hungry and you gave me food to eat. I was thirsty and you gave me drink. I was

ʷ Q. 2:203

ˣ see footnote

---

* ᵛ Q. 2:196; 3:11; 8:13; 10:27; 13:6; 24:40; 25:27; 40:3; 59:4

† ˣ Q. 3:9, 158; 4:87; 5:96; 6:12; 8:24; 10:28; 11:103; 15:25; 17:97; 18:100; 19:68; 20:102; 23:79; 25:17; 27:83, 87; 30:14, 43; 34:40; 36:59; 37:22; 41:19; 42:7; 44:40; 45:26, 28; 46:6; 56:50; 58:9; 64:9; 67:15; 77:14, 38; 78:17, 18; 99:6

a stranger and you took me in. [36]I was naked and you clothed me. I was sick and you visited me. I was in prison and you came to me.'[y]* [37]"Then the righteous will answer him, saying, 'Lord, when did we see you hungry and feed you, or thirsty and give you a drink? [38]When did we see you as a stranger and take you in, or naked and clothe you? [39]When did we see you sick or in prison and come to you?' [40]"The King will answer them, 'Most certainly I tell you, because you did it to one of the least of these my brothers, you did it to me.'

[41]Then he will say also to those on the left hand, 'Depart from me, you cursed, into the eternal fire which is prepared for the devil and his angels[z]†; [42]for I was hungry, and you didn't give me food to eat; I was thirsty, and you gave me no drink; [43]I was a stranger, and you didn't take me in; naked, and you didn't clothe me; sick, and in prison, and you didn't visit me.' "Then they will also answer, saying, 'Lord, when did we see you hungry, or thirsty, or a stranger, or naked, or sick, or in prison, and didn't help you?' "Then he will answer them, saying, 'Most certainly I tell you, because you didn't do it to one of the least of these,[a] you didn't do it to me.' [46]These will go away into eternal punishment, but the righteous into eternal life."[b]‡

[y] see footnote

[z] see footnote

[a] Q. 74:44

[b] see footnote

---

* [y] Q. 3:180; 16:30, 32; 18:108; 44:56; 56:8, 38; 56:90, 91; 65:11; 69:19; 74:39; 76:8, 20; 77:43; 90:18

† [z] Q. 2:7; 3:4; 5:18; 7:38; 8:14; 9:3; 11:3; 12:107; 13:34; 15:50; 16:63, 85; 17:8, 11, 63; 18:55; 90:19; 22:2, 22; 24:11, 19; 25:19; 26:135; 27:5; 29:23; 30:16; 31:6; 32:14; 33:8, 64; 34:5; 35:7; 37:9; 38:8; 39:13, 32; 40:7, 52; 41:15; 42:16; 43:39; 45:8; 46:18; 48:6; 50:26; 51:37; 56:9, 41; 57:20; 58:4; 59:3; 61:10; 64:5; 65:10; 67:5; 68:33; 69:25; 70:1; 71:1; 72:17; 73:13; 76:31; 78:30; 82:16; 84:24; 85:10; 88:24; 98:6; 99:6

‡ [b] Q. 2:7; 3:4, 107, 136; 5:18; 8:14; 9:3; 11:4; 12:107; 13:34; 15:50; 16:63; 17:11; 18:3, 55; 22:2, 22; 24:11, 19; 25:19; 26:135; 27:5, 90; 29:23; 30:16; 31:6; 32:14; 34:5; 35:7, 36; 37:9; 38:8; 39:13, 72; 40:7; 41:15; 42:16; 43:39; 44:57; 45:8; 46:18; 48:6; 50:26; 51:37; 52:13; 57:20; 58:4; 59:3; 61:10; 64:5; 65:10, 11; 67:5; 68:33; 69:25; 70:1; 71:1; 72:17, 23; 73:13; 76:31; 78:23, 30; 84:24; 85:10; 88:24; 99:6

26

¹When Jesus had finished all these words, he said to his disciples, ²"You know that after two days the Passover is coming, and the Son of Man will be delivered up to be crucified."

³Then the chief priests, the scribes, and the elders of the people were gathered together in the court of the high priest, who was called Caiaphas. ⁴They took counsel together that they might take Jesus by deceit and kill him. ⁵But they said, "Not during the feast, lest a riot occur among the people."

⁶Now when Jesus was in Bethany, in the house of Simon the leper, ⁷a woman came to him having an alabaster jar of very expensive ointment, and she poured it on his head as he sat at the table. ⁸But when his disciples saw this, they were indignant, saying, "Why this waste? ⁹For this ointment might have been sold for much and given to the poor." ¹⁰However, knowing this, Jesus said to them, "Why do you trouble the woman? She has done a good work for me. ¹¹For you always have the poor with you, but you don't always have me. ¹²For in pouring this ointment on my body, she did it to prepare me for burial. ¹³Most certainly I tell you, wherever this Good News is preached in the whole world, what this woman has done will also be spoken of as a memorial of her."

¹⁴Then one of the twelve, who was called Judas Iscariot, went to the chief priests ¹⁵and said, "What are you willing to give me if I deliver him to you?" So they weighed out for him thirty pieces of silver. ¹⁶From that time he sought opportunity to betray him.

¹⁷Now on the first day of unleavened bread, the disciples came to Jesus, saying to him, "Where do you want us to prepare for you to eat the Passover?" ¹⁸He said, "Go into the city to a certain person, and tell him, 'The Teacher says, "My time is at hand. I will keep the Passover at your house

with my disciples." [19]The disciples did as Jesus commanded them, and they prepared the Passover.

[20]Now when evening had come, he was reclining at the table with the twelve disciples. [21]As they were eating, he said, "Most certainly I tell you that one of you will betray me." They were exceedingly sorrowful, and each began to ask him, "It isn't me, is it, Lord?" He answered, "He who dipped his hand with me in the dish will betray me. [24]The Son of Man goes even as it is written of him, but woe to that man through whom the Son of Man is betrayed! It would be better for that man if he had not been born." [25]Judas, who betrayed him, answered, "It isn't me, is it, Rabbi?" He said to him, "You said it."

[26]As they were eating, Jesus took bread, gave thanks for[*] it, and broke it. He gave to the disciples and said, "Take, eat; this is my body." [27]He took the cup, gave thanks, and gave to them, saying, "All of you drink it, [28]for this is my blood of the new covenant, which is poured out for many for the remission of sins. [29]But I tell you that I will not drink of this fruit of the vine from now on, until that day when I drink it anew[c] with you in my Father's Kingdom."

[c] Q. 56:17; 76:19

[30]When they had sung a hymn, they went out to the Mount of Olives. Then Jesus said to them, "All of you will be made to stumble because of me tonight, for it is written, 'I will strike the shepherd, and the sheep of the flock will be scattered.'[d†] [32]But after I am raised up, I will go before you into Galilee." [33]But Peter answered him, "Even if all will be made to stumble because of you, I will never be made to stumble." [34]Jesus said to him, "Most certainly I tell you that tonight, before the rooster crows, you will deny me three times." [35]Peter said to him, "Even if I must die with you, I will not deny you." All of the disciples also said likewise.

[d] Q. 2:203

---

[*] 26:26 TR reads "blessed" instead of "gave thanks for"

[†] 26:31 Zechariah 13:7

³⁶Then Jesus came with them to a place called Gethsemane, and said to his disciples, "Sit here, while I go there and pray." ³⁷He took with him Peter and the two sons of Zebedee, and began to be sorrowful and severely troubled. ³⁸Then he said to them, "My soul is exceedingly sorrowful, even to death. Stay here and watch with me." ³⁹He went forward a little, fell on his face, and prayed, saying, "My Father, if it is possible, let this cup pass away from me; nevertheless, not what I desire, but what you desire." ⁴⁰He came to the disciples and found them sleeping, and said to Peter, "What, couldn't you watch with me for one hour? ⁴¹Watch and pray,[e] that you don't enter into temptation. The spirit indeed is willing, but the flesh is weak." ⁴²Again, a second time he went away and prayed, saying, "My Father, if this cup can't pass away from me unless I drink it, your desire be done." He came again and found them sleeping, for their eyes were heavy. ⁴⁴He left them again, went away, and prayed a third time, saying the same words. ⁴⁵Then he came to his disciples and said to them, "Are you still sleeping and resting? Behold, the hour is at hand, and the Son of Man is betrayed into the hands of sinners. ⁴⁶Arise, let's be going. Behold, he who betrays me is at hand."

⁴⁷While he was still speaking, behold, Judas, one of the twelve, came, and with him a great multitude with swords and clubs, from the chief priests and elders of the people. ⁴⁸Now he who betrayed[f] him had given them a sign, saying, "Whoever I kiss, he is the one. Seize him." ⁴⁹Immediately he came to Jesus, and said, "Greetings, Rabbi!" and kissed him. ⁵⁰Jesus said to him, "Friend, why are you here?" Then they came and laid hands on Jesus, and took him. ⁵¹Behold, one of those who were with Jesus stretched out his hand and drew his sword, and struck the servant of the high priest, and cut off his ear. ⁵²Then Jesus said to him, "Put your sword back into its place, for all those who take the sword will die by the sword.[g] ⁵³Or do you think that I couldn't ask

[e] Q. 17:79

[f] Q. 2:61; 3:21; 4:155; 5:70

[g] Q. 2:178

h Q.
3:124;
8:9;
37:173;
74:31

my Father, and he would even now send me more than twelve legions of angels?[h] [54]How then would the Scriptures be fulfilled that it must be so?" [55]In that hour Jesus said to the multitudes, "Have you come out as against a robber with swords and clubs to seize me? I sat daily in the temple teaching, and you didn't arrest me. [56]But all this has happened that the Scriptures of the prophets might be fulfilled." Then all the disciples left him and fled.

[57]Those who had taken Jesus led him away to Caiaphas the high priest, where the scribes and the elders were gathered together. [58]But Peter followed him from a distance to the court of the high priest, and entered in and sat with the officers, to see the end.

[59]Now the chief priests, the elders, and the whole council sought false testimony against Jesus, that they might put him to death, [60]and they found none. Even though many false witnesses came forward, they found none. But at last two false witnesses came forward [61]and said, "This man said, 'I am able to destroy the temple of God, and to build it in three days.' " [62]The high priest stood up and said to him, "Have you no answer? What is this that these testify against you?" [63]But Jesus stayed silent. The high priest answered him, "I adjure you by the living God that you tell us whether you are the Christ, the Son of God." Jesus said to him, [64]"You have said so. Nevertheless, I tell you, after this you will see the Son of Man sitting at the right hand of Power,[i] and coming on the clouds of the sky." [65]Then the high priest tore his clothing, saying, "He has spoken blasphemy! Why do we need any more witnesses? Behold, now you have heard his blasphemy. [66]What do you think?" They answered, "He is worthy of death!" [67]Then they spat in his face and beat him with their fists, and some slapped him, [68]saying, "Prophesy to us, you Christ! Who hit you?"

i Q.
2:54

[69]Now Peter was sitting outside in the court, and a maid came to him, saying, "You were also with Jesus, the

Galilean!" ⁷⁰But he denied it before them all, saying, "I don't know what you are talking about." ⁷¹When he had gone out onto the porch, someone else saw him and said to those who were there, "This man also was with Jesus of Nazareth." ⁷²Again he denied it with an oath, "I don't know the man." ⁷³After a little while those who stood by came and said to Peter, "Surely you are also one of them, for your speech makes you known." ⁷⁴Then he began to curse and to swear, "I don't know the man!" Immediately the rooster crowed. ⁷⁵Peter remembered the word which Jesus had said to him, "Before the rooster crows, you will deny me three times." Then he went out and wept bitterly.

27

¹Now when morning had come, all the chief priests and the elders of the people took counsel against Jesus to put him to death. ²They bound him, led him away, and delivered him up to Pontius Pilate, the governor.

³Then Judas, who betrayed him, when he saw that Jesus was condemned, felt remorse, and brought back the thirty pieces of silver to the chief priests and elders, ⁴saying, "I have sinned in that I betrayed blood." But they said, "What is that to us? You see to it." ⁵He threw down the pieces of silver in the sanctuary and departed. Then he went away and hanged himself. ⁶The chief priests took the pieces of silver and said, "It's not lawful to put them into the treasury, since it is the price of blood." ⁷They took counsel, and bought the potter's field with them to bury strangers in. ⁸Therefore that field has been called "The Field of Blood" to this day. ⁹Then that which was spoken through Jeremiah⁺ the prophet was fulfilled, saying, "They took the thirty pieces of silver, the price of him upon whom a price had been set, whom some of the children of Israel

---

*27:9 some manuscripts omit "Jeremiah"

68

priced, [10]and they gave them for the potter's field, as the Lord commanded me."*

[11]Now Jesus stood before the governor; and the governor asked him, saying, "Are you the King of the Jews?" Jesus said to him, "So you say." [12]When he was accused by the chief priests and elders, he answered nothing. [13]Then Pilate said to him, "Don't you hear how many things they testify against you?" [14]He gave him no answer, not even one word, so that the governor marveled greatly.

[15]Now at the feast the governor was accustomed to release to the multitude one prisoner whom they desired. [16]They had then a notable prisoner called Barabbas. [17]When therefore they were gathered together, Pilate said to them, "Whom do you want me to release to you? Barabbas, or Jesus who is called Christ?" [18]For he knew that because of envy they had delivered him up. [19]While he was sitting on the judgment seat, his wife sent to him, saying, "Have nothing to do with that righteous man, for I have suffered many things today in a dream because of him." [20]Now the chief priests and the elders persuaded the multitudes to ask for Barabbas and destroy Jesus. [21]But the governor answered them, "Which of the two do you want me to release to you?" They said, "Barabbas!" [22]Pilate said to them, "What then shall I do to Jesus who is called Christ?" They all said to him, "Let him be crucified!" [23]But the governor said, "Why? What evil has he done?" But they cried out exceedingly, saying, "Let him be crucified!"

[24]So when Pilate saw that nothing was being gained, but rather that a disturbance was starting, he took water and washed his hands before the multitude, saying, "I am innocent of the blood of this righteous person. You see to it." [25]All the people answered, "May his blood be on us and on our children!" [26]Then he released Barabbas to them, but Jesus he flogged and delivered to be crucified.

---

* 27:10 Zechariah 11:12-13; Jeremiah 19:1-13; 32:6-9

²⁷Then the governor's soldiers took Jesus into the Praetorium, and gathered the whole garrison together against him. ²⁸They stripped him and put a scarlet robe on him. ²⁹They braided a crown of thorns and put it on his head, and a reed in his right hand; and they kneeled down before him and mocked[j] him, saying, "Hail, King of the Jews!" ³⁰They spat on him, and took the reed and struck him on the head. ³¹When they had mocked[k†] him, they took the robe off him, and put his clothes on him, and led him away to crucify him.

³²As they came out, they found a man of Cyrene, Simon by name, and they compelled him to go with them, that he might carry his cross. ³³When they came to a place called "Golgotha", that is to say, "The place of a skull," ³⁴they gave him sour wine[‡] to drink mixed with gall.[§] When he had tasted it, he would not drink. ³⁵When they had crucified him, they divided his clothing among them, casting lots,[l**] ³⁶and they sat and watched him there. ³⁷They set up over his head the accusation against him written, "THIS IS JESUS, THE KING OF THE JEWS." ³⁸Then there were two robbers crucified with him, one on his right hand and one on the left. ³⁹Those who passed by blasphemed him, wagging their heads ⁴⁰and saying, "You who destroy the temple and build it in three days, save yourself! If you are the Son of God, come down from the cross!" ⁴¹Likewise the chief priests also mocking[m] with the scribes, the Pharisees,[††] and the elders, said, ⁴²"He saved others, but he can't save himself. If he is the King of Israel, let him come down from the cross now, and we will

[j] see footnote

[k] see footnote

[l] Q. 2:219

[m] Q. 6:10; 13:32; 15:11; 21:41; 36:30; 43:7

---

*j Q. 6:10; 13:32; 15:11; 21:41; 36:30; 43:7
†k Q. 6:10; 13:32; 15:11; 21:41; 36:30; 43:7
‡ 27:34 or, vinegar
§ 27:34 Gall is a bitter-tasting, dark green oil from a wormwood plant that is alcoholic in its effect
** 27:35 TR adds "that it might be fulfilled which was spoken by the prophet: 'They divided my garments among them, and for my clothing they cast lots;' " [see Psalm 22:18 and John 19:24]
†† 27:41 TR omits "the Pharisees"

believe in him. [43]He trusts in God. Let God deliver him now, if he wants him; for he said, 'I am the Son of God'". [44]The robbers also who were crucified with him cast on him the same reproach.

[45]Now from the sixth hour[*] there was darkness over all the land until the ninth hour.[†] [46]About the ninth hour Jesus cried with a loud voice, saying, "Eli, Eli, lima[‡] sabachthani?" That is, "My God, my God, why have you forsaken me?"[§] [47]Some of them who stood there, when they heard it, said, "This man is calling Elijah." [48]Immediately one of them ran and took a sponge, filled it with vinegar, put it on a reed, and gave him a drink. [49]The rest said, "Let him be. Let's see whether Elijah comes to save him." [50]Jesus cried again with a loud voice, and yielded up his spirit.[n]

[n] Q. 4:157

[51]Behold, the veil of the temple was torn in two from the top to the bottom. The earth quaked[o] and the rocks were split. [52]The tombs were opened, and many bodies of the saints who had fallen asleep were raised[p]; [53]and coming out of the tombs after his resurrection, they entered into the holy city and appeared to many. [54]Now the centurion and those who were with him watching Jesus, when they saw the earthquake[q] and the things that were done, were terrified, saying, "Truly this was the Son of God!"

[o] Q. 99:1

[p] Q. 82:4

[q] Q. 33:11

[55]Many women were there watching from afar, who had followed Jesus from Galilee, serving him. [56]Among them were Mary Magdalene, Mary the mother of James and Joseph, and the mother of the sons of Zebedee.

[57]When evening had come, a rich man from Arimathaea named Joseph, who himself was also Jesus' disciple, came.

---

[*] 27:45 noon

[†] 27:45 3:00 p.m.

[‡] 27:46 TR reads "lama" instead of "lima"

[§] 27:46 Psalm 22:1

[58]This man went to Pilate and asked for Jesus' body. Then Pilate commanded the body to be given up. [59]Joseph took the body and wrapped it in a clean linen cloth [60]and laid it in his own new tomb[r], which he had cut out in the rock. Then he rolled a large stone against the door of the tomb, and departed. [61]Mary Magdalene was there, and the other Mary, sitting opposite the tomb.

[62]Now on the next day, which was the day after the Preparation Day, the chief priests and the Pharisees were gathered together to Pilate, [63]saying, "Sir, we remember what that deceiver said while he was still alive: 'After three days I will rise again.' [64]Command therefore that the tomb be made secure until the third day, lest perhaps his disciples come at night and steal him away, and tell the people, 'He is risen from the dead;' and the last deception will be worse than the first." [65]Pilate said to them, "You have a guard. Go, make it as secure as you can." [66]So they went with the guard and made the tomb secure, sealing the stone.[s]

[r] Q. 4:157

[s] Q. 2:74

28

[1]Now after the Sabbath, as it began to dawn on the first day of the week, Mary Magdalene and the other Mary came to see the tomb. [2]Behold, there was a great earthquake, for an angel of the Lord descended from the sky and came and rolled away the stone from the door and sat on it. [3]His appearance was like lightning, and his clothing white as snow. [4]For fear of him, the guards shook, and became like dead men. [5]The angel answered the women, "Don't be afraid, for I know that you seek Jesus, who has been crucified. [6]He is not here, for he has risen,[t] just like he said. Come, see the place where the Lord was lying. [7]Go quickly and tell his disciples, 'He has risen from the dead, and behold, he goes before you into Galilee; there you will see him.' Behold, I have told you." [8]They departed

[t] Q. 19:33; 99:1

quickly from the tomb with fear and great joy, and ran to bring his disciples word. [9]As they went to tell his disciples, behold, Jesus met them, saying, "Rejoice!" They came and took hold of his feet, and worshiped him. [10]Then Jesus said to them, "Don't be afraid. Go tell my brothers[*] that they should go into Galilee, and there they will see me."

[11]Now while they were going, behold, some of the guards came into the city and told the chief priests all the things that had happened. [12]When they were assembled with the elders and had taken counsel, they gave a large amount of silver to the soldiers, [13]saying, "Say that his disciples came by night and stole him away while we slept. [14]If this comes to the governor's ears, we will persuade him and make you free of worry." [15]So they took the money and did as they were told. This saying was spread abroad among the Jews, and continues until today.

[16]But the eleven disciples went into Galilee, to the mountain where Jesus had sent them. [17]When they saw him, they bowed down to him; but some doubted. [18]Jesus came to them and spoke to them, saying, "All authority has been given to me in heaven and on earth.[u] [19]Go[†] and make disciples of all nations, baptizing them in the name of the Father and of the Son and of the Holy Spirit, [20]teaching them to observe all things that I commanded you. Behold, I am with you always, even to the end of the age." Amen.

[u] Q. 14:22; 15:24; 16:99; 17:65; 21:91; 34:21

---

[*] 28:10 The word for "brothers" here may be also correctly translated "brothers and sisters" or "siblings."
[†]28:19 TR and NU add "therefore"

The Good News According to Mark

1

¹The beginning of the Good News of Jesus Christ, the Son of God.

²As it is written in the prophets,

"Behold,* I send my messenger before your face, who will prepare your way before you:†

³the voice of one crying in the wilderness, 'Make ready the way of the Lord!

Make his paths straight!' "‡

⁴John came baptizing§ in the wilderness and preaching the baptism of repentance for forgiveness of sins. ⁵All the country of Judea and all those of Jerusalem went out to him. They were baptized by him in the Jordan river, confessing their sins. ⁶John was clothed with camel's hair and a leather belt around his waist. He ate locusts and wild honey. ⁷He preached, saying, "After me comes he who is mightier than I, the thong of whose sandals I am not worthy to stoop down and loosen. ⁸I baptized you in** water, but he will baptize you in the Holy Spirit."

⁹In those days,ᵃ†† Jesus came from Nazareth of Galilee, and was baptized by John in the Jordan. ¹⁰Immediately coming up from the water, he saw the heavens parting and the Spirit descending on him like a dove. ¹¹A voice came out of the sky, "You are my beloved Son, in whom I am well

ᵃ see footnote

---

* 1:2 "Behold", from "ἰδοὺ", means look at, take notice, observe, see, or gaze at. It is often used as an interjection.

† 1:2 Malachi 3:1

‡ 1:3 Isaiah 40:3

§ 1:4 or, immersing

** 1:8 The Greek word (en) translated here as "in" could also be translated as "with" in some contexts.

†† ᵃ Q. 2:87, 253; 3:52; 5:112; 19:30; 43:63

footnote

pleased."b*

¹²Immediately the Spirit drove him out into the wilderness. ¹³He was there in the wilderness forty days, tempted by Satan. He was with the wild animals; and the angels were serving him.

¹⁴Now after John was taken into custody, Jesus came into Galilee, preaching the Good News of God's Kingdom, ¹⁵and saying, "The time is fulfilled, and God's Kingdom is at hand! Repent, and believe in the Good News."

¹⁶Passing along by the sea of Galilee, he saw Simon and Andrew, the brother of Simon, casting a net into the sea, for they were fishermen. ¹⁷Jesus said to them, "Come after me, and I will make you into fishers for men."

¹⁸Immediately they left their nets, and followed him. ¹⁹Going on a little further from there, he saw James the son of Zebedee, and John his brother, who were also in the boat mending the nets. ²⁰Immediately he called them, and they left their father, Zebedee, in the boat with the hired servants, and went after him.

²¹They went into Capernaum, and immediately on the Sabbath day he entered into the synagogue and taught. ²²They were astonished at his teaching, for he taught them as having authority, and not as the scribes. ²³Immediately there was in their synagogue a man with an unclean spirit, and he cried out, ²⁴saying, "Ha! What do we have to do with you, Jesus, you Nazarene? Have you come to destroy us? I know you who you are: the Holy One of God!" ²⁵Jesus rebuked him, saying, "Be quiet, and come out of him!" ²⁶The unclean spirit, convulsing him and crying with a loud voice, came out of him. ²⁷They were all amazed, so that they questioned among themselves, saying, "What is this? A new teaching? For with authority he commands even the unclean spirits, and they obey him!" ²⁸The report of him went out immediately everywhere into all the region of

---

* b Q. 2:87, 253; 3:52; 5:110, 112; 19:21, 30; 43:63

Galilee and its surrounding area.

²⁹Immediately, when they had come out of the synagogue, they came into the house of Simon and Andrew, with James and John. ³⁰Now Simon's wife's mother lay sick with a fever, and immediately they told him about her. ³¹He came and took her by the hand and raised her up. The fever left her immediately*, and she served them.

³²At evening, when the sun had set, they brought to him all who were sick and those who were possessed by demons. ³³All the city was gathered together at the door. ³⁴He healed many who were sick with various diseases^c and cast out many demons. He didn't allow the demons to speak, because they knew him.

^c Q. 3:49

³⁵Early in the morning, while it was still dark, he rose up and went out, and departed into a deserted place, and prayed there. ³⁶Simon and those who were with him searched for him. ³⁷They found him and told him, "Everyone is looking for you." ³⁸He said to them, "Let's go elsewhere into the next towns, that I may preach there also, because I came out for this reason." ³⁹He went into their synagogues throughout all Galilee, preaching and casting out demons.

⁴⁰A leper came to him, begging him, kneeling down to him, and saying to him, "If you want to, you can make me clean." ⁴¹Being moved with compassion, he stretched out his hand, and touched him, and said to him, "I want to. Be made clean." ⁴²When he had said this, immediately the leprosy departed from him and he was made clean. ⁴³He strictly warned him and immediately sent him out, ⁴⁴and said to him, "See that you say nothing to anybody, but go show yourself to the priest and offer for your cleansing the things which Moses commanded, for a testimony to them." ⁴⁵But he went out, and began to proclaim it much, and to spread about the matter, so that Jesus could no more openly enter into a city, but was outside in desert places.

---

* 1:31 NU omits "immediately".

People came to him from everywhere.

2

¹When he entered again into Capernaum after some days, it was heard that he was at home. ²Immediately many were gathered together, so that there was no more room, not even around the door; and he spoke the word to them. ³Four people came, carrying a paralytic to him. ⁴When they could not come near to him for the crowd, they removed the roof where he was. When they had broken it up, they let down the mat that the paralytic was lying on. ⁵Jesus, seeing their faith, said to the paralytic, "Son, your sins are forgiven you." ⁶But there were some of the scribes sitting there and reasoning in their hearts, ⁷"Why does this man speak blasphemies like that? Who can forgive sins but God alone?"ᵈ ⁸Immediately Jesus, perceiving in his spirit that they so reasoned within themselves, said to them, "Why do you reason these things in your hearts? ⁹Which is easier, to tell the paralytic, 'Your sins are forgiven;' or to say, 'Arise, and take up your bed, and walk?' ¹⁰But that you may know that the Son of Man has authority on earth to forgive sins"—he said to the paralytic— ¹¹"I tell you, arise, take up your mat, and go to your house." ¹²He arose, and immediately took up the mat and went out in front of them all, so that they were all amazed and glorified God, saying, "We never saw anything like this!"

¹³He went out again by the seaside. All the multitude came to him, and he taught them. ¹⁴As he passed by, he saw Levi the son of Alphaeus sitting at the tax office. He said to him, "Follow me." And he arose and followed him.

¹⁵He was reclining at the table in his house, and many tax collectors and sinners sat down with Jesus and his disciples, for there were many, and they followed him. ¹⁶The scribes and the Pharisees, when they saw that he was eating

ᵈ Q. 3:135

with the sinners and tax collectors, said to his disciples, "Why is it that he eats and drinks with tax collectors and sinners?" [17]When Jesus heard it, he said to them, "Those who are healthy have no need for a physician, but those who are sick. I came not to call the righteous, but sinners to repentance."

[18]John's disciples and the Pharisees were fasting, and they came and asked him, "Why do John's disciples and the disciples of the Pharisees fast, but your disciples don't fast?" [19]Jesus said to them, "Can the groomsmen fast while the bridegroom is with them? As long as they have the bridegroom with them, they can't fast. [20]But the days will come when the bridegroom will be taken away from them, and then they will fast[e] in that day. [21]No one sews a piece of unshrunk cloth on an old garment, or else the patch shrinks and the new tears away from the old, and a worse hole is made. [22]No one puts new wine into old wineskins; or else the new wine will burst the skins, and the wine pours out, and the skins will be destroyed; but they put new wine into fresh wineskins."

[23]He was going on the Sabbath day through the grain fields; and his disciples began, as they went, to pluck the ears of grain. [24]The Pharisees said to him, "Behold, why do they do that which is not lawful on the Sabbath day?" [25]He said to them, "Did you never read what David did when he had need and was hungry—he, and those who were with him? [26]How he entered into God's house at the time of Abiathar the high priest, and ate the show bread, which is not lawful to eat except for the priests, and gave also to those who were with him?" [27]He said to them, "The Sabbath was made for man, not man for the Sabbath.[f] [28]Therefore the Son of Man is lord even of the Sabbath."

[e] Q. 2:183

[f] see footnote

---

* [f] Q. 2:65; 4:47, 154; 7:163; 16:124

3

^g Q
3:49

¹He entered again into the synagogue, and there was a man there whose hand was withered. ²They watched him, whether he would heal^g him on the Sabbath day, that they might accuse him. ³He said to the man whose hand was withered, "Stand up." ⁴He said to them, "Is it lawful on the Sabbath day to do good or to do harm? To save a life or to kill?" But they were silent. ⁵When he had looked around at them with anger, being grieved at the hardening of their hearts, he said to the man, "Stretch out your hand." He stretched it out, and his hand was restored as healthy as the other. ⁶The Pharisees went out, and immediately conspired with the Herodians against him, how they might destroy him.

⁷Jesus withdrew to the sea with his disciples; and a great multitude followed him from Galilee, from Judea, ⁸from Jerusalem, from Idumaea, beyond the Jordan, and those from around Tyre and Sidon. A great multitude, hearing what great things he did, came to him. ⁹He spoke to his disciples that a little boat should stay near him because of the crowd, so that they wouldn't press on him. ¹⁰For he had healed^h many, so that as many as had diseases pressed on him that they might touch him. ¹¹The unclean spirits, whenever they saw him, fell down before him and cried, "You are the Son of God!" ¹²He sternly warned them that they should not make him known.

^h Q.
3:49

¹³He went up into the mountain and called to himself those whom he wanted, and they went to him. ¹⁴He appointed twelve, that they might be with him, and that he might send them out to preach ¹⁵and to have authority to heal sicknesses and to cast out demons: ¹⁶Simon (to whom he gave the name Peter); ¹⁷James the son of Zebedee; and John, the brother of James, (whom he called Boanerges, which means, Sons of Thunder); ¹⁸Andrew; Philip; Bartholomew; Matthew; Thomas; James, the son of

Alphaeus; Thaddaeus; Simon the Zealot; ¹⁹and Judas Iscariot, who also betrayed him.

²⁰Then he came into a house. The multitude came together again, so that they could not so much as eat bread. ²¹When his friends heard it, they went out to seize him; for they said, "He is insane."

²²The scribes who came down from Jerusalem said, "He has Beelzebul," and, "By the prince of the demons he casts out the demons." ²³He summoned them and said to them in parables, "How can Satan cast out Satan? ²⁴If a kingdom is divided against itself, that kingdom cannot stand. ²⁵If a house is divided against itself, that house cannot stand. ²⁶If Satan has risen up against himself, and is divided, he can't stand, but has an end. ²⁷But no one can enter into the house of the strong man to plunder unless he first binds[i] the strong man; then he will plunder his house.

²⁸"Most certainly I tell you, all sins of the descendants of man will be forgiven[j], including their blasphemies with which they may blaspheme; ²⁹but whoever may blaspheme against the Holy Spirit never has forgiveness, but is subject to eternal condemnation."* ³⁰—because they said, "He has an unclean spirit."

³¹His mother and his brothers came, and standing outside, they sent to him, calling him. ³²A multitude was sitting around him, and they told him, "Behold, your mother, your brothers, and your sisters† are outside looking for you." ³³He answered them, "Who are my mother and my brothers?" ³⁴Looking around at those who sat around him, he said, "Behold, my mother and my brothers! ³⁵For whoever does the will of God is my brother, my sister, and mother."

[i] Q. 38:38

[j] Q. 39:53

* 3:29 NU reads, guilty of an eternal sin.
† 3:32 TR omits "your sisters"

4

¹Again he began to teach by the seaside. A great multitude was gathered to him, so that he entered into a boat in the sea and sat down. All the multitude were on the land by the sea. ²He taught them many things in parables, and told them in his teaching, ³"Listen! Behold, the farmer went out to sow. ⁴As he sowed, some seed fell by the road, and the birds* came and devoured it. ⁵Others fell on the rocky ground, where it had little soil, and immediately it sprang up, because it had no depth of soil. ⁶When the sun had risen, it was scorched; and because it had no root, it withered away. ⁷Others fell among the thorns, and the thorns grew up and choked it, and it yielded no fruit. ⁸Others fell into the good ground and yielded fruit, growing up and increasing. Some produced thirty times, some sixty times, and some one hundred times as much." ⁹He said, "Whoever has ears to hear, let him hear."

¹⁰When he was alone, those who were around him with the twelve asked him about the parables. ¹¹He said to them, "To you is given the mystery of God's Kingdom, but to those who are outside, all things are done in parables, ¹²that

'seeing they may see and not perceive, and hearing they may hear and not understand, lest perhaps they should turn again, and their sins should be forgiven them.' "†

¹³He said to them, "Don't you understand this parable? How will you understand all of the parables? ¹⁴The farmer sows the word. ¹⁵The ones by the road are the ones where the word is sown; and when they have heard, immediately Satan comes and takes away the word which has been sown in them.ᵏ ¹⁶These in the same way are those who are sown on the rocky places, who, when they have

ᵏ Q. 58:19

---

* 4:4 TR adds "of the air
† 4:12 Isaiah 6:9-10

heard the word, immediately receive it with joy. [17]They have no root in themselves, but are short-lived. When oppression or persecution arises because of the word, immediately they stumble. [18]Others are those who are sown among the thorns. These are those who have heard the word, [19]and the cares of this age, and the deceitfulness of riches, and the lusts of other things entering in choke the word, and it becomes unfruitful. [20]Those which were sown on the good ground are those who hear the word, accept it, and bear fruit, some thirty times, some sixty times, and some one hundred times."

[21]He said to them, "Is a lamp brought to be put under a basket[*] or under a bed? Isn't it put on a stand? [22]For there is nothing hidden[1] except that it should be made known, neither was anything made secret but that it should come to light. [23]If any man has ears to hear, let him hear." [24]He said to them, "Take heed what you hear. With whatever measure you measure, it will be measured to you; and more will be given to you who hear. [25]For whoever has, to him more will be given; and he who doesn't have, even that which he has will be taken away from him."

[26]He said, "God's Kingdom is as if a man should cast seed on the earth, [27]and should sleep and rise night and day, and the seed should spring up and grow, though he doesn't know how.[m] [28]For the earth bears fruit by itself: first the blade, then the ear, then the full grain in the ear. [29]But when the fruit is ripe, immediately he puts in the sickle, because the harvest has come."

[30]He said, "How will we liken God's Kingdom? Or with what parable will we illustrate it? [31]It's like a grain of mustard seed[n], which, when it is sown in the earth, though it is less than all the seeds that are on the earth, [32]yet when it is sown, grows up and becomes greater than all the herbs, and puts out great branches, so that the birds of the

[1] Q. 3:5

[m] Q. 10:24

[n] Q. 31:16

---

[*] 4:21 literally, a modion, a dry measuring basket containing about a peck (about 9 liters)

sky can lodge under its shadow."

³³With many such parables he spoke the word to them, as they were able to hear it. ³⁴Without a parable he didn't speak to them; but privately to his own disciples he explained everything.

³⁵On that day, when evening had come, he said to them, "Let's go over to the other side." ³⁶Leaving the multitude, they took him with them, even as he was, in the boat. Other small boats were also with him. ³⁷A big wind storm arose, and the waves beat into the boat, so much that the boat was already filled. ³⁸He himself was in the stern, asleep on the cushion; and they woke him up and asked him, "Teacher, don't you care that we are dying?" ³⁹He awoke and rebuked the wind, and said to the sea, "Peace! Be still!" The wind ceased and there was a great calm.° ⁴⁰He said to them, "Why are you so afraid? How is it that you have no faith?" ⁴¹They were greatly afraid and said to one another, "Who then is this, that even the wind and the sea obey him?"

° Q.
10:22

5

¹They came to the other side of the sea, into the country of the Gadarenes. ²When he had come out of the boat, immediately a man with an unclean spirit met him out of the tombs. ³He lived in the tombs. Nobody could bind him any more, not even with chains, ⁴because he had been often bound with fetters and chains, and the chains had been torn apart by him, and the fetters broken in pieces. Nobody had the strength to tame him. ⁵Always, night and day, in the tombs and in the mountains, he was crying out, and cutting himself with stones. ⁶When he saw Jesus from afar, he ran and bowed down to him, ⁷and crying out with a loud voice, he said, "What have I to do with you, Jesus, you Son of the Most High God? I adjure you by God, don't torment me." ⁸For he said to him, "Come out of the man, you unclean spirit!" ⁹He asked him, "What is your

name?" He said to him, "My name is Legion, for we are many."ᵖ ¹⁰He begged him much that he would not send them away out of the country. ¹¹Now on the mountainside there was a great herd of pigs feeding. ¹²All the demons begged him, saying, "Send us into the pigs, that we may enter into them." ¹³At once Jesus gave them permission. The unclean spirits came out and entered into the pigs. The herd of about two thousand rushed down the steep bank into the sea, and they were drowned in the sea.

ᵖ Q.
6:128

¹⁴Those who fed the pigs fled, and told it in the city and in the country. The people came to see what it was that had happened. ¹⁵They came to Jesus, and saw him who had been possessed by demons sitting, clothed, and in his right mind, even him who had the legion; and they were afraid. ¹⁶Those who saw it declared to them what happened to him who was possessed by demons, and about the pigs. ¹⁷They began to beg him to depart from their region. ¹⁸As he was entering into the boat, he who had been possessed by demons begged him that he might be with him. ¹⁹He didn't allow him, but said to him, "Go to your house, to your friends, and tell them what great things the Lord has done for you and how he had mercy on you." ²⁰He went his way, and began to proclaim in Decapolis how Jesus had done great things for him, and everyone marveled.

²¹When Jesus had crossed back over in the boat to the other side, a great multitude was gathered to him; and he was by the sea. ²²Behold, one of the rulers of the synagogue, Jairus by name, came; and seeing him, he fell at his feet ²³and begged him much, saying, "My little daughter is at the point of death. Please come and lay your hands on her, that she may be made healthy, and live." ²⁴He went with him,

and a great multitude followed him, and they pressed upon him on all sides. ²⁵A certain woman who had a discharge of blood for twelve years, ²⁶and had suffered many things by many physicians, and had spent all that she had, and was no better, but rather grew worse, ²⁷having heard the things concerning Jesus, came up behind him in the crowd and touched his clothes. [28]For she said, "If I just touch his clothes, I will be made well." [29]Immediately the flow of her blood was dried up, and she felt in her body that she was healed[q] of her affliction. [30]Immediately Jesus, perceiving in himself that the power had gone out from him, turned around in the crowd and asked, "Who touched my clothes?" [31]His disciples said to him, "You see the multitude pressing against you, and you say, 'Who touched me?'" He looked around to see her who had done this thing. [33]But the woman, fearing and trembling, knowing what had been done to her, came and fell down before him, and told him all the truth. [34]He said to her, "Daughter, your faith has made you well. Go in peace, and be cured of your disease."

[35]Why bother the Teacher any more?" [36]But Jesus, when he heard the message spoken, immediately said to the ruler of the synagogue, "Don't be afraid, only believe." [37]He allowed no one to follow him except Peter, James, and John the brother of James. [38]He came to the synagogue ruler's house, and he saw an uproar, weeping, and great wailing. [39]When he had entered in, he said to them, "Why do you make an uproar and weep? The child is not dead, but is asleep." [40]They ridiculed him. But he, having put them all out, took the father of the child, her mother, and those who were with him, and went in where the child was lying. [41]Taking the child by the hand, he said to her, "Talitha cumi!" which means, being interpreted, "Girl, I tell you, get up!" [42]Immediately the girl rose up and walked, for she was twelve years old. They were amazed with great amazement. [43]He strictly ordered them that no one should know this, and commanded that something should be given to her to eat.

[q] Q. 3:49

6

[1]He went out from there. He came into his own country, and his disciples followed him. [2]When the Sabbath had come, he began to teach[r] in the synagogue, and many hearing him were astonished, saying, "Where did this man get these things?" and, "What is the wisdom that is given to this man, that such mighty works come about by his hands? [3]Isn't this the carpenter, the son of Mary[s] and brother of James, Joses, Judah, and Simon? Aren't his sisters here with us?" So they were offended at him. [4]Jesus said to them, "A prophet is not without honor, except in his own country, and among his own relatives, and in his own house." [5]He could do no mighty work there, except that he laid his hands on a few sick people and healed[t] them. [6]He marveled because of their unbelief.

He went around the villages teaching.

[7]He called to himself the twelve, and began to send them out two by two; and he gave them authority over the unclean spirits.[u]* [8]He commanded them that they should take nothing for their journey, except a staff only: no bread, no wallet, no money in their purse, [9]but to wear sandals, and not put on two tunics. [10]He said to them, "Wherever you enter into a house, stay there until you depart from there. [11]Whoever will not receive you nor hear you, as you depart from there, shake off the dust that is under your feet for a testimony against them. Assuredly, I tell you, it will be more tolerable for Sodom and Gomorrah in the day of judgment than for that city!" [12]They went out and preached that people should repent. [13]They cast out many demons, and anointed many with oil who were sick and healed them.

[14]King Herod heard this, for his name had become known, and he said, "John the Baptizer has risen from the dead, and therefore these powers are at work in him." [15]But

[r] Q. 3:164; 43:63

[s] Q. 43:57; 23:50

[t] Q. 3:49

[u] see footnote

---

* [u] Q. 14:22; 15:42; 16:99; 17:65; 34:21

others said, "He is Elijah." Others said, "He is a prophet, or like one of the prophets." [16]But Herod, when he heard this, said, "This is John, whom I beheaded. He has risen from the dead." [17]For Herod himself had sent out and arrested John and bound him in prison for the sake of Herodias, his brother Philip's wife, for he had married her. [18]For John had said to Herod, "It is not lawful for you to have your brother's wife." [19]Herodias set herself against him and desired to kill him, but she couldn't, [20]for Herod feared John, knowing that he was a righteous and holy man, and kept him safe. When he heard him, he did many things, and he heard him gladly.

[21]Then a convenient day came when Herod on his birthday made a supper for his nobles, the high officers, and the chief men of Galilee. [22]When the daughter of Herodias herself came in and danced, she pleased Herod and those sitting with him. The king said to the young lady, "Ask me whatever you want, and I will give it to you." [23]He swore to her, "Whatever you ask of me, I will give you, up to half of my kingdom." [24]She went out and said to her mother, "What shall I ask?" She said, "The head of John the Baptizer." [25]She came in immediately with haste to the king and requested, "I want you to give me right now the head of John the Baptizer on a platter." [26]The king was exceedingly sorry, but for the sake of his oaths and of his dinner guests, he didn't wish to refuse her. [27]Immediately the king sent out a soldier of his guard and commanded to bring John's head; and he went and beheaded him in the prison, [28]and brought his head on a platter, and gave it to the young lady; and the young lady gave it to her mother. [29]When his disciples heard this, they came and took up his corpse and laid it in a tomb.

[30]The apostles gathered themselves together to Jesus, and they told him all things, whatever they had done, and whatever they had taught. [31]He said to them, "Come away into a deserted place, and rest awhile." For there were

many coming and going, and they had no leisure so much as to eat. ³²They went away in the boat to a deserted place by themselves. ³³They* saw them going, and many recognized him and ran there on foot from all the cities. They arrived before them and came together to him. ³⁴Jesus came out, saw a great multitude, and he had compassion on them because they were like sheep without a shepherd; and he began to teach them many things. ³⁵When it was late in the day, his disciples came to him and said, "This place is deserted, and it is late in the day. ³⁶Send them away, that they may go into the surrounding country and villages and buy themselves bread, for they have nothing to eat." ³⁷But he answered them, "You give them something to eat."ᵛ They asked him, "Shall we go and buy two hundred denarii† worth of bread and give them something to eat?" ³⁸He said to them, "How many loaves do you have? Go see." When they knew, they said, "Five, and two fish." ³⁹He commanded them that everyone should sit down in groups on the green grass. ⁴⁰They sat down in ranks, by hundreds and by fifties. ⁴¹He took the five loaves and the two fish; and looking up to heaven, he blessed and broke the loaves, and he gave to his disciples to set before them, and he divided the two fish among them all. ⁴²They all ate and were filled. ⁴³They took up twelve baskets full of broken pieces and also of the fish. ⁴⁴Those who ate the loaves were‡ five thousand men.

⁴⁵Immediately he made his disciples get into the boat and go ahead to the other side, to Bethsaida, while he himself sent the multitude away. ⁴⁶After he had taken leave of them, he went up the mountain to pray. ⁴⁷When evening had come, the boat was in the middle of the sea, and he was alone on the land. ⁴⁸Seeing them distressed in rowing, for the wind was contrary to them, about the fourth watch of

ᵛ Q. 5:112

---

* 6:33 TR reads "The multitudes" instead of "They"
† 6:37 200 denarii was about 7 or 8 months wages for an agricultural laborer
‡ 6:44 TR adds "about"

the night he came to them, walking on the sea;[*] and he would have passed by them, ⁴⁹but they, when they saw him walking on the sea, supposed that it was a ghost, and cried out; ⁵⁰for they all saw him and were troubled. But he immediately spoke with them and said to them, "Cheer up! It is I![†] Don't be afraid." ⁵¹He got into the boat with them; and the wind ceased, and they were very amazed among themselves, and marveled; ⁵²for they hadn't understood about the loaves, but their hearts were hardened.

⁵³When they had crossed over, they came to land at Gennesaret and moored to the shore. ⁵⁴When they had come out of the boat, immediately the people recognized him, ⁵⁵and ran around that whole region, and began to bring those who were sick on their mats to where they heard he was. ⁵⁶Wherever he entered—into villages, or into cities, or into the country—they laid the sick in the marketplaces and begged him that they might just touch the fringe[‡] of his garment; and as many as touched him were made well.

7

¹Then the Pharisees and some of the scribes gathered together to him, having come from Jerusalem. ²Now when they saw some of his disciples eating bread with defiled, that is unwashed, hands, they found fault.^w ³(For the Pharisees and all the Jews don't eat unless they wash their hands and forearms, holding to the tradition of the elders. ⁴They don't eat when they come from the marketplace unless they bathe themselves, and there are many other things which they have received to hold to: washings of cups, pitchers, bronze vessels, and couches.) ⁵The Pharisees and the scribes asked him, "Why don't

^w Q. 18:55

---

[*] 6:48 See Job 9:8
[†]6:50 or, "I AM!"
[‡] 6:56 or, tassel

your disciples walk according to the tradition of the elders, but eat their bread with unwashed hands?" [6]He answered them, "Well did Isaiah prophesy of you hypocrites, as it is written,

'This people honors me with their lips,
but their heart is far from me.
[7]They worship me in vain,
teaching as doctrines the commandments of men.'[*]

[8]"For you set aside the commandment of God, and hold tightly to the tradition of men—the washing of pitchers and cups, and you do many other such things." [9]He said to them, "Full well do you reject the commandment of God, that you may keep your tradition! [10]For Moses said, 'Honor your father and your mother;'[†] and, 'He who speaks evil of father or mother, let him be put to death.'[‡] [11]But you say, 'If a man tells his father or his mother, "Whatever profit you might have received from me is Corban,"'[§] that is to say, given to God, [12]"then you no longer allow him to do anything for his father or his mother, [13]making void the word of God by your tradition which you have handed down. You do many things like this."

[14]He called all the multitude to himself and said to them, "Hear me, all of you, and understand. [15]There is nothing from outside of the man that going into him can defile him; but the things which proceed out of the man are those that defile the man. [16]If anyone has ears to hear, let him hear!"[**] [17]When he had entered into a house away from the multitude, his disciples asked him about the parable. [18]He said to them, "Are you also without understanding? Don't you perceive that whatever goes into the man from outside can't defile him, [19]because it doesn't

---

[*] 7:7 Isaiah 29:13
[†] 7:10 Exodus 20:12; Deuteronomy 5:16
[‡] 7:10 21:17; Leviticus 20:9
[§] 7:11 Corban is a Hebrew word for an offering devoted to God.
[**] 7:16 NU omits verse 16

90

go into his heart, but into his stomach, then into the latrine, making all foods clean?"ˣ* ²⁰He said, "That which proceeds out of the man, that defiles the man. ²¹For from within, out of the hearts of men, proceed evil thoughts, adulteries, sexual sins, murders, thefts, ²²covetings, wickedness, deceit, lustful desires, an evil eye, blasphemy, pride, and foolishness. ²³All these evil things come from within and defile the man."ʸ†

²⁴From there he arose and went away into the borders of Tyre and Sidon. He entered into a house and didn't want anyone to know it, but he couldn't escape notice. ²⁵For a woman whose little daughter had an unclean spirit, having heard of him, came and fell down at his feet. ²⁶Now the woman was a Greek, a Syrophoenician by race. She begged him that he would cast the demon out of her daughter. ²⁷But Jesus said to her, "Let the children be filled first, for it is not appropriate to take the children's bread and throw it to the dogs." ²⁸But she answered him, "Yes, Lord. Yet even the dogs under the table eat the children's crumbs." ²⁹He said to her, "For this saying, go your way. The demon has gone out of your daughter." ³⁰She went away to her house, and found the child having been laid on the bed, with the demon gone out.

³¹Again he departed from the borders of Tyre and Sidon, and came to the sea of Galilee through the middle of the region of Decapolis. ³²They brought to him one who was deaf and had an impediment in his speech. They begged him to lay his hand on him. ³³He took him aside from the multitude privately and put his fingers into his ears; and he spat and touched his tongue. ³⁴Looking up to heaven, he sighed, and said to him, "Ephphatha!" that is, "Be opened!" ³⁵Immediately his ears were opened, and the impediment of

ˣ Q. 3:50; 5:3, 4

ʸ see footnote

* 7:19 NU ends quote and question after "latrine", ending the verse with "Thus he declared all foods clean.
† ʸ Q. 10:44; 12:53; 14:34; 16:62; 22:62; 29:40; 33:72; 42:48; 43:18; 80:17; 91:8-10; 103:2

his tongue was released, and he spoke clearly. ³⁶He commanded them that they should tell no one, but the more he commanded them, so much the more widely they proclaimed it. ³⁷They were astonished beyond measure, saying, "He has done all things well. He makes even the deaf hear and the mute speak!"ᶻ

ᶻ Q. 10:42; 27:93

8

¹In those days, when there was a very great multitude, and they had nothing to eat, Jesus called his disciples to himself and said to them, ²"I have compassion on the multitude, because they have stayed with me now three days and have nothing to eat. ³If I send them away fasting to their home, they will faint on the way, for some of them have come a long way." ⁴His disciples answered him, "From where could one satisfy these people with bread here in a deserted place?" ⁵He asked them, "How many loaves do you have?" They said, "Seven." ⁶He commanded the multitude to sit down on the ground, and he took the seven loaves. Having given thanks, he broke them and gave them to his disciples to serve, and they served the multitude. ⁷They also had a few small fish. Having blessed them, he said to serve these also. ⁸They ate and were filled. They took up seven baskets of broken pieces that were left over. ⁹Those who had eaten were about four thousand. Then he sent them away. ¹⁰Immediately he entered into the boat with his disciples and came into the region of Dalmanutha.

¹¹The Pharisees came out and began to question him, seeking from him a sign from heavenᵃ and testing him. ¹²He sighed deeply in his spirit and said, "Why does this generation* seek a sign? Most certainly I tell you, no sign will be given to this generation." ¹³He left them, and again

ᵃ Q. 13:7

---

* 8:12 The word translated "generation" here (genea) could also be translated "people", "race", or "family".

entering into the boat, departed to the other side.

¹⁴They forgot to take bread; and they didn't have more than one loaf in the boat with them. ¹⁵He warned them, saying, "Take heed: beware of the yeast of the Pharisees and the yeast of Herod." ¹⁶They reasoned with one another, saying, "It's because we have no bread." ¹⁷Jesus, perceiving it, said to them, "Why do you reason that it's because you have no bread? Don't you perceive yet or understand?ᵇ Is your heart still hardened? ¹⁸Having eyes, don't you see? Having ears, don't you hear? Don't you remember? ¹⁹When I broke the five loaves among the five thousand, how many baskets full of broken pieces did you take up?" They told him, "Twelve." ²⁰"When the seven loaves fed the four thousand, how many baskets full of broken pieces did you take up?" They told him, "Seven." ²¹He asked them, "Don't you understand yet?"

²²He came to Bethsaida. They brought a blind man to him and begged him to touch him. ²³He took hold of the blind man by the hand, and brought him out of the village. When he had spat on his eyes, and laid his hands on him, he asked him if he saw anything. ²⁴He looked up, and said, "I see men, but I see them like walking trees." ²⁵Then again he laid his hands on his eyes. He looked intently, and was restored, and saw everyone clearly. ²⁶He sent him away to his house, saying, "Don't enter into the village, nor tell anyone in the village."

²⁷Jesus went out, with his disciples, into the villages of Caesarea Philippi. On the way he asked his disciples, "Who do men say that I am?" ²⁸They told him, "John the Baptizer, and others say Elijah, but others, one of the prophets." ²⁹He said to them, "But who do you say that I am?" Peter answered, "You are the Christ." ³⁰He commanded them that they should tell no one about him.

³¹He began to teach them that the Son of Man must suffer many things, and be rejected by the elders, the chief priests, and the scribes, and be killed, and after three days

rise again. ³²He spoke to them openly. Peter took him and began to rebuke him. ³³But he, turning around and seeing his disciples, rebuked Peter, and said, "Get behind me, Satan! For you have in mind not the things of God, but the things of men."

³⁴He called the multitude to himself with his disciples and said to them, "Whoever wants to come after me, let him deny himself, and take up his cross, and follow me. ³⁵For whoever wants to save his life will lose it; and whoever will lose his life for my sake and the sake of the Good News will save it. ³⁶For what does it profit a man to gain the whole world and forfeit his life?ᶜ ³⁷For what will a man give in exchange for his life? ³⁸For whoever will be ashamed of me and of my words in this adulterous and sinful generation, the Son of Man also will be ashamed of him when he comes in his Father's glory with the holy angels."

ᶜ Q. 42:36

9

¹He said to them, "Most certainly I tell you, there are some standing here who will in no way taste death until they see God's Kingdom come with power."

²After six days Jesus took with him Peter, James, and John, and brought them up onto a high mountain privately by themselves, and he was changed into another form in front of them. ³His clothing became glistening, exceedingly white, like snow, such as no launderer on earth can whiten them. ⁴Elijah and Moses appeared to them, and they were talking with Jesus. ⁵Peter answered Jesus, "Rabbi, it is good for us to be here. Let's make three tents: one for you, one for Moses, and one for Elijah." ⁶For he didn't know what to say, for they were very afraid. ⁷A cloud came, overshadowing them, and a voice came out of the cloud, "This is my beloved Son. Listen to him." ⁸Suddenly looking around, they saw no one with them any more, except Jesus only.

⁹As they were coming down from the mountain, he commanded them that they should tell no one what things they had seen, until after the Son of Man had risen from the dead. ¹⁰They kept this saying to themselves, questioning what the "rising from the dead" meant. ¹¹They asked him, saying, "Why do the scribes say that Elijah must come first?" ¹²He said to them, "Elijah indeed comes first, and restores all things. How is it written about the Son of Man, that he should suffer many things and be despised? ¹³But I tell you that Elijah has come, and they have also done to him whatever they wanted to, even as it is written about him."

¹⁴Coming to the disciples, he saw a great multitude around them, and scribes questioning them. ¹⁵Immediately all the multitude, when they saw him, were greatly amazed, and running to him, greeted him. ¹⁶He asked the scribes, "What are you asking them?" ¹⁷One of the multitude answered, "Teacher, I brought to you my son, who has a mute spirit; ¹⁸and wherever it seizes him, it throws him down; and he foams at the mouth, grinds his teeth, and becomes rigid. I asked your disciples to cast it out, and they weren't able." ¹⁹He answered him, "Unbelieving generation, how long shall I be with you? How long shall I bear with you? Bring him to me." ²⁰They brought him to him, and when he saw him, immediately the spirit convulsed him and he fell on the ground, wallowing and foaming at the mouth. ²¹He asked his father, "How long has it been since this has been happening to him?" He said, "From childhood. ²²Often it has cast him both into the fire and into the water to destroy him. But if you can do anything, have compassion on us and help us." ²³Jesus said to him, "If you can believe, all things are possible to him who believes." ²⁴Immediately the father of the child cried out with tears, "I believe. Help my unbelief!" ²⁵When Jesus saw that a multitude came running together, he rebuked the unclean spirit, saying to him, "You mute and deaf spirit, I command you, come out of him, and

never enter him again!" ²⁶After crying out and convulsing him greatly, it came out of him. The boy became like one dead, so much that most of them said, "He is dead." ²⁷But Jesus took him by the hand and raised him up; and he arose.^d ²⁸When he had come into the house, his disciples asked him privately, "Why couldn't we cast it out?" ²⁹He said to them, "This kind can come out by nothing but by prayer and fasting."

^d Q. 2:260

³⁰They went out from there and passed through Galilee. He didn't want anyone to know it, ³¹for he was teaching his disciples, and said to them, "The Son of Man is being handed over to the hands of men, and they will kill him; and when he is killed, on the third day he will rise again." ³²But they didn't understand the saying, and were afraid to ask him.

³³He came to Capernaum, and when he was in the house he asked them, "What were you arguing among yourselves on the way?" ³⁴But they were silent, for they had disputed with one another on the way about who was the greatest. ³⁵He sat down and called the twelve; and he said to them, "If any man wants to be first, he shall be last of all, and servant of all." ³⁶He took a little child and set him in the middle of them. Taking him in his arms, he said to them, ³⁷"Whoever receives one such little child in my name receives me; and whoever receives me, doesn't receive me, but him who sent me."

³⁸John said to him, "Teacher, we saw someone who doesn't follow us casting out demons in your name; and we forbade him, because he doesn't follow us." ³⁹But Jesus said, "Don't forbid him, for there is no one who will do a mighty work in my name and be able quickly to speak evil of me. ⁴⁰For whoever is not against^e us is on our side. ⁴¹For whoever will give you a cup of water to drink in my name because you are Christ's, most certainly I tell you, he will in no way lose his reward.

^e Q. 58:14

⁴²"Whoever will cause one of these little ones who believe in me to stumble, it would be better for him if he

were thrown into the sea with a millstone hung around his neck. [43]If your hand causes you to stumble, cut it off. It is better for you to enter into life maimed, rather than having your two hands to go into Gehenna,[f*] into the unquenchable fire, [44]'where their worm doesn't die, and the fire is not quenched.'[†] [45]If your foot causes you to stumble, cut it off. It is better for you to enter into life lame, rather than having your two feet to be cast into Gehenna,[‡]into the fire that will never be quenched [46]'where their worm doesn't die, and the fire is not quenched.'[§] [47]If your eye causes you to stumble, throw it out. It is better for you to enter into God's Kingdom with one eye, rather than having two eyes to be cast into the Gehenna[**] of fire[g††], [48]'where their worm doesn't die, and the fire is not quenched.'[‡‡] [49]For everyone will be salted with fire, and every sacrifice will be seasoned with salt. [50]Salt is good, but if the salt has lost its saltiness, with what will you season it? Have salt in yourselves, and be at peace with one another."

[f] Q. 13:35; 101:11;

[g] Q. see footnote

10

[1]He arose from there and came into the borders of Judea and beyond the Jordan. Multitudes came together to him again. As he usually did, he was again teaching them.

[2]Pharisees came to him testing him, and asked him, "Is it lawful for a man to divorce his wife?" [3]He answered, "What did Moses command you?" [4]They said, "Moses allowed a certificate of divorce to be written, and to

---

[*] 9:43 or, Hel
[†] 9:44 Isaiah 66:24; NU omits verse 44.
[‡] 9:45 or, Hell
[§] 9:46 NU omits verse 46
[**] 9:47 or, Hell
[††] [g] Q. 2:196; 3:11; 5:2; 8:13; 13:6; 40:3; 59:4
[‡‡] 9:48 Isaiah 66:24

divorce her." ⁵But Jesus said to them, "For your hardness of heart, he wrote you this commandment. ⁶But from the beginning of the creation, God made them male and female.* ⁷For this cause a man will leave his father and mother, and will join to his wife, ⁸and the two will become one flesh,† so that they are no longer two, but one flesh. ⁹What therefore God has joined together, let no man separate."

¹⁰In the house, his disciples asked him again about the same matter. ¹¹He said to them, "Whoever divorcesʰ his wife and marries another commits adultery against her. ¹²If a woman herself divorces her husband and marries another, she commits adultery."

ʰ Q. 65:1

¹³They were bringing to him little children, that he should touch them, but the disciples rebuked those who were bringing them. ¹⁴But when Jesus saw it, he was moved with indignation and said to them, "Allow the little children to come to me! Don't forbid them, for God's Kingdom belongs to such as these. ¹⁵Most certainly I tell you, whoever will not receive God's Kingdom like a little child, he will in no way enter into it." ¹⁶He took them in his arms and blessed them, laying his hands on them.

¹⁷As he was going out into the way, one ran to him, knelt before him, and asked him, "Good Teacher, what shall I do that I may inherit eternal life?" ¹⁸Jesus said to him, "Why do you call me good? No one is good except one—God. ¹⁹You know the commandments: 'Do not murder,' 'Do not commit adultery,' 'Do not steal,' 'Do not give false testimony,' 'Do not defraud,' 'Honor your father and mother.'"‡ ²⁰He said to him, "Teacher, I have observed all these things from my youth." ²¹Jesus looking at him loved him, and said to him, "One thing you lack. Go, sell whatever you have and give to the poor,ⁱand you will have treasure in heaven; and come,

ⁱ Q. 2:177

---

* 10:6 Genesis 1:27
† 10:8 Genesis 2:24
‡ 10:19 Exodus 20:12-16; Deuteronomy 6:16-20

98

follow me, taking up the cross." ²²But his face fell at that saying, and he went away sorrowful, for he was one who had great possessions.

²³Jesus looked around and said to his disciples, "How difficult it is for those who have riches to enter into God's Kingdom!" The disciples were amazed at his words. But Jesus answered again, "Children, how hard it is for those who trust in riches to enter into God's Kingdom! ²⁵It is easier for a camel to go through a needle's eye^j than for a rich man to enter into God's Kingdom." ²⁶They were exceedingly astonished, saying to him, "Then who can be saved?" ²⁷Jesus, looking at them, said, "With men it is impossible, but not with God, for all things are possible with God."^k* ²⁸Peter began to tell him, "Behold, we have left all and have followed you." ²⁹Jesus said, "Most certainly I tell you, there is no one who has left house, or brothers, or sisters, or father, or mother, or wife, or children, or land, for my sake, and for the sake of the Good News, ³⁰but he will receive one hundred times more^l now in this time: houses, brothers, sisters, mothers, children, and land, with persecutions; and in the age to come eternal life.^m† ³¹But many who are first will be last, and the last first."

³²They were on the way, going up to Jerusalem; and Jesus was going in front of them, and they were amazed; and those who followed were afraid. He again took the twelve, and began to tell them the things that were going to happen to him. ³³"Behold, we are going up to Jerusalem. The Son of Man will be delivered to the chief priests and the scribes. They will condemn him to death, and will deliver him to the Gentiles. ³⁴They will mock him, spit on him, scourge him, and kill him. On the third day he will rise again."

^j Q. 7:40

^k see footnote

^l Q. 28:84

^m see footnote

* ^k Q. 2:20, 106, 109, 148, 259, 284; 3:26; 5:17, 19; 6:17; 8:41; 9:39; 11:4; 16:77; 18:45; 22:6; 24:45; 29:20; 30:50; 33:27; 35:1; 41:39; 42:9; 46:33; 48:21; 57:2; 59:6; 64:1; 65:12; 66:8; 67:1
† ^m Q. 3:107, 136, 148; 16:30, 41; 39:10; 50:35

³⁵James and John, the sons of Zebedee, came near to him, saying, "Teacher, we want you to do for us whatever we will ask." ³⁶He said to them, "What do you want me to do for you?" ³⁷They said to him, "Grant to us that we may sit, one at your right hand and one at your left hand, in your glory." ³⁸But Jesus said to them, "You don't know what you are asking. Are you able to drink the cup that I drink, and to be baptized with the baptism that I am baptized with?" ³⁹They said to him, "We are able." Jesus said to them, "You shall indeed drink the cup that I drink, and you shall be baptized with the baptism that I am baptized with; ⁴⁰but to sit at my right hand and at my left hand is not mine to give, but for whom it has been prepared." ⁴¹When the ten heard it, they began to be indignant toward James and John. ⁴²Jesus summoned them and said to them, "You know that they who are recognized as rulers over the nations lord it over them, and their great ones exercise authority over them. ⁴³But it shall not be so among you, but whoever wants to become great among you shall be your servant. ⁴⁴Whoever of you wants to become first among you shall be bondservant of all. ⁴⁵For the Son of Man also came not to be served but to serve, and to give his life as a ransom for many."

⁴⁶They came to Jericho. As he went out from Jericho with his disciples and a great multitude, the son of Timaeus, Bartimaeus, a blind beggar, was sitting by the road. ⁴⁷When he heard that it was Jesus the Nazarene, he began to cry out and say, "Jesus, you son of David, have mercy on me!" ⁴⁸Many rebuked him, that he should be quiet, but he cried out much more, "You son of David, have mercy on me!" Jesus stood still and said, "Call him." They called the blind man, saying to him, "Cheer up! Get up. He is calling you!" He, casting away his cloak, sprang up, and came to Jesus. ⁵¹Jesus asked him, "What do you want me to do for you?"

The blind man said to him, "Rabboni,[*] that I may see again." ⁵²Jesus said to him, "Go your way. Your faith has made you well." Immediately he received his sight and followed Jesus on the way.

11

¹When they came near to Jerusalem, to Bethsphage[†] and Bethany, at the Mount of Olives, he sent two of his disciples ²and said to them, "Go your way into the village that is opposite you. Immediately as you enter into it, you will find a young donkey tied, on which no one has sat. Untie him and bring him. ³If anyone asks you, 'Why are you doing this?' say, 'The Lord needs him;' and immediately he will send him back here." ⁴They went away, and found a young donkey tied at the door outside in the open street, and they untied him. ⁵Some of those who stood there asked them, "What are you doing, untying the young donkey?" ⁶They said to them just as Jesus had said, and they let them go. ⁷They brought the young donkey to Jesus and threw their garments on it, and Jesus sat on it. ⁸Many spread their garments on the way, and others were cutting down branches from the trees and spreading them on the road. ⁹Those who went in front and those who followed cried out, "Hosanna![‡] Blessed is he who comes in the name of the Lord![§] ¹⁰Blessed is the kingdom of our father David that is coming in the name of the Lord! Hosanna in the highest!"

¹¹Jesus entered into the temple in Jerusalem. When he had looked around at everything, it being now evening, he went out to Bethany with the twelve.

¹²The next day, when they had come out from Bethany,

---

[*] 10:51 Rabboni is a literal transliteration of the Hebrew word for "great teacher."

[†] 11:1 TR & NU read "Bethphage" instead of "Bethsphage"

[‡] 11:9 "Hosanna" means "save us" or "help us, we pray"

[§] 11:9 Psalm 118:25-26

he was hungry. [13]Seeing a fig tree afar off having leaves, he came to see if perhaps he might find anything on it. When he came to it, he found nothing but leaves, for it was not the season for figs. [14]Jesus told it, "May no one ever eat fruit from you again!" and his disciples heard it.

[15]They came to Jerusalem, and Jesus entered into the temple and began to throw out those who sold and those who bought in the temple, and overthrew the money changers' tables and the seats of those who sold the doves. [16]He would not allow anyone to carry a container through the temple. [17]He taught, saying to them, "Isn't it written, 'My house will be called a house of prayer for all the nations?'* But you have made it a den of robbers!"† [18]The chief priests and the scribes heard it, and sought how they might destroy him. For they feared him, because all the multitude was astonished at his teaching. When evening came, he went out of the city.

[20]As they passed by in the morning, they saw the fig tree withered away from the roots. [21]Peter, remembering, said to him, "Rabbi, look! The fig tree which you cursed[n] has withered away." [22]Jesus answered them, "Have faith in God. [23]For most certainly I tell you, whoever may tell this mountain, 'Be taken up and cast into the sea,'[o] and doesn't doubt in his heart, but believes that what he says is happening, he shall have whatever he says. [24]Therefore I tell you, all things whatever you pray and ask for,[p] believe that you have received them, and you shall have them. [25]Whenever you stand praying, forgive, if you have anything against anyone; so that your Father, who is in heaven, may also forgive you your transgressions. [26]But if you do not forgive, neither will your Father in heaven forgive your transgressions."‡

[27]They came again to Jerusalem, and as he was walking in

[n] Q. 17:60

[o] Q. 13:31

[p] Q. 27:62

---

* 11:17 Isaiah 56:7

† 11:17 Jeremiah 7:11

‡ 11:26 NU omits verse 26.

the temple, the chief priests, the scribes, and the elders came to him, [28]and they began saying to him, "By what authority do you do these things? Or who gave you this authority to do these things?" [29]Jesus said to them, "I will ask you one question. Answer me, and I will tell you by what authority I do these things. [30]The baptism of John—was it from heaven, or from men? Answer me." [31]They reasoned with themselves, saying, "If we should say, 'From heaven;' he will say, 'Why then did you not believe him?' [32]If we should say, 'From men' "—they feared the people, for all held John to really be a prophet. [33]They answered Jesus, "We don't know." Jesus said to them, "Neither will I tell you by what authority I do these things."

12

[1]He began to speak to them in parables. "A man planted a vineyard, put a hedge around it, dug a pit for the wine press, built a tower, rented it out to a farmer, and went into another country. [2]When it was time, he sent a servant to the farmer to get from the farmer his share of the fruit of the vineyard. [3]They took him, beat him, and sent him away empty. [4]Again, he sent another servant to them; and they threw stones at him, wounded him in the head, and sent him away shamefully treated. [5]Again he sent another, and they killed him, and many others, beating some, and killing some. [6]Therefore still having one, his beloved son, he sent him last to them, saying, 'They will respect my son.' [7]But those farmers said among themselves, 'This is the heir. Come, let's kill him, and the inheritance will be ours.' [8]They took him, killed him, and cast him out of the vineyard. [9]What therefore will the lord of the vineyard do? He will come and destroy the farmers, and will give the vineyard to others. [10]Haven't you even read this Scripture:

'The stone which the builders rejected

was made the head of the corner.

11This was from the Lord.

It is marvelous in our eyes'?"*

12They tried to seize him, but they feared the multitude; for they perceived that he spoke the parable against them. They left him and went away.

13They sent some of the Pharisees and the Herodians to him, that they might trap him with words. 14When they had come, they asked him, "Teacher, we know that you are honest, and don't defer to anyone; for you aren't partial to anyone, but truly teach the way of God. Is it lawful to pay taxes to Caesar, or not? Shall we give, or shall we not give?" 15But he, knowing their hypocrisy, said to them, "Why do you test me? Bring me a denarius, that I may see it." 16They brought it. He said to them, "Whose is this image and inscription?" They said to him, "Caesar's." 17Jesus answered them, "Render to Caesar the things that are Caesar's, and to God the things that are God's." They marveled greatly at him.

18Some Sadducees, who say that there is no resurrection, came to him. They asked him, saying, 19"Teacher, Moses wrote to us, 'If a man's brother dies and leaves a wife behind him, and leaves no children, that his brother should take his wife and raise up offspring for his brother.' 20There were seven brothers. The first took a wife, and dying left no offspring. 21The second took her, and died, leaving no children behind him. The third likewise; 22and the seven took her and left no children. Last of all the woman also died. 23In the resurrection, when they rise, whose wife will she be of them? For the seven had her as a wife."

24Jesus answered them, "Isn't this because you are mistaken, not knowing the Scriptures nor the power of God? 25For when they will rise from the dead, they neither marry nor are given in marriage, but are like angels in

---

* 12:11 Psalm 118:22-23

heaven. [26]But about the dead, that they are raised, haven't you read in the book of Moses about the Bush, how God spoke to him, saying, 'I am the God of Abraham, the God of Isaac, and the God of Jacob'?[*] [27]He is not the God of the dead, but of the living. You are therefore badly mistaken."

[28]One of the scribes came and heard them questioning together, and knowing that he had answered them well, asked him, "Which commandment is the greatest of all?" [29]Jesus answered, "The greatest is: 'Hear, Israel, the Lord our God, the Lord is one.[q][†] [30]You shall love the Lord your God with all your heart, with all your soul, with all your mind, and with all your strength.'[‡] This is the first commandment. [31]The second is like this: 'You shall love your neighbor as yourself.'[§] There is no other commandment greater than these." [32]The scribe said to him, "Truly, teacher, you have said well that he is one, and there is none other but he; [33]and to love him with all the heart, with all the understanding, all the soul, and with all the strength, and to love his neighbor as himself, is more important than all whole burnt offerings and sacrifices." [34]When Jesus saw that he answered wisely, he said to him, "You are not far from God's Kingdom." No one dared ask him any question after that.

[35]Jesus responded, as he taught in the temple, "How is it that the scribes say that the Christ is the son of David? [36]For David himself said in the Holy Spirit,

'The Lord said to my Lord, "Sit at my right hand,
until I make your enemies the footstool of your
feet."'[**]

[37]Therefore David himself calls him Lord, so how can he be his son?" The common people heard him gladly.

[q] see footnote

---

[*] 12:26 Exodus 3:6
[†] [q] Q. 3:51, 64; 5:72, 117; 6:19; 9:31; 18:110; 19:36; 29:46; 112:1
[‡] 12:30 Deuteronomy 6:4-5
[§] 12:31 Leviticus 19:18
[**] 12:36 Psalm 110:1

³⁸In his teaching he said to them, "Beware of the scribed, who like to walk in long robes, and to get greetings in the marketplaces, ³⁹and to get the best seats in the synagogues and the best places at feasts, ⁴⁰those who devour widows' houses, and for a pretense make long prayers. These will receive greater condemnation."

⁴¹Jesus sat down opposite the treasury and saw how the multitude cast money into the treasury. Many who were rich cast in much. ⁴²A poor widow came and she cast in two small brass coins,* which equal a quadrans coin.† ⁴³He called his disciples to himself and said to them, "Most certainly I tell you, this poor widow gave more than all those who are giving into the treasury, ⁴⁴for they all gave out of their abundance, but she, out of her poverty, gave all that she had to live on."ʳ

ʳ Q.
2:177;
49:18

13

¹As he went out of the temple, one of his disciples said to him, "Teacher, see what kind of stones and what kind of buildings!" ²Jesus said to him, "Do you see these great buildings? There will not be left here one stone on another, which will not be thrown down."

³As he sat on the Mount of Olives opposite the temple, Peter, James, John, and Andrew asked him privately, ⁴"Tell us, when will these things be?ˢ What is the sign that these things are all about to be fulfilled?" ⁵Jesus, answering, began to tell them, "Be careful that no one leads you astray. ⁶For many will come in my name, saying, 'I am he!'‡ and will lead many astray. ⁷"When you hear of

ˢ Q.
51:12

---

* 12:42 literally, lepta (or widow's mites). Lepta are very small brass coins worth half a quadrans each, which is a quarter of the copper assarion. Lepta are worth less than 1% of an agricultural worker's daily wages.
† 12:42 A quadrans is a coin worth about 1/64 of a denarius. A denarius is about one day's wages for an agricultural laborer
‡ 13:6 or, "I AM!"

wars and rumors of wars, don't be troubled. For those must happen, but the end is not yet. [8]For nation will rise against nation, and kingdom against kingdom. There will be earthquakes in various places. There will be famines and troubles. These things are the beginning of birth pains.

[9]"But watch yourselves, for they will deliver you up to councils. You will be beaten in synagogues. You will stand before rulers and kings for my sake, for a testimony to them. [10]The Good News must first be preached to all the nations. [11]When they lead you away and deliver you up, don't be anxious beforehand or premeditate what you will say, but say whatever will be given you in that hour. For it is not you who speak, but the Holy Spirit. [12]"Brother will deliver up brother to death, and the father his child. Children will rise up against parents and cause them to be put to death. [13]You will be hated by all men for my name's sake, but he who endures to the end will be saved.

[14]"But when you see the abomination of desolation,[*] spoken of by Daniel the prophet, standing where it ought not" (let the reader understand), "then let those who are in Judea flee to the mountains, [15]and let him who is on the housetop not go down, nor enter in, to take anything out of his house. [16]Let him who is in the field not return back to take his cloak. [17]But woe to those who are with child and to those who nurse babies in those days! [18]Pray that your flight won't be in the winter. [19]For in those days there will be oppression, such as there has not been the like from the beginning of the creation which God created until now, and never will be. [20]Unless the Lord had shortened the days, no flesh would have been saved; but for the sake of the chosen ones, whom he picked out, he shortened the days. [21]Then if anyone tells you, 'Look, here is the Christ!' or, 'Look, there!' don't believe it. [22]For false christs and false prophets will arise and will show signs and wonders, that

---

[*] 13:14 Daniel 9:17; 11:31; 12:11

they may lead astray, if possible, even the chosen ones. ²³But you watch. "Behold, I have told you all things beforehand.ᵗ

²⁴But in those days, after that oppression, the sun will be darkened, the moon will not give its light, ²⁵the starsᵘ will be falling from the sky, and the powers that are in the heavens will be shaken.* ²⁶Then they will see the Son of Man coming in clouds with great power and glory. ²⁷Then he will send out his angelsᵛ, and will gather together his chosen ones from the four winds, from the ends of the earth to the ends of the sky.

²⁸"Now from the fig tree, learn this parable. When the branch has now become tender and produces its leaves, you know that the summer is near; ²⁹even so you also, when you see these things coming to pass, know that it is near, at the doors. ³⁰Most certainly I say to you, this generation† will not pass away until all these things happen. ³¹Heaven and earth will pass away, but my words will not pass away.

³²"But of that day or that hour no one knows—not even the angels in heaven, nor the Son, but only the Father.ʷ ³³Watch, keep alert, and pray; for you don't know when the time is. ³⁴"It is like a man traveling to another country, having left his house and given authority to his servants, and to each one his work, and also commanded the doorkeeper to keep watch. ³⁵Watch therefore, for you don't know when the lord of the house is coming—whether at evening, or at midnight, or when the rooster crows, or in the morning; ³⁶lest, coming suddenly, he might find you sleeping.ˣ ³⁷What I tell you, I tell all: Watch!"

ᵗ Q. 17:5, 7
ᵘ Q. 56:75
ᵛ Q. 89:22
ʷ Q. 7:187; 31:34; 67:26
ˣ Q. 3:154

---

* 13:25 Isaiah 13:10; 34:4
† 13:30 The word translated "generation" (genea) could also be translated "race", "family", or "people".

14

¹It was now two days before the Passover and the Feast of Unleavened Bread, and the chief priests and the scribes sought how they might seize him by deception and kill him. ²For they said, "Not during the feast, because there might be a riot among the people."

³While he was at Bethany, in the house of Simon the leper, as he sat at the table, a woman came having an alabaster jar of ointment of pure nard—very costly. She broke the jar and poured it over his head. ⁴But there were some who were indignant among themselves, saying, "Why has this ointment been wasted? ⁵For this might have been sold for more than three hundred denarii* and given to the poor." So they grumbled against her. ⁶But Jesus said, "Leave her alone. Why do you trouble her? She has done a good work for me. ⁷For you always have the poor with you, and whenever you want to, you can do them good; but you will not always have me. ⁸She has done what she could. She has anointed my body beforehand for the burying. ⁹Most certainly I tell you, wherever this Good News may be preached throughout the whole world, that which this woman has done will also be spoken of for a memorial of her."

¹⁰Judas Iscariot, who was one of the twelve, went away to the chief priests, that he might deliver him to them. ¹¹They, when they heard it, were glad, and promised to give him money. He sought how he might conveniently deliver him.

¹²On the first day of unleavened bread, when they sacrificed the Passover, his disciples asked him, "Where do you want us to go and prepare that you may eat the Passover?" ¹³He sent two of his disciples and said to them, "Go into the city, and there a man carrying a pitcher of water will meet you. Follow him, ¹⁴and wherever he enters in, tell

---

* 14:5 300 denarii was about a year's wages for an agricultural laborer

the master of the house, 'The Teacher says, "Where is the guest room, where I may eat the Passover with my disciples?"' 15He will himself show you a large upper room furnished and ready. Get ready for us there." 16His disciples went out, and came into the city, and found things as he had said to them, and they prepared the Passover.

17When it was evening he came with the twelve. 18As they sat and were eating, Jesus said, "Most certainly I tell you, one of you will betray me—he who eats with me." 19They began to be sorrowful, and to ask him one by one, "Surely not I?" And another said, "Surely not I?" 20He answered them, "It is one of the twelve, he who dips with me in the dish. 21For the Son of Man goes as it is written about him, but woe to that man by whom the Son of Man is betrayed! It would be better for that man if he had not been born."

22As they were eating, Jesus took bread, and when he had blessed it, he broke it and gave to them, and said, "Take, eat. This is my body." 23He took the cup, and when he had given thanks, he gave to them. They all drank of it. 24He said to them, "This is my blood of the new covenant, which is poured out for many. 25Most certainly I tell you, I will no more drink of the fruit of the vine until that day when I drink it anew in God's Kingdom."

26When they had sung a hymn, they went out to the Mount of Olives. 27Jesus said to them, "All of you will be made to stumble because of me tonight, for it is written, 'I will strike the shepherd, and the sheep will be scattered.'* 28However, after I am raised up, I will go before you into Galilee." 29But Peter said to him, "Although all will be offended, yet I will not." 30Jesus said to him, "Most certainly I tell you that you today, even this night, before the rooster crows twice, you will deny me three times." 31But he spoke all the more, "If I must die with you, I will not deny

---

* 14:27 Zechariah 13:7

you." They all said the same thing.

³²They came to a place which was named Gethsemane. He said to his disciples, "Sit here while I pray." ³³He took with him Peter, James, and John, and began to be greatly troubled and distressed. ³⁴He said to them, "My soul is exceedingly sorrowful, even to death. Stay here and watch." ³⁵He went forward a little, and fell on the ground, and prayed that if it were possible, the hour might pass away from him. ³⁶He said, "Abba,* Father, all things are possible to you. Please remove this cup from me. However, not what I desire, but what you desire." ³⁷He came and found them sleeping, and said to Peter, "Simon, are you sleeping? Couldn't you watch one hour? ³⁸Watch and pray, that you may not enter into temptation. The spirit indeed is willing, but the flesh is weak." ³⁹Again he went away and prayed, saying the same words. ⁴⁰Again he returned and found them sleeping, for their eyes were very heavy; and they didn't know what to answer him. ⁴¹He came the third time and said to them, "Sleep on now, and take your rest. It is enough. The hour has come. Behold, the Son of Man is betrayed into the hands of sinners. ⁴²Arise! Let's get going. Behold, he who betrays me is at hand."

⁴³Immediately, while he was still speaking, Judas, one of the twelve, came —and with him a multitude with swords and clubs, from the chief priests, the scribes, and the elders. ⁴⁴Now he who betrayed him had given them a sign, saying, "Whomever I will kiss, that is he. Seize him, and lead him away safely." ⁴⁵When he had come, immediately he came to him and said, "Rabbi! Rabbi!" and kissed him. ⁴⁶They laid their hands on him and seized him. ⁴⁷But a certain one of those who stood by drew his sword and struck the servant of the high priest, and cut off his ear. ⁴⁸Jesus answered them, "Have you come out, as against a robber, with swords and clubs to seize me? ⁴⁹I was daily with you in

---

* 14:36 Abba is a Greek spelling for the Aramaic word for "Father" or "Daddy" used in a familiar, respectful, and loving way

the temple teaching, and you didn't arrest me. But this is so that the Scriptures might be fulfilled." ⁵⁰They all left him, and fled.

⁵¹A certain young man followed him, having a linen cloth thrown around himself over his naked body. The young men grabbed him, ⁵²but he left the linen cloth and fled from them naked.

⁵³They led Jesus away to the high priest. All the chief priests, the elders, and the scribes came together with him. ⁵⁴Peter had followed him from a distance, until he came into the court of the high priest. He was sitting with the officers, and warming himself in the light of the fire. ⁵⁵Now the chief priests and the whole council sought witnesses against Jesus to put him to death, and found none. ⁵⁶For many gave false testimony against him, and their testimony didn't agree with each other. ⁵⁷Some stood up and gave false testimony against him, saying, ⁵⁸"We heard him say, 'I will destroy this temple that is made with hands, and in three days I will build another made without hands.' " ⁵⁹Even so, their testimony didn't agree. ⁶⁰The high priest stood up in the middle, and asked Jesus, "Have you no answer? What is it which these testify against you?" ⁶¹But he stayed quiet, and answered nothing. Again the high priest asked him, "Are you the Christ, the Son of the Blessed?" Jesus said, "I am. You will see the Son of Man sitting at the right hand of Power, and coming with the clouds of the sky." ⁶³The high priest tore his clothes and said, "What further need have we of witnesses? ⁶⁴You have heard the blasphemy! What do you think?" They all condemned him to be worthy of death. ⁶⁵Some began to spit on him, and to cover his face, and to beat him with fists, and to tell him, "Prophesy!" The officers struck him with the palms of their hands.

⁶⁶As Peter was in the courtyard below, one of the maids of the high priest came, ⁶⁷and seeing Peter warming himself, she looked at him and said, "You were also with the

Nazarene, Jesus!" [68]But he denied it, saying, "I neither know nor under- stand what you are saying." He went out on the porch, and the rooster crowed. [69]The maid saw him and began again to tell those who stood by, "This is one of them." [70]But he again denied it. After a little while again those who stood by said to Peter, "You truly are one of them, for you are a Galilean, and your speech shows it." [71]But he began to curse and to swear, "I don't know this man of whom you speak!" [72]The rooster crowed the second time. Peter remembered the words that Jesus said to him, "Before the rooster crows twice, you will deny me three times." When he thought about that, he wept.

15

[1]Immediately in the morning the chief priests, with the elders, scribes, and the whole council, held a consultation, bound Jesus, carried him away, and delivered him up to Pilate. [2]Pilate asked him, "Are you the King of the Jews?" He answered, "So you say." [3]The chief priests accused him of many things. [4]Pilate again asked him, "Have you no answer? See how many things they testify against you!" [5]But Jesus made no further answer, so that Pilate marveled.

[6]Now at the feast he used to release to them one prisoner, whomever they asked of him. [7]There was one called Barabbas, bound with his fellow insurgents, men who in the insurrection had committed murder. [8]The multitude, crying aloud, began to ask him to do as he always did for them. [9]Pilate answered them, saying, "Do you want me to release to you the King of the Jews?" [10]For he perceived that for envy the chief priests had delivered him up. [11]But the chief priests stirred up the multitude, that he should release Barabbas to them instead. [12]Pilate again asked them, "What then should I do to him whom you call the King of the Jews?" They cried out again, "Crucify him!"

¹⁴Pilate said to them, "Why, what evil has he done?" But they cried out exceedingly, "Crucify him!" ¹⁵Pilate, wishing to please the multitude, released Barabbas to them, and handed over Jesus, when he had flogged him, to be crucified.

¹⁶The soldiers led him away within the court, which is the Praetorium; and they called together the whole cohort. ¹⁷They clothed him with purple; and weaving a crown of thorns, they put it on him. ¹⁸They began to salute him, "Hail, King of the Jews!" ¹⁹They struck his head with a reed and spat on him, and bowing their knees, did homage to him. ²⁰When they had mocked^{y*} him, they took the purple cloak off him, and put his own garments on him. They led him out to crucify him.

ʸ see footnote

²¹They compelled one passing by, coming from the country, Simon of Cyrene, the father of Alexander and Rufus, to go with them that he might bear his cross. ²²They brought him to the place called Golgotha, which is, being interpreted, "The place of a skull." ²³They offered him wine mixed with myrrh to drink, but he didn't take it. ²⁴Crucifying him, they parted his garments among them, casting lots^z on them, what each should take. ²⁵It was the third hour† when they crucified him. ²⁶The superscription of his accusation was written over him: "THE KING OF THE JEWS." ²⁷With him they crucified two robbers, one on his right hand, and one on his left. ²⁸The Scripture was fulfilled which says, "He was counted with transgressors."‡ ²⁹Those who passed by blasphemed him, wagging their heads and saying, "Ha! You who destroy the temple and build it in three days, ³⁰save yourself, and come down from the cross!" ³¹Likewise, also the chief priests mocking^{a§} among them-selves with the scribes said, "He saved others.

^{z} Q. 2:219

^{a} see footnote

---

* ʸ Q. 6:10; 13:32; 15:11; 36:30; 43:7; 21:41
† 15:25 9:00 a.m.
‡ 15:28 NU omits verse 28
§ ᵃ Q. 6:10; 13:32; 15:11; 36:30; 43:7; 21:41

He can't save himself. [32]Let the Christ, the King of Israel, now come down from the cross, that we may see and believe him."[*] Those who were crucified with him also insulted him.

[33]When the sixth hour[†] had come, there was darkness over the whole land until the ninth hour.[‡] [34]At the ninth hour Jesus cried with a loud voice, saying, "Eloi, Eloi, lama sabachthani?" which is, being interpreted, "My God, my God, why have you forsaken me?"[§] [35]Some of those who stood by, when they heard it, said, "Behold, he is calling Elijah." [36]One ran, and filling a sponge full of vinegar, put it on a reed and gave it to him to drink, saying, "Let him be. Let's see whether Elijah comes to take him down." [37]Jesus cried out with a loud voice, and gave up the spirit. [38]The veil of the temple was torn in two from the top to the bottom. [39]When the centurion, who stood by opposite him, saw that he cried out like this and breathed his last, he said, "Truly this man was the Son of God!"

[40]There were also women watching from afar, among whom were both Mary Magdalene and Mary the mother of James the less and of Joses, and Salome; [41]who, when he was in Galilee, followed him and served him; and many other women who came up with him to Jerusalem.

[42]When evening had now come, because it was the Preparation Day, that is, the day before the Sabbath, [43]Joseph of Arimathaea, a prominent council member who also himself was looking for God's Kingdom, came. He boldly went in to Pilate, and asked for Jesus' body. [44]Pilate was surprised to hear that he was already dead; and summoning the centurion, he asked him whether he had been dead long. [45]When he found out from the centurion, he granted the body to Joseph. [46]He bought a linen cloth,

---

[*] 15:32 TR omits "him"

[†] 15:33 or, noon

[‡] 15:33 3:00 p.m.

[§] 15:34 Psalm 22:1

and taking him down, wound him in the linen cloth and laid him in a tomb which had been cut out of a rock. He rolled a stone against the door of the tomb. [47]Mary Magdalene and Mary the mother of Joses, saw where he was laid.

16

[1]When the Sabbath was past, Mary Magdalene, and Mary the mother of James, and Salome bought spices, that they might come and anoint him. [2]Very early on the first day of the week, they came to the tomb when the sun had risen. [3]They were saying among themselves, "Who will roll away the stone from the door of the tomb for us?" [4]for it was very big. Looking up, they saw that the stone was rolled back. [5]Entering into the tomb, they saw a young man sitting on the right side, dressed in a white robe; and they were amazed. [6]He said to them, "Don't be amazed. You seek Jesus, the Nazarene, who has been crucified. He has risen! He is not here. See the place where they laid him! [7]But go, tell his disciples and Peter, 'He goes before you into Galilee. There you will see him, as he said to you.' " [8]They went out,[*] and fled from the tomb, for trembling and astonishment had come on them. They said nothing to anyone; for they were afraid.[†]

[9][‡]Now when he had risen early on the first day of the week, he appeared first to Mary Magdalene, from whom he had cast out seven demons. [10]She went and told those who

---

[*] 16:8 TR adds "quickly"

[†] 16:8 One isolated manuscript omits verses 9-20 but adds this "short ending of Mark" to the end of verse 8: They told all that had been commanded them briefly to those around Peter. After that, Jesus himself sent them out, from east to west, with the sacred and imperishable proclamation of eternal salvation

[‡] 16:9 NU includes the text of verses 9-20, but mentions in a footnote that a few manuscripts omitted it. The translators of the World English Bible regard Mark 16:9-20 as reliable based on an overwhelming majority of textual evidence, including not only the authoritative Greek Majority Text New Testament, but also the TR and many of the manuscripts cited in the NU text

116

had been with him, as they mourned and wept. ¹¹When they heard that he was alive and had been seen by her, they disbelieved.

¹²After these things he was revealed in another form to two of them as they walked, on their way into the country. ¹³They went away and told it to the rest. They didn't believe them, either.

¹⁴Afterward he was revealed to the eleven themselves as they sat at the table; and he rebuked them for their unbelief and hardness of heart, because they didn't believe those who had seen him after he had risen. ¹⁵He said to them, "Go into all the world and preach the Good News to the whole creation. ¹⁶He who believes and is baptized will be saved; but he who disbelieves will be condemned. ¹⁷These signs will accompany those who believe: in my name they will cast out demons; they will speak with new languages; ¹⁸they will take up serpents; and if they drink any deadly thing, it will in no way hurt them; they will lay hands on the sick, and they will recover."

¹⁹So then the Lord,* after he had spoken to them, was received up into heaven and sat down at the right hand of God. ²⁰They went out and preached everywhere, the Lord working with them and confirming the word by the signs that followed. Amen.

---

* 16:19 NU adds "Jesus"

The Good News According to Luke[a]

1

[1]Since many have undertaken to set in order a narrative concerning those matters which have been fulfilled among us, [2]even as those who from the beginning were eyewitnesses and servants of the word delivered them to us, [3]it seemed good to me also, having traced the course of all things accurately from the first, to write to you in order, most excellent Theophilus; [4]that you might know the certainty concerning the things in which you were instructed.

[5]There was in the days of Herod, the king of Judea, a certain priest named Zacharias[b], of the priestly division of Abijah. He had a wife of the daughters of Aaron[c], and her name was Elizabeth. [6]They were both righteous before God, walking blamelessly in all the commandments and ordinances of the Lord. [7]But they had no child,[d] because Elizabeth was barren, and they both were well advanced in years.[e]

[8]Now while he executed the priest's office before God in the order of his division [9]according to the custom of the priest's office, his lot was to enter into the temple of the Lord and burn incense. [10]The whole multitude of the people were praying outside at the hour of incense.[f] [11]An angel of the Lord appeared to him, standing on the right side of the altar of incense. [12]Zacharias was troubled when he saw him, and fear fell upon him. [13]but the angel said to him, "Don't be afraid, Zacharias, because your request has been heard. Your wife, Elizabeth, will bear you a son, and you

g see
footnote

shall call his name John.^g* ¹⁴You will have joy and gladness, and many will rejoice at his birth. ¹⁵For he will be great in the sight of the Lord, and he will drink no wine nor strong drink. He will be filled with the Holy Spirit, even from his mother's womb. ¹⁶He will turn many of the children of Israel to the Lord their God. ¹⁷He will go before him in the spirit and power of Elijah^h, 'to turn the hearts of the fathers to the children,'[†] and the disobedient to the wisdom of the just; to prepare a people prepared for the Lord."

h Q.
19:6

¹⁸Zacharias said to the angel, "How can I be sure of this? For I am an old man, and my wife is well advanced in years."ⁱ ¹⁹The angel answered him, "I am Gabriel, who stands in the presence of God. I was sent to speak to you and to bring you this good news. ²⁰Behold,[‡] you will be silent and not able to speak until the day that these things will happen^j, because you didn't believe my words, which will be fulfilled in their proper time." ²¹The people were waiting for Zacharias, and they marveled that he delayed in the temple. ²²When he came out, he could not speak to them. They perceived that he had seen a vision in the temple. He continued making signs to them^k, and remained mute. ²³When the days of his service were fulfilled, he departed to his house.

i Q.
3:40,
41;
19:8,
10

j Q.
3:41;
19:10

k Q.
19:11

²⁴After these days Elizabeth his wife conceived^l, and she hid herself five months, saying, ²⁵"Thus has the Lord done to me in the days in which he looked at me, to take away my reproach among men.

l Q.
21:90

²⁶Now in the sixth month, the angel Gabriel was sent from God to a city of Galilee named Nazareth, ²⁷to a virgin pledged to be married to a man whose name was Joseph, of David's house. The virgin's name was Mary.^m ²⁸Having come in, the angel said to her, "Rejoice, you highly

m Q.
19:16,
17

---

* ^g Q. 19:7; 21:89, 90

[†] 1:17 Malachi 4:6

[‡] 1:20 "Behold", from "ἰδού", means look at, take notice, observe, see, or gaze at. It is often used as an interjection

favored one! The Lord is with you. Blessed are you among women!"[n] [29]But when she saw him, she was greatly troubled at the saying, and considered what kind of salutation this might be. [30]The angel said to her, "Don't be afraid, Mary, for you have found favor with God.[o] [31]Behold, you will conceive in your womb and give birth to a son,[p] and shall name him 'Jesus.' [32]He will be great and will be called the Son of the Most High. The Lord God will give him the throne of his father David, [33]and he will reign over the house of Jacob forever. There will be no end to his Kingdom."

[34]Mary said to the angel, "How can this be, seeing I am a virgin?"[q][*]

[35]The angel answered her, "The Holy Spirit will come on you, and the power of the Most High will overshadow you.[r][†] Therefore also the holy one who is born from you will be called the Son of God. [36]Behold, Elizabeth your relative also has conceived a son in her old age[s]; and this is the sixth month with her who was called barren. [37]For nothing spoken by God is impossible.[t][‡] [38]Mary said, "Behold, the servant of the Lord; let it be done to me according to your word."[u] Then the angel departed from her.

[39]Mary arose in those days and went into the hill country with haste, into a city of Judah,[v] [40]and entered into the house of Zacharias and greeted Elizabeth. [41]When Elizabeth heard Mary's greeting, the baby leaped in her womb; and Elizabeth was filled with the Holy Spirit. [42]She called out with a loud voice and said, "Blessed are you among women,[w] and blessed is the fruit of your womb! [43]Why am I so favored, that the mother of my Lord should

[n] Q. 3:37
[o] Q. 3:42; 19:18
[p] Q. 3:42, 19:19
[q] see footnote
[r] see footnote
[s] Q. 3:35; 19:7
[t] see footnote
[u] Q. 19:22; 66:12
[v] Q. 19:16, 22
[w] Q. 3:42

[*] [q] Q. 3:47; 19:20; 21:91; 66:12
[†] [r] Q. 3:47; 19:20-22; 21:91; 66:12
[‡] [t] Q. 2:106, 109, 148, 259, 284; 3:26; 5:17, 19; 6:17; 9:39; 11:4; 14:20; 16:77; 18:45; 19:9, 21; 22:6; 24:45; 29:20; 30:50; 33:27; 35:1; 41:39; 42:9; 46:33; 48:21; 57:2; 59:6; 64:1; 65:12; 66:8; 67:1

come to me? 44For behold, when the voice of your greeting came into my ears, the baby leaped in my womb for joy! 45Blessed is she who believed, for there will be a fulfillment of the things which have been spoken to her from the Lord!"x

46Mary said,

"My soul magnifies the Lord.
47My spirit has rejoiced in God my Savior,y*
48for he has looked at the humble state of his servant.

For behold, from now on, all generations will call me blessed.
49For he who is mighty has done great things for me.z

Holy is his name.
50His mercy is for generations and generations on those who fear him.
51He has shown strength with his arm.

He has scattered the proud in the imagination of their hearts.
52He has put down princes from their thrones, and has exalted the lowly.
53He has filled the hungry with good things.

He has sent the rich away empty.
54He has given help to Israel, his servant, that he might remember mercy,
55as he spoke to our fathers, to Abraham and his offspring‡ forever."

56Mary stayed with her about three months, and then returned to her house.

57Now the time that Elizabeth should give birth was fulfilled, and she gave birth to a son.a 58Her neighbors and her relatives heard that the Lord had magnified his mercy toward her, and they rejoiced with her. 59On the eighth day, they came to circumcise the child; and they would

x Q. 3:37; 66:12

y see footnote

z Q. 3:37

a Q. 19:15

---

* y Q. 2:107; 3:150; 8:40; 9:116; 29:22; 42:31
‡ 1:55 or, seed

have called him Zacharias[b], after the name of his father. [60]His mother answered, "Not so; but he will be called John." [61]They said to her, "There is no one among your relatives who is called by this name." [62]They made signs to his father, what he would have him called. [63]He asked for a writing tablet, and wrote, "His name is John."[c] They all marveled. [64]His mouth was opened immediately and his tongue freed, and he spoke, blessing God. [65]Fear came on all who lived around them, and all these sayings were talked about throughout all the hill country of Judea. [66]All who heard them laid them up in their heart, saying, "What then will this child be?" The hand of the Lord was with him.

[67]His father Zacharias was filled with the Holy Spirit,
and prophesied, saying,
[68]"Blessed be the Lord, the God of Israel,
for he has visited and redeemed his people;
[69]and has raised up a horn of salvation for us in the house
of his servant David
[70](as he spoke by the mouth of his holy prophets who
have been from of old),[d]
[71]salvation from our enemies and from the hand of
all who hate us;
[72]to show mercy toward our fathers,
to remember his holy covenant,
[73]the oath which he swore to Abraham our father,
to grant to us
[74]that we, being delivered out of the
hand of our enemies,
should serve him without fear,
[75]in holiness and righteousness before him all the
days of our life.
[76]And you, child, will be called a prophet of the Most High[e];
for you will go before the face of the Lord to prepare
his ways,
[77]to give knowledge of salvation to his people by the
remission of their sins,

[b] Q. 19:2

[c] Q. 19:7

[d] Q. 17:55

[e] Q. 3:39

[78]because of the tender mercy of our God,

by which the dawn from on high will visit us,

[79]to shine on those who sit in darkness and the shadow of death;

to guide our feet into the way of peace."

[80]The child was growing and becoming strong in spirit, and was in the desert until the day of his public appearance to Israel.

2[f*]

[f] see footnote

[1]Now in those days, a decree went out from Caesar Augustus that all the world should be enrolled. [2]This was the first enrollment made when Quirinius was governor of Syria. [3]All went to enroll themselves, everyone to his own city. [4]Joseph also went up from Galilee, out of the city of Nazareth, into Judea, to David's city, which is called Bethlehem, because he was of the house and family of David, [5]to enroll himself with Mary, who was pledged to be married to him as wife, being pregnant. [g] [6]While they were there, the day had come for her to give birth. [7]She gave birth to her firstborn son. She wrapped him in bands of cloth and laid him in a feeding trough, because there was no room for them in the inn.

[g] Q. 19:16

[8]There were shepherds in the same country staying in the field, and keeping watch by night over their flock. [9]Behold, an angel of the Lord stood by them[h], and the glory of the Lord shone around them, and they were terrified. [10]The angel said to them, "Don't be afraid, for behold, I bring you good news of great joy which will be to all the people. [11]For there is born to you today, in David's city, a Savior, who is Christ[†] the Lord.[i] [12]This is the sign to you: you will find a baby wrapped in strips of cloth, lying in a

[h] Q. 97:4

[i] Q. 3:55

---

[*] [f] Q. 2:87, 253; 3:45; 5:110; 19:30; 43:63

[†] 2:11 "Christ" means "Anointed One".

feeding trough." ¹³Suddenly, there was with the angel a multitude of the heavenly army praising God and saying,

¹⁴"Glory to God in the highest,
on earth peace, good will toward men."ʲ

¹⁵When the angels went away from them into the sky, the shepherds said to one another, "Let's go to Bethlehem, now, and see this thing that has happened, which the Lord has made known to us."ᵏ ¹⁶They came with haste and found both Mary and Joseph, and the baby was lying in the feeding trough. ¹⁷When they saw it, they publicized widely the saying which was spoken to them about this child. ¹⁸All who heard it wondered at the things which were spoken to them by the shepherds. ¹⁹But Mary kept all these sayings, pondering them in her heart. ²⁰The shepherds returned, glorifying and praising

²¹God for all the things that they had heard and seen, just as it was told them. When eight days were fulfilled for the circumcision of the child, his name was called Jesus, which was given by the angel before he was conceived in the womb.

²²When the days of their purification according to the law of Moses were fulfilled, they brought him up to Jerusalem to present him to the Lord ²³(as it is written in the law of the Lord, "Every male who opens the womb shall be called holy to the Lord"),* ²⁴and to offer a sacrifice according to that which is said in the law of the Lord, "A pair of turtledoves, or two young pigeons."† ²⁵Behold, there was a man in Jerusalem whose name was Simeon. This man was righteous and devout, looking for the consolation of Israel, and the Holy Spirit was on him. ²⁶It had been revealed to him by the Holy Spirit that he should not see death before he had seen the Lord's Christ.‡ ²⁷He came in the Spirit into the temple. When the parents

ʲ Q. 27:59

ᵏ Q. 44:3

---

* 2:23 Exodus 13:2,12
† 2:24 Leviticus 12:8
‡ 2:26 "Christ" (Greek) and "Messiah" (Hebrew) both mean "Anointed One"

brought in the child, Jesus, that they might do concerning him according to the custom of the law, ²⁸then he received him into his arms and blessed God, and said,

²⁹"Now you are releasing your servant, Master, according to your word, in peace;

³⁰for my eyes have seen your salvation,

³¹which you have prepared before the face of all peoples;

³²a light for revelation to the nations, and the glory of your people Israel."

³³Joseph and his mother were marveling at the things which were spoken concerning him. ³⁴Simeon blessed them, and said to Mary, his mother, "Behold, this child is appointed for the falling and the rising of many in Israel,^l and for a sign which is spoken against. ³⁵Yes, a sword will pierce through your own soul, that the thoughts of many hearts may be revealed."

^l Q. 43:59

³⁶There was one Anna, a prophetess, the daughter of Phanuel, of the tribe of Asher (she was of a great age, having lived with a husband seven years from her virginity, ³⁷and she had been a widow for about eighty-four years), who didn't depart from the temple, worshiping with fastings^m and petitions night and day. ³⁸Coming up at that very hour, she gave thanks to the Lord, and spoke of him to all those who were looking for redemption in Jerusalem.

^m Q. 2:183

³⁹When they had accomplished all things that were according to the law of the Lord, they returned into Galilee, to their own city, Nazareth. ⁴⁰The child was growing, and was becoming strong in spirit, being filled with wisdom, and the grace of God was upon him.

⁴¹His parents went every year to Jerusalem at the feast of the Passover. ⁴²When he was twelve years old, they went up to Jerusalem according to the custom of the feast; ⁴³and when they had fulfilled the days, as they were returning, the boy Jesus stayed behind in Jerusalem. Joseph and his mother didn't know it, ⁴⁴but supposing

him to be in the company, they went a day's journey; and they looked for him among their relatives and acquaintances. [45]When they didn't find him, they returned to Jerusalem, looking for him. [46]After three days they found him in the temple, sitting in the middle of the teachers, both listening to them and asking them questions. [47]All who heard him were amazed at his understanding and his answers. [48]When they saw him, they were astonished; and his mother said to him, "Son, why have you treated us this way? Behold, your father and I were anxiously looking for you." [49]He said to them, "Why were you looking for me? Didn't you know that I must be in my Father's house?" [50]They didn't understand the saying which he spoke to them. [51]And he went down with them and came to Nazareth. He was subject to them, and his mother kept all these sayings in her heart.

[52]And Jesus increased in wisdom and stature, and in favor with God and men.

3

[1]Now in the fifteenth year of the reign of Tiberius Caesar, Pontius Pilate being governor of Judea, and Herod being tetrarch of Galilee, and his brother Philip tetrarch of the region of Ituraea and Trachonitis, and Lysanias tetrarch of Abilene, [2]during the high priesthood of Annas and Caiaphas, the word of God came to John, the son of Zacharias, in the wilderness. [3]He came into all the region around the Jordan, preaching the baptism of repentance

for remission of sins. [4]As it is written in the book of the words of Isaiah the prophet,

"The voice of one crying in the wilderness, 'Make ready the way of the Lord.

Make his paths straight.[n]

[5]Every valley will be filled.

Every mountain and hill will be brought low.

[n] Q. 11:19

The crooked will become straight, and the rough ways smooth.

⁶All flesh will see God's salvation.' "*

⁷He said therefore to the multitudes who went out to be baptized by him, "You offspring of vipers, who warned you to flee from the wrath to come? ⁸Therefore produce fruits worthy of repentance, and don't begin to say among yourselves, 'We have Abraham for our father;' for I tell you that God is able to raise up children to Abraham from these stones!° ⁹Even now the ax also lies at the root of the trees. Every tree therefore that doesn't produce good fruit is cut down and thrown into the fire."

° Q.
35:16

¹⁰The multitudes asked him, "What then must we do?" ¹¹He answered them, "He who has two coats, let him give to him who has none. He who has food, let him do likewise." ¹²Tax collectors also came to be baptized, and they said to him, "Teacher, what must we do?" ¹³He said to them, "Collect no more than that which is appointed to you." ¹⁴Soldiers also asked him, saying, "What about us? What must we do?" He said to them, "Extort from no one by violence, neither accuse anyone wrongfully. Be content with your wages."

¹⁵As the people were in expectation, and all men reasoned in their hearts concerning John, whether perhaps he was the Christ, ¹⁶John answered them all, "I indeed baptize you with water, but he comes who is mightier than I, the strap of whose sandals I am not worthy to loosen. He will baptize you in the Holy Spirit and fire. ¹⁷His winnowing fan is in his hand, and he will thoroughly cleanse his threshing floor, and will gather the wheat into his barn; but he will burn up the chaff with unquenchable fire."ᵖ

ᵖ Q.
88:4

¹⁸Then with many other exhortations he preached good news to the people, ¹⁹but Herod the tetrarch,† being

---

* 3:6 Isaiah 40:3-5
† 3:19 a tetrarch is one of four governors of a province

reproved by him for Herodias, his brother's[*] wife, and for all the evil things which Herod had done, [20]added this also to them all, that he shut up John in prison.

[21]Now when all the people were baptized, Jesus also had been baptized and was praying. The sky was opened, [22]and the Holy Spirit descended in a bodily form like a dove on him; and a voice came out of the sky, saying "You are my beloved Son. In you I am well pleased."

[23]Jesus himself, when he began to teach[q], was about thirty years old, being the son (as was supposed) of Joseph, the son of Heli, [24]the son of Matthat, the son of Levi, the son of Melchi, the son of Jannai, the son of Joseph, [25]the son of Mattathias, the son of Amos, the son of Nahum, the son of Esli, the son of Naggai, [26]the son of Maath, the son of Mattathias, the son of Semein, the son of Joseph, the son of Judah, [27]the son of Joanan, the son of Rhesa, the son of Zerubbabel, the son of Shealtiel, the son of Neri, [28]the son of Melchi, the son of Addi, the son of Cosam, the son of Elmodam, the son of Er, [29]the son of Jose, the son of Eliezer, the son of Jorim, the son of Matthat, the son of Levi, [30]the son of Simeon, the son of Judah, the son of Joseph, the son of Jonan, the son of Eliakim, [31]the son of Melea, the son of Menan, the son of Mattatha, the son of Nathan, the son of David, [32]the son of Jesse, the son of Obed, the son of Boaz, the son of Salmon, the son of Nahshon, [33]the son of Amminadab, the son of Aram,[†] the son of Hezron, the son of Perez, the son of Judah, [34]the son of Jacob, the son of Isaac, the son of Abraham, the son of Terah, the son of Nahor, [35]the son of Serug, the son of Reu, the son of Peleg, the son of Eber, the son of Shelah[r‡], [36]the son of Cainan, the son of Arphaxad, the son of Shem, the son of Noah, the son of Lamech, [37]the son of Methuselah, the son of Enoch, the son of Jared, the son of Mahalaleel, the son of Cainan, [38]the son of Enos, the son of

[q] Q. 3:46

[r] Q. see footnote

[*] 3:19 TR reads "brother Philip's" instead of "brother's"
[†] 3:33 NU reads "Admin, the son of Arni" instead of "Aram"
[‡][r] Q. 7:73; 11:61; 26:142; 27:45

128

Seth, the son of Adam, the son of God.

^s Q.
see
footnote

^t Q.
2:87,
253;
5:110

^u Q.
25:7

^v Q.
3:79

4^{s*}

¹Jesus, full of the Holy Spirit,^t returned from the Jordan and was led by the Spirit into the wilderness ²for forty days, being tempted by the devil. He ate nothing in those days.^u Afterward, when they were completed, he was hungry. ³The devil said to him, "If you are the Son of God, command this stone to become bread." ⁴Jesus answered him, saying, "It is written, 'Man shall not live by bread alone, but by every word of God.' "[†] ⁵The devil, leading him up on a high mountain, showed him all the kingdoms of the world in a moment of time. ⁶The devil said to him, "I will give you all this authority and their glory, for it has been delivered to me, and I give it to whomever I want. ⁷If you therefore will worship before me, it will all be yours." ⁸Jesus answered him,

"Get behind me, Satan! For it is written, 'You shall worship the Lord your God, and you shall serve him only.' "^{v‡}

⁹He led him to Jerusalem and set him on the pinnacle of the temple, and said to him, "If you are the Son of God, cast yourself down from here, ¹⁰for it is written,

'He will put his angels in charge of you, to guard you;'
¹¹and,

'On their hands they will bear you up,
lest perhaps you dash your foot against a stone.' "[§]

¹²Jesus answering, said to him, "It has been said, 'You shall not tempt the Lord your God.' "^{**} ¹³When the devil had completed every temptation, he departed from him

---

[*] ^s Q. 2:87, 253; 3:49, 52; 5:110, 112; 19:30-34; 43:63
[†] 4:4 Deuteronomy 8:3
[‡] 4:8 Deuteronomy 6:13
[§] 4:11 Psalm 91:11-12
^{**} 4:12 Deuteronomy 6:16

until another time.

¹⁴Jesus returned in the power of the Spirit[w] into Galilee, and news about him spread through all the surrounding area. ¹⁵He taught in their synagogues, being glorified by all.

¹⁶He came to Nazareth, where he had been brought up. He entered, as was his custom, into the synagogue on the Sabbath[x] day, and stood up to read. ¹⁷The book of the prophet Isaiah was handed to him. He opened the book, and found the place where it was written,

¹⁸"The Spirit of the Lord is on me,[y]

because he has anointed me to preach good news to the poor.

He has sent me to heal the broken hearted,[*] to proclaim release to the captives, recovering of sight to the blind,

to deliver those who are crushed,

¹⁹and to proclaim the acceptable year of the Lord."[†]

²⁰He closed the book, gave it back to the attendant, and sat down. The eyes of all in the synagogue were fastened on him. ²¹He began to tell them, "Today, this Scripture has been fulfilled in your hearing." ²²All testified about him and wondered at the gracious words which proceeded out of his mouth; and they said," Is not this Joseph's son?" ²³"He said to them, "Doubtless you will tell me this proverb, 'Physician , heal yourself! Whatever we have heard done at Capernaum, do also here in your hometown.' " ²⁴He said, "Most certainly I tell you, no prophet is acceptable in his hometown. ²⁵But truly I tell you, there were many widows in Israel in the days of Elijah, when the sky was shut up three years and six months, when a great famine came over all the land. ²⁶Elijah was sent to none of them, except to Zarephath, in the land of Sidon, to a woman who was a widow. ²⁷There were many lepers in Israel in the time of Elisha the prophet, yet not one of them was cleansed, except Naaman, the

[w] Q. 5:110

[x] Q. 4:47

[y] Q. 5:110

---

* 4:18 NU omits "to heal the broken hearted"
† 4:19 Isaiah 61:1-2

Syrian." ²⁸They were all filled with wrath in the synagogue as they heard these things. ²⁹They rose up, threw him out of the city, and led him to the brow of the hill that their city was built on, that they might throw him off the cliff. ³⁰But he, passing through the middle of them, went his way.

³¹He came down to Capernaum, a city of Galilee. He was teaching them on the Sabbath day, ³²and they were astonished at his teaching, for his word was with authority. ³³In the synagogue there was a man who had a spirit of an unclean demon; and he cried out with a loud voice, ³⁴saying, "Ah! what have we to do with you, Jesus of Nazareth? Have you come to destroy us? I know who you are: the Holy One of God!" ³⁵Jesus rebuked him, saying, "Be silent and come out of him!" When the demon had thrown him down in the middle of them, he came out of him, having done him no harm. ³⁶Amazement came on all and they spoke together, one with another, saying, "What is this word? For with authority and power he commands the unclean spirits, and they come out!" ³⁷News about him went out into every place of the surrounding region.

³⁸He rose up from the synagogue and entered into Simon's house. Simon's mother-in-law was afflicted with a great fever, and they begged him to help her. ³⁹He stood over her and rebuked the fever, and it left her. Immediately she rose up and served them.

⁴⁰When the sun was setting, all those who had any sick[z] with various diseases brought them to him; and he laid his hands on every one of them, and healed them. ⁴¹Demons also came out of many, crying out and saying, "You are the Christ, the Son of God!" Rebuking them, he didn't allow them to speak, because they knew that he was the Christ.

⁴²When it was day, he departed and went into an uninhabited place and the multitudes looked for him, and came to him, and held on to him, so that he wouldn't go away from them. ⁴³But he said to them, "I must preach the good news of God's Kingdom to the other cities also. For

[z] Q. 3:49

this reason I have been sent." 44He was preaching in the synagogues of Galilee.

5a*

1Now while the multitude pressed on him and heard the word of God, he was standing by the lake of Gennesaret. 2He saw two boats standing by the lake, but the fishermen had gone out of them and were washing their nets. 3He entered into one of the boats, which was Simon's, and asked him to put out a little from the land. He sat down and taught the multitudes from the boat. 4When he had finished speaking, he said to Simon, "Put out into the deep and let down your nets for a catch." 5Simon answered him, "Master, we worked all night and caught nothing; but at your word I will let down the net." 6When they had done this, they caught a great multitude of fish, and their net was breaking. 7They beckoned to their partners in the other boat, that they should come and help them. They came and filled both boats, so that they began to sink. 8But Simon Peter, when he saw it, fell down at Jesus' knees, saying, "Depart from me, for I am a sinful man, Lord." 9For he was amazed, and all who were with him, at the catch of fish which they had caught; 10and so also were James and John, sons of Zebedee, who were partners with Simon. Jesus said to Simon, "Don't be afraid. From now on you will be catching people alive." 11When they had brought their boats to land, they left everything, and followed him.

12While he was in one of the cities, behold, there was a man full of leprosy. When he saw Jesus, he fell on his face and begged him, saying, "Lord, if you want to, you can make me clean." 13He stretched out his hand and touched him, saying, "I want to. Be made clean." Immediately the leprosy left him. 14He commanded him to tell no one, "But

---

* a Q. 2:87, 253; 3:49, 52; 5:110, 112; 19:30; 43:63

go your way and show yourself to the priest, and offer for your cleansing according to what Moses commanded, for a testimony to them." ¹⁵But the report concerning him spread much more, and great multitudes came together to hear and to be healed by him of their infirmities. ¹⁶But he withdrew himself into the desert and prayed.

¹⁷On one of those days, he was teaching; and there were Pharisees and teachers of the law sitting by who had come out of every village of Galilee, Judea, and Jerusalem. The power of the Lord was with him to heal them.ᵇ ¹⁸Behold, men brought a paralyzed man on a cot, and they sought to bring him in to lay before Jesus. ¹⁹Not finding a way to bring him in because of the multitude, they went up to the housetop and let him down through the tiles with his cot into the middle before Jesus. ²⁰Seeing their faith, he said to him, "Man, your sins are forgiven you." The scribes and the Pharisees began to reason, saying, "Who is this who speaks blasphemies? Who can forgive sins, but God alone?"ᶜ But Jesus, perceiving their thoughts, answered them, "Why are you reasoning so in your hearts? ²³Which is easier to say, 'Your sins are forgiven you,' or to say, 'Arise and walk?' ²⁴But that you may know that the Son of Man has authority on earth to forgive sins," he said to the paralyzed man, "I tell you, arise, take up your cot, and go to your house." ²⁵Immediately he rose up before them, and took up that which he was laying on, and departed to his house, glorifying God. ²⁶Amazement took hold on all, and they glorified God. They were filled with fear, saying, "We have seen strange things today."

²⁷After these things he went out and saw a tax collector named Levi sitting at the tax office, and said to him, "Follow me!" ²⁸He left everything, and rose up and followed him.

²⁹Levi made a great feast for him in his house. There was a great crowd of tax collectors and others who were reclining with them. ³⁰Their scribes and the Pharisees

ᵇ Q. 3:49

ᶜ Q. 3:135

murmured against his disciples, saying, "Why do you eat and drink with the tax collectors and sinners?" ³¹Jesus answered them, "Those who are healthy have no need for a physician, but those who are sick do. ³²I have not come to call the righteous, but sinners, to repentance."

³³They said to him, "Why do John's disciples often fast and pray, likewise also the disciples of the Pharisees, but yours eat and drink?" ³⁴He said to them, "Can you make the friends of the bridegroom fast while the bridegroom is with them? ³⁵But the days will come when the bridegroom will be taken away from them. Then they will fast in those days." ³⁶He also told a parable to them. "No one puts a piece from a new garment on an old garment, or else he will tear the new, and also the piece from the new will not match the old. ³⁷No one puts new wine into old wine skins, or else the new wine will burst the skins, and it will be spilled and the skins will be destroyed. ³⁸But new wine must be put into fresh wine skins, and both are preserved. ³⁹No man having drunk old wine immediately desires new, for he says, 'The old is better.' "

6ᵈ*

ᵈ see footnote

¹Now on the second Sabbath after the first, he was going through the grain fields. His disciples plucked the heads of grain and ate, rubbing them in their hands. ²But some of the Pharisees said to them, "Why do you do that which is not lawful to do on the Sabbath day?" ³Jesus, answering them, said, "Haven't you read what David did when he was hungry, he and those who were with him, ⁴how he entered into God's house, and took and ate the show bread, and gave also to those who were with him, which is not lawful to eat except for the priests alone?" ⁵He said to them, "The Son of Man is lord of the Sabbath."

* ᵈ Q. 2:87, 253; 3:49, 52; 5:110, 112; 19:30; 43:63

⁶It also happened on another Sabbath that he entered into the synagogue and taught. There was a man there, and his right hand was withered. ⁷The scribes and the Pharisees watched him, to see whether he would heal on the Sabbath, that they might find an accusation against him. ⁸But he knew their thoughts^e; and he said to the man who had the withered hand, "Rise up and stand in the middle." He arose and stood. ⁹Then Jesus said to them, "I will ask you something: Is it lawful on the Sabbath to do good, or to do harm? To save a life, or to kill?" ¹⁰He looked around at them all, and said to the man, "Stretch out your hand." He did, and his hand was restored as sound as the other. ¹¹But they were filled with rage, and talked with one another about what they might do to Jesus.

¹²In these days, he went out to the mountain to pray, and he continued all night in prayer to God. ¹³When it was day, he called his disciples, and from them he chose twelve, whom he also named apostles: ¹⁴Simon, whom he also named Peter; Andrew, his brother; James; John; Philip; Bartholomew; ¹⁵Matthew; Thomas; James the son of Alphaeus; Simon who was called the Zealot; ¹⁶Judas the son of James; and Judas Iscariot, who also became a traitor.

¹⁷He came down with them and stood on a level place, with a crowd of his disciples and a great number of the people from all Judea and Jerusalem and the sea coast of Tyre and Sidon, who came to hear him and to be healed^f of their diseases, ¹⁸as well as those who were troubled by unclean spirits; and they were being healed. ¹⁹All the multitude sought to touch him, for power came out of him and healed them all.

²⁰He lifted up his eyes to his disciples, and said:

"Blessed are you who are poor^g, for God's Kingdom is yours.

²¹Blessed are you who hunger^h now, for you will be filled. Blessed are you who weep now, for you will laugh.

²²Blessed are you when men hate you, and when they

e Q.
3:49;
72:26

f Q.
3:49

g Q.
2:177

h Q.
2:177

exclude and mock you, and throw out your name as evil, for the Son of Man's sake. [23]Rejoice in that day and leap for joy, for behold, your reward[i] is great in heaven, for their fathers did the same thing to the prophets.

[24]"But woe to you who are rich! For you have received your consolation.

[25]Woe[j] to you, you who are full now, for you will be hungry.

Woe to you who laugh now, for you will mourn and weep.

[26]Woe,[*] when[†] men speak well of you, for their fathers did the same thing to the false prophets.[k]

[27]"But I tell you who hear: love your enemies, do good to those who hate you, [28]bless those who curse you[l], and pray for those who mistreat you. [29]To him who strikes you on the cheek, offer also the other; and from him who takes away your cloak, don't withhold your coat also. [30]Give to everyone who asks you, and don't ask him who takes away your goods to give them back again. [31]"As you would like people to do to you, do exactly so to them.

[32]"If you love those who love you, what credit is that to you? For even sinners love those who love them. [33]If you do good to those who do good to you, what credit is that to you? For even sinners do the same. [34]If you lend to those from whom you hope to receive, what credit is that to you? Even sinners lend to sinners, to receive back as much. [35]But love your enemies, and do good, and lend, expecting nothing back; and your reward will be great[m], and you will be children of the Most High; for he is kind toward the unthankful and evil. [36]"Therefore be merciful, even as your Father is also merciful.[n]

[37]Don't judge, and you won't be judged. Don't condemn, and you won't be condemned. Set free, and you will be set free. [38]"Give, and it will be given to you: good measure,

[i] Q. 3:57, 144

[j] Q. 53:43

[k] Q. 25:31

[l] Q. 3:159

[m] Q. 3:57, 144; 35:7; 46:14

[n] Q. 42:40

---

[*] 6:26 TR adds "to you"
[†] 6:26 TR adds "all"

pressed down, shaken together, and running over, will be given to you.* For with the same measure you measure it will be measured back to you."

³⁹He spoke a parable to them. "Can the blind guide the blind? Won't they both fall into a pit? ⁴⁰A disciple is not above his teacher, but everyone when he is fully trained will be like his teacher. ⁴¹Why do you see the speck of chaff that is in your brother's eye, but don't consider the beam that is in your own eye? ⁴²Or how can you tell your brother, 'Brother, let me remove the speck of chaff that is in your eye,' when you yourself don't see the beam that is in your own eye? You hypocrite! First remove the beam from your own eye, and then you can see clearly to remove the speck of chaff that is in your brother's eye.

⁴³"For there is no good tree that produces rotten fruit, nor again a rotten tree that produces good fruit. ⁴⁴For each tree is known by its own fruit. For people don't gather figs from thorns, nor do they gather grapes from a bramble bush. ⁴⁵The good man out of the good treasure of his heart brings out that which is good, and the evil man out of the evil treasure of his heart brings out that which is evil, for out of the abundance of the heart, his mouth speaks.

⁴⁶"Why do you call me, 'Lord, Lord,' and don't do the things which I say? ⁴⁷Everyone who comes to me, and hears my words and does them, I will show you who he is like. ⁴⁸He is like a man building a house, who dug and went deep and laid a foundation on the rock. When a flood arose, the stream broke against that house, and could not shake it, because it was founded on the rock. ⁴⁹But he who hears and doesn't do, is like a man who built a house on the earth without a foundation, against which the stream broke, and immediately it fell; and the ruin of that house was great."

---

* 6:38 literally, into your bosom.

7°*

° see footnote

¹After he had finished speaking in the hearing of the people, he entered into Capernaum. ²A certain centurion's servant, who was dear to him, was sick and at the point of death. ³When he heard about Jesus, he sent to him elders of the Jews, asking him to come and save his servant. ⁴When they came to Jesus, they begged him earnestly, saying, "He is worthy for you to do this for him, ⁵for he loves our nation, and he built our synagogue for us." ⁶Jesus went with them. When he was now not far from the house, the centurion sent friends to him, saying to him, "Lord, don't trouble yourself, for I am not worthy for you to come under my roof. ⁷Therefore I didn't even think myself worthy to come to you; but say the word, and my servant will be healed.ᵖ ⁸For I also am a man placed under authority, having under myself soldiers. I tell this one, 'Go!' and he goes; and to another, 'Come!' and he comes; and to my servant, 'Do this,' and he does it." ⁹When Jesus heard these things, he marveled at him, and turned and said to the multitude who followed him, "I tell you, I have not found such great faith, no, not in Israel." ¹⁰Those who were sent, returning to the house, found that the servant who had been sick was well.

ᵖ Q. 3:49

¹¹Soon afterwards, he went to a city called Nain. Many of his disciples, along with a great multitude, went with him. ¹²Now when he came near to the gate of the city, behold, one who was dead was carried out, the only born† son of his mother, and she was a widow. Many people of the city were with her. ¹³When the Lord saw her, he had compassion on her and said to her, "Don't cry." ¹⁴He came near and touched the coffin, and the bearers stood still. He said, "Young man, I tell you, arise!"�q ¹⁵He who was dead sat up and began to speak.ʳ Then he gave him to his mother. ¹⁶Fear took hold of

q Q. 5:110

ʳ Q. 3:49

---

* ° Q. 2:87, 253; 3:49, 52; 5:110, 112; 19:30; 43:63
† 7:12 The phrase "only born" is from the Greek word "μονογενη", which is sometimes translated "only begotten" or "one and only".

138

all, and they glorified God, saying, "A great prophet has arisen among us!" and, "God has visited his people!" [17]This report went out concerning him in the whole of Judea and in all the surrounding region.

[18]The disciples of John told him about all these things. [19]John, calling to himself two of his disciples, sent them to Jesus, saying, "Are you the one who is coming, or should we look for another?" [20]When the men had come to him, they said, "John the Baptizer has sent us to you, saying, 'Are you he who comes, or should we look for another?' " [21]In that hour he cured many of diseases and plagues and evil spirits; and to many who were blind he gave sight. [22]Jesus answered them, "Go and tell John the things which you have seen and heard: that the blind receive their sight, the lame walk, the lepers are cleansed, the deaf hear[s], the dead are raised up, and the poor have good news preached to them. [23]Blessed is he who finds no occasion for stumbling in me."

[24]When John's messengers had departed, he began to tell the multitudes about John, "What did you go out into the wilderness to see? A reed shaken by the wind? [25]But what did you go out to see? A man clothed in soft clothing? Behold, those who are gorgeously dressed and live delicately are in kings' courts. [26]But what did you go out to see? A prophet? Yes, I tell you, and much more than a prophet. [27]This is he of whom it is written,

'Behold, I send my messenger[t] before your face, who will prepare your way before you.'[*]

[28]"For I tell you, among those who are born of women there is not a greater prophet than John the Baptizer; yet he who is least in God's Kingdom is greater than he." [29]When all the people and the tax collectors heard this, they declared God to be just, having been baptized with John's baptism. [30]But the Pharisees and the lawyers rejected the

[s] Q. 10:42

[t] Q. 64:12

---

[*] 7:27 Malachi 3:1

counsel of God, not being baptized by him themselves.

^{31*}"To what then should I compare the people of this generation? What are they like? ³²They are like children who sit in the marketplace and call to one another, saying,

'We piped to you, and you didn't dance.

We mourned, and you didn't weep.'

³³For John the Baptizer came neither eating bread nor drinking wine, and you say, 'He has a demon.' ³⁴The Son of Man has come eating and drinking, and you say, 'Behold, a glutton and a drunkard, a friend of tax collectors and sinners!' ³⁵Wisdom is justified by all her children.'"

³⁶One of the Pharisees invited him to eat with him. He entered into the Pharisee's house and sat at the table. ³⁷Behold, a woman in the city who was a sinner, when she knew that he was reclining in the Pharisee's house, brought an alabaster jar of ointment. ³⁸Standing behind at his feet weeping, she began to wet his feet with her tears, and she wiped them with the hair of her head, kissed his feet, and anointed them with the ointment. ³⁹Now when the Pharisee who had invited him saw it, he said to himself, "This man, if he were a prophet, would have perceived who and what kind of woman this is who touches him, that she is a sinner." ⁴⁰Jesus answered him, "Simon, I have something to tell you." He said, "Teacher, say on."

⁴¹"A certain lender had two debtors. The one owed five hundred denarii, and the other fifty. ⁴²When they couldn't pay, he forgave them both. Which of them therefore will love him most?" ⁴³Simon answered, "He, I suppose, to whom he forgave the most." He said to him, "You have judged correctly." ⁴⁴Turning to the woman, he said to Simon, "Do you see this woman? I entered into your house, and you gave me no water for my feet, but she has wet my feet with her tears, and wiped them with the hair of her head. ⁴⁵You gave me no kiss, but she, since the time I came in,

---

* 7:31 TR adds "But the Lord said,"

has not ceased to kiss my feet. [46]You didn't anoint my head with oil, but she has anointed my feet with ointment. [47]Therefore I tell you, her sins, which are many, are forgiven, for she loved much. But one to whom little is forgiven, loves little." [48]He said to her, "Your sins are forgiven." Those who sat at the table with him began to say to themselves, "Who is this who even forgives sins?" He said to the woman, "Your faith has saved you. Go in peace."

8[u*]

[u] see footnote

[1]Soon afterwards, he went about through cities and villages, preaching and bringing the good news of God's Kingdom. With him were the twelve, [2]and certain women who had been healed[v] of evil spirits and infirmities: Mary who was called Magdalene, from whom seven demons had gone out; [3]and Joanna, the wife of Chuzas, Herod's steward; Susanna; and many others who served them[†] from their possessions.

[v] Q. 3:49

[4]When a great multitude came together and people from every city were coming to him, he spoke by a parable: [5]"The farmer went out to sow his seed. As he sowed, some fell along the road, and it was trampled under foot, and the birds of the sky devoured it. [6]Other seed fell on the rock, and as soon as it grew, it withered away, because it had no moisture. [7]Other fell amid the thorns, and the thorns grew with it and choked it. [8]Other fell into the good ground and grew and produced one hundred times as much fruit." As he said these things, he called out, "He who has ears to hear, let him hear!"

[9]Then his disciples asked him, "What does this parable mean?" [10]He said, "To you it is given to know the mysteries of God's Kingdom[w], but to the rest it is given in parables, that 'seeing they may not see, and hearing they

[w] Q. 3:13

---

* [u] Q. 2:87, 253; 3:49, 52; 5:110, 112; 19:30; 43:63
[†] 8:3 TR reads "him" instead of "them

may not understand.'* 11"Now the parable is this: The seed is the word of God. 12Those along the road are those who hear; then the devil comes and takes away the word from their heart, that they may not believe and be saved. 13Those on the rock are they who, when they hear, receive the word with joy; but these have no root. They believe for a while, then fall away in time of temptation. 14What fell among the thorns, these are those who have heard, and as they go on their way they are choked with cares, riches, and pleasures of life; and they bring no fruit to maturity. 15Those in the good ground, these are those who with an honest and good heart, having heard the word, hold it tightly, and produce fruit with perseverance.

16"No one, when he has lit a lamp, covers it with a container or puts it under a bed; but puts it on a stand, that those who enter in may see the light.x 17For nothing is hidden y that will not be revealed, nor anything secret that will not be known and come to light. 18Be careful therefore how you hear. For whoever has, to him will be given; and whoever doesn't have, from him will be taken away even that which he thinks he has."

x Q. 29:10

y Q. 36:76

19His mother and brothers came to him, and they could not come near him for the crowd. 20Some people told him, "Your mother and your brothers stand outside, desiring to see you." 21But he answered them, "My mother and my brothers are these who hear the word of God and do it."

22Now on one of those days, he entered into a boat, himself and his disciples, and he said to them, "Let's go over to the other side of the lake." So they launched out. 23But as they sailed, he fell asleep. A wind storm came down on the lake, and they were taking on dangerous amounts of water. 24They came to him and awoke him, saying, "Master, Master, we are dying!" He awoke and rebuked the wind and the raging of the water; then they

---

* 8:10 Isaiah 6:9

ceased, and it was calm.[*] ²⁵He said to them, "Where is your faith?" Being afraid, they marveled, saying to one another, "Who is this then, that he commands even the winds and the water, and they obey him?"

²⁶Then they arrived at the country of the Gadarenes, which is opposite Galilee. ²⁷When Jesus stepped ashore, a certain man out of the city who had demons for a long time met him. He wore no clothes, and didn't live in a house, but in the tombs. ²⁸When he saw Jesus, he cried out and fell down before him, and with a loud voice said, "What do I have to do with you, Jesus, you Son of the Most High God? I beg you, don't torment me!" ²⁹For Jesus was commanding the unclean spirit to come out of the man. For the unclean spirit had often seized the man. He was kept under guard and bound with chains and fetters. Breaking the bonds apart, he was driven by the demon into the desert. ³⁰Jesus asked him, "What is your name?" He said, "Legion," for many demons had entered into him. ³¹They begged him that he would not command them to go into the abyss. ³²Now there was there a herd of many pigs feeding on the mountain, and they begged him that he would allow them to enter into those. Then he allowed them. ³³The demons came out of the man and entered into the pigs, and the herd rushed down the steep bank into the lake and were drowned.

³⁴When those who fed them saw what had happened, they fled and told it in the city and in the country. ³⁵People went out to see what had happened. They came to Jesus and found the man from whom the demons had gone out, sitting at Jesus' feet, clothed and in his right mind; and they were afraid. ³⁶Those who saw it told them how he who had been possessed by demons was healed. ³⁷All the people of the surrounding country of the Gadarenes asked him to depart from them, for they were very much afraid.

---

[*] 8:24 See Psalm 107:29

Then he entered into the boat and returned. ³⁸But the man from whom the demons had gone out begged him that he might go with him, but Jesus sent him away, saying, ³⁹"Return to your house, and declare what great things God has done for you."ᶻ He went his way, proclaiming throughout the whole city what great things Jesus had done for him.

ᶻ Q.
3:49

⁴⁰When Jesus returned, the multitude welcomed him, for they were all waiting for him. ⁴¹Behold, a man named Jairus came. He was a ruler of the synagogue. He fell down at Jesus' feet and begged him to come into his house, ⁴²for he had an only born* daughter, about twelve years of age, and she was dying.ᵃ But as he went, the multitudes pressed against him. ⁴³A woman who had a flow of blood for twelve years, who had spent all her living on physicians and could not be healed by any, ⁴⁴came behind him and touched the fringe† of his cloak. Immediately the flow of her blood stopped.ᵇ ⁴⁵Jesus said, "Who touched me?" When all denied it, Peter and those with him said, "Master, the multitudes press and jostle you, and you say, 'Who touched me?'" ⁴⁶But Jesus said, "Someone did touch me, for I perceived that power has gone out of me." ⁴⁷When the woman saw that she was not hidden, she came trembling; and falling down before him declared to him in the presence of all the people the reason why she had touched him, and how she was healed immediately. ⁴⁸He said to her, "Daughter, cheer up. Your faith has made you well. Go in peace."

ᵃ Q.
5:110

ᵇ Q.
3:49

⁴⁹While he still spoke, one from the ruler of the synagogue's house came, saying to him, "Your daughter is dead. Don't trouble the Teacher." But Jesus hearing it, answered him, "Don't be afraid. Only believe, and she will be healed." When he came to the house, he didn't allow anyone to enter in, except Peter, John, James, the father of

---

* 8:42 The phrase "only born" is from the Greek word "μονογενη", which is sometimes translated "only begotten" or "one and only".
† 8:44 or, tassel

144

the child, and her mother. [52]All were weeping and mourning her, but he said, "Don't weep. She isn't dead, but sleeping." [53]They were ridiculing him, knowing that she was dead. [54]But he put them all outside, and taking her by the hand, he called, saying, "Child, arise!" [55]Her spirit returned, and she rose up immediately. He commanded that something be given to her to eat. [56]Her parents were amazed, but he commanded them to tell no one what had been done.

9[c][*]

[c] see footnote

[1]He called the twelve[†] together and gave them power and authority over all demons, and to cure diseases. [2]He sent them out to preach God's Kingdom and to heal the sick. [3]He said to them, "Take nothing for your journey no staffs, nor wallet, nor bread, nor money. Don't have two tunics each. [4]Into whatever house you enter, stay there, and depart from there. [5]As many as don't receive you, when you depart from that city, shake off even the dust from your feet for a testimony against them." [6]They departed and went throughout the villages, preaching the Good News and healing everywhere.

[7]Now Herod the tetrarch heard of all that was done by him; and he was very perplexed, because it was said by some that John had risen from the dead, [8]and by some that Elijah had appeared, and by others that one of the old prophets had risen again. [9]Herod said, "I beheaded John, but who is this about whom I hear such things?" He sought to see him.

[10]The apostles, when they had returned, told him what things they had done. He took them and withdrew apart to a desert region of[‡] a city called Bethsaida. [11]But the multitudes, perceiving it, followed him. He welcomed

---

[*] [c] Q. 2:87, 253; 3:49, 52; 5:110, 112; 19:30; 43:63

[†] 9:1 TR reads "his twelve disciples" instead of "the twelve"

[‡] 9:10 NU omits "a desert region of ".

them, spoke to them of God's Kingdom, and he cured those who needed healing. [12]The day began to wear away; and the twelve came and said to him, "Send the multitude away, that they may go into the surrounding villages and farms and lodge and get food, for we are here in a deserted place." [13]But he said to them, "You give them something to eat." They said, "We have no more than five loaves and two fish, unless we should go and buy food for all these people." [14]For they were about five thousand men. He said to his disciples, "Make them sit down in groups of about fifty each." [15]They did so, and made them all sit down. [16]He took the five loaves and the two fish, and looking up to the sky, he blessed them, broke them, and gave them to the disciples to set before the multitude.[d] [17]They ate and were all filled. They gathered up twelve baskets of broken pieces that were left over.

[d] Q. 3:49; 5:112

[18]As he was praying alone, the disciples were near him, and he asked them, "Who do the multitudes say that I am?" [19]They answered, "'John the Baptizer,' but others say, 'Elijah,' and others, that one of the old prophets has risen again." [20]He said to them, "But who do you say that I am?" Peter answered, "The Christ of God."

[21]But he warned them and commanded them to tell this to no one, [22]saying, "The Son of Man must suffer many things, and be rejected by the elders, chief priests, and scribes, and be killed, and the third day be raised up."

[23]He said to all, "If anyone desires to come after me, let him deny himself, take up his cross,[*] and follow me. [24]For whoever desires to save his life will lose it, but whoever will lose his life for my sake will save it. [25]For what does it profit a man if he gains the whole world, and loses or forfeits his own self? [26]For whoever will be ashamed of me and of my words, of him will the Son of Man be ashamed when he comes in his glory, and the glory of the Father, and of the

---

[*] 9:23 TR, NU add "daily"

holy angels. 27But I tell you the truth: There are some of those who stand here who will in no way taste of death until they see God's Kingdom."

28About eight days after these sayings, he took with him Peter, John, and James, and went up onto the mountain to pray. 29As he was praying, the appearance of his face was altered, and his clothing became white and dazzling. 30Behold, two men were talking with him, who were Moses and Elijah, 31who appeared in glory and spoke of his departure,* which he was about to accomplish at Jerusalem. 32Now Peter and those who were with him were heavy with sleep, but when they were fully awake, they saw his glory, and the two men who stood with him. 33As they were parting from him, Peter said to Jesus, "Master, it is good for us to be here. Let's make three tents: one for you, one for Moses, and one for Elijah," not knowing what he said. 34While he said these things, a cloud came and overshadowed them, and they were afraid as they entered into the cloud. 35A voice came out of the cloud, saying, "This is my beloved Son. Listen to him!" 36When the voice came, Jesus was found alone. They were silent, and told no one in those days any of the things which they had seen.

37On the next day, when they had come down from the mountain, a great multitude met him. 38Behold, a man from the crowd called out, saying, "Teacher, I beg you to look at my son, for he is my only born† child. 39Behold, a spirit takes him, he suddenly cries out, and it convulses him so that he foams; and it hardly departs from him, bruising him severely. 40I begged your disciples to cast it out, and they couldn't." Jesus answered, "Faithless and perverse generation, how long shall I be with you and bear with you? Bring your son here." While he was still

* 9:31 literally, "exodus"

† 9:38 The phrase "only born" is from the Greek word "μονογενη", which is sometimes translated "only begotten" or "one and only". 9:38 The phrase "only born" is from the Greek word "μονογενη", which is sometimes translated "only begotten" or "one and only".

coming, the demon threw him down and convulsed him violently. But Jesus rebuked the unclean spirit, healed the boy, and gave him back to his father. [43]They were all astonished at the majesty of God.

But while all were marveling at all the things which Jesus did, he said to his disciples, [44]"Let these words sink into your ears, for the Son of Man will be delivered up into the hands of men." [45]But they didn't understand this saying. It was concealed from them, that they should not perceive it, and they were afraid to ask him about this saying.

[46]An argument arose among them about which of them was the greatest. [47]Jesus, perceiving the reasoning of their hearts, took a little child, and set him by his side, [48]and said to them, "Whoever receives this little child in my name receives me. Whoever receives me receives him who sent me. For whoever is least among you all, this one will be great."

[49]John answered, "Master, we saw someone casting out demons in your name, and we forbade him, because he doesn't follow with us." [50]Jesus said to him, "Don't forbid him, for he who is not against[e] us is for us."

[51]It came to pass, when the days were near that he should be taken up, he intently set his face to go to Jerusalem [52]and sent messengers before his face. They went and entered into a village of the Samaritans, so as to prepare for him. [53]They didn't receive him, because he was traveling with his face set toward Jerusalem. [54]When his disciples, James and John, saw this, they said, "Lord, do you want us to command fire to come down from the sky[f] and destroy them, just as Elijah did?" [55]But he turned and rebuked them, "You don't know of what kind of spirit you are. [56]For the Son of Man didn't come to destroy men's lives, but to save them." They went to another village.

[57]As they went on the way, a certain man said to him, "I want to follow you wherever you go, Lord." [58]Jesus

[e] Q. 58:14

[f] Q. 3:183

148

said to him, "The foxes have holes and the birds of the sky have nests, but the Son of Man has no place to lay his head." 59He said to another, "Follow me!" But he said, "Lord, allow me first to go and bury my father." 60But Jesus said to him, "Leave the dead to bury their own dead, but you go and announce God's Kingdom." 61Another also said, "I want to follow you, Lord, but first allow me to say goodbye to those who are at my house." 62But Jesus said to him, "No one, having put his hand to the plow and looking back, is fit for God's Kingdom."

10

1Now after these things, the Lord also appointed seventy others, and sent them two by two ahead of him* into every city and place where he was about to come. 2Then he said to them, "The harvest is indeed plentiful, but the laborers are few. Pray therefore to the Lord of the harvest, that he may send out laborers into his harvest. 3Go your ways. Behold, I send you out as lambs among wolves. 4Carry no purse, nor wallet, nor sandals. Greet no one on the way. 5Into whatever house you enter, first say, 'Peace be to this house.' 6If a son of peace is there, your peace will rest on him; but if not, it will return to you. 7Remain in that same house, eating and drinking the things they give, for the laborer is worthy of his wages. Don't go from house to house. 8Into whatever city you enter and they receive you, eat the things that are set before you. 9Heal the sick who are there and tell them, 'God's Kingdom has come near to you.' 10But into whatever city you enter and they don't receive you, go out into its streets and say, 11'Even the dust from your city that clings to us, we wipe off against you. Nevertheless know this, that God's Kingdom has come near to you.' 12I tell you, it will

* 10:1 literally, "before his face"

be more tolerable in that day for Sodom than for that city.

¹³"Woe to you, Chorazin! Woe to you, Bethsaida! For if the mighty works had been done in Tyre and Sidon which were done in you, they would have repented long ago, sitting in sackcloth and ashes. ¹⁴But it will be more tolerable for Tyre and Sidon in the judgment than for you. ¹⁵You, Capernaum, who are exalted to heaven, will be brought down to Hades.* ¹⁶Whoever listens to you listens to me, and whoever rejects you rejects me. Whoever rejects me rejects him who sent me."

¹⁷The seventy returned with joy, saying, "Lord, even the demons are subject to us in your name!" He said to them, "I saw Satan having fallen^g like lightning from heaven. ¹⁹Behold, I give you authority^h to tread on serpents and scorpions, and over all the power of the enemy. Nothing will in any way hurt you. ²⁰Nevertheless, don't rejoice in this, that the spirits are subject to you, but rejoice that your names are written in heaven."

²¹In that same hour, Jesus rejoiced in the Holy Spirit,^i and said, "I thank you, O Father, Lord of heaven and earth, that you have hidden these things from the wise and understanding, and revealed them to little children. Yes, Father, for so it was well-pleasing in your sight." ²²Turning to the disciples, he said, "All things have been delivered to me by my Father. No one knows who the Son is, except the Father, and who the Father is, except the Son, and he to whomever the Son desires to reveal him."

²³Turning to the disciples, he said privately, "Blessed are the eyes which see the things that you see, ²⁴for I tell you that many prophets and kings desired to see the things which you see, and didn't see them, and to hear the things which you hear, and didn't hear them."

²⁵Behold, a certain lawyer stood up and tested him, saying, "Teacher, what shall I do to inherit eternal life?"

^g Q. 22:31

^h Q. 14:22; 15:42; 16:99; 17:65

^i Q. 2:87, 253; 5:110

---

* 10:15 Hades is the lower realm of the dead, or Hell

²⁶He said to him, "What is written in the law? How do you read it?" ²⁷He answered, "You shall love the Lord your God with all your heart, with all your soul, with all your strength, and with all your mind;* and your neighbor as yourself."† ²⁸He said to him, "You have answered correctly. Do this, and you will live."

²⁹But he, desiring to justify himself, asked Jesus, "Who is my neighbor?" ³⁰Jesus answered, "A certain man was going down from Jerusalem to Jericho, and he fell among robbers, who both stripped him and beat him, and departed, leaving him half dead. ³¹By chance a certain priest was going down that way. When he saw him, he passed by on the other side. ³²In the same way a Levite also, when he came to the place and saw him, passed by on the other side. ³³But a certain Samaritan, as he traveled, came where he was. When he saw him, he was moved with compassion, ³⁴came to him, and bound up his wounds, pouring on oil and wine. He set him on his own animal, brought him to an inn, and took care of him. ³⁵On the next day, when he departed, he took out two denarii, gave them to the host, and said to him, 'Take care of him. Whatever you spend beyond that, I will repay you when I return.' ³⁶Now which of these three do you think seemed to be a neighbor to him who fell among the robbers?" ³⁷He said, "He who showed mercy on him." Then Jesus said to him, "Go and do likewise."

³⁸As they went on their way, he entered into a certain village, and a certain woman named Martha received him into her house. ³⁹She had a sister called Mary, who also sat at Jesus' feet and heard his word. ⁴⁰But Martha was distracted with much serving, and she came up to him, and said, "Lord, don't you care that my sister left me to serve alone? Ask her therefore to help me." ⁴¹Jesus answered her, "Martha, Martha, you are anxious and troubled about many things, ⁴²but one thing is needed.

---

* 10:27 Deuteronomy 6:5
† 10:27 Leviticus 19:18

Mary has chosen the good part, which will not be taken away from her."

11[j]

[j] Q. 3:49; 5:110; 19:30

[1]When he finished praying in a certain place, one of his disciples said to him, "Lord, teach us to pray, just as John also taught his disciples." [2]He said to them, "When you pray, say,

'Our Father in heaven,
may your name be kept holy.
May your Kingdom come.
May your will be done on earth, as it is in heaven.
[3]Give us day by day our daily bread.
[4]Forgive us our sins,[k*]

[k] see footnote

for we ourselves also forgive everyone who is indebted to us.

Bring us not into temptation,
but deliver us from the evil one.'"

[5]He said to them, "Which of you, if you go to a friend at midnight and tell him, 'Friend, lend me three loaves of bread, [6]for a friend of mine has come to me from a journey, and I have nothing to set before him,' [7]and he from within will answer and say, 'Don't bother me. The door is now shut, and my children are with me in bed. I can't get up and give it to you'? [8]I tell you, although he will not rise and give it to him because he is his friend, yet because of his persistence, he will get up and give him as many as he needs. [9]"I tell you, keep asking, and it will be given you. Keep seeking, and you will find. Keep knocking, and it will be opened to you. [10]For everyone who asks receives. He who seeks finds. To him who knocks it will be opened. [11]"Which of you fathers, if your son asks for bread, will give him a stone? Or if he asks for a fish, he won't give

---

* [k] Q. 3:16, 135, 147, 193; 71:4

him a snake instead of a fish, will he? [12]Or if he asks for an egg, he won't give him a scorpion, will he? [13]If you then, being evil, know how to give good gifts to your children, how much more will your heavenly Father give the Holy Spirit to those who ask him?"

[14]He was casting out a demon, and it was mute. When the demon had gone out, the mute man spoke[1]; and the multitudes marveled. [15]But some of them said, "He casts out demons by Beelzebul, the prince of the demons." [16]Others, testing him, sought from him a sign from heaven.[m] [17]But he, knowing their thoughts, said to them, "Every kingdom divided against itself is brought to desolation. A house divided against itself falls. [18]If Satan also is divided against himself, how will his kingdom stand? For you say that I cast out demons by Beelzebul. [19]But if I cast out demons by Beelzebul, by whom do your children cast them out? Therefore they will be your judges. [20]But if I by God's finger cast out demons, then God's Kingdom has come to you. [21]"When the strong man, fully armed, guards his own dwelling, his goods are safe. [22]But when someone stronger attacks him and overcomes him, he takes from him his whole armor in which he trusted, and divides his plunder. [23]"He who is not with me is against me. He who doesn't gather with me scatters.

[24]The unclean spirit, when he has gone out of the man, passes through dry places, seeking rest; and finding none, he says, 'I will turn back to my house from which I came out.' [25]When he returns, he finds it swept and put in order. [26]Then he goes and takes seven other spirits more evil than himself, and they enter in and dwell there. The last state of that man becomes worse than the first."

[27]It came to pass, as he said these things, a certain woman out of the multitude lifted up her voice and said to him, "Blessed is the womb that bore you, and the breasts which nursed you!"[n] [28]But he said, "On the contrary, blessed are those who hear the word of God, and keep it."

[1] Q. 3:49

[m] Q. 13:7

[n] Q. 4:1

²⁹When the multitudes were gathering together to him, he began to say, "This is an evil generation. It seeks after a sign. No sign will be given to it but the sign of Jonah the prophet. ³⁰For even as Jonah became a sign to the Ninevites, so the Son of Man will also be to this generation. ³¹The Queen of the South will rise up in the judgment with the men of this generation and will condemn them, for she came from the ends of the earth to hear the wisdom of Solomon; and behold, one greater than Solomon is here. ³²The men of Nineveh will stand up in the judgment with this generation, and will condemn it, for they repented at the preaching of Jonah; and behold, one greater than Jonah is here.

³³"No one, when he has lit a lamp, puts it in a cellar or under a basket, but on a stand, that those who come in may see the light. ³⁴The lamp of the body is the eye. Therefore when your eye is good, your whole body is also full of light; but when it is evil, your body also is full of darkness. ³⁵Therefore see whether the light that is in you isn't darkness. ³⁶If therefore your whole body is full of light, having no part dark, it will be wholly full of light, as when the lamp with its bright shining gives you light."

³⁷Now as he spoke, a certain Pharisee asked him to dine with him. He went in and sat at the table. ³⁸When the Pharisee saw it, he marveled that he had not first washed himself before dinner. ³⁹The Lord said to him, "Now you Pharisees cleanse the outside of the cup and of the platter, but your inward part is full of extortion and wickedness. ⁴⁰You foolish ones, didn't he who made the outside make the inside also? ⁴¹But give for gifts to the needy those things which are within, and behold, all things will be clean to you.

⁴²But woe to you Pharisees! For you tithe mint and rue and every herb, but you bypass justice and God's love.^o You ought to have done these, and not to have left the other undone. ⁴³Woe to you Pharisees! For you love the best

^o Q. 98:5

seats in the synagogues and the greetings in the marketplaces. ⁴⁴Woe to you, scribes and Pharisees, hypocrites! For you are like hidden graves, and the men who walk over them don't know it."

⁴⁵One of the lawyers answered him, "Teacher, in saying this you insult us also." ⁴⁶He said, "Woe to you lawyers also! For you load men with burdens that are difficult to carry, and you yourselves won't even lift one finger to help carry those burdens. ⁴⁷Woe to you! For you build the tombs of the prophets, and your fathers killed them.ᵖ ⁴⁸So you testify and consent to the works of your fathers. For they killed them, and you build their tombs. ⁴⁹Therefore also the wisdom of God said, 'I will send to them prophets and apostlesq; and some of them they will kill and persecute, ⁵⁰that the blood of all the prophets, which was shed from the foundation of the world, may be required of this generation, ⁵¹from the blood of Abel to the blood of Zachariah, who perished between the altar and the sanctuary.' Yes, I tell you, it will be required of this generation. ⁵²Woe to you lawyers! For you took away the key of knowledge. You didn't enter in yourselves, and those who were entering in, you hindered."r*

⁵³As he said these things to them, the scribes and the Pharisees began to be terribly angry, and to draw many things out of him, ⁵⁴lying in wait for him, and seeking to catch him in something he might say, that they might accuse him.

12

¹Meanwhile, when a multitude of many thousands had gathered together, so much so that they trampled on each other, he began to tell his disciples first of all, "Beware of the

ᵖ Q. 2:61; 3:21; 4:155; 5:70

q Q. 3:164

r see footnote

---

* r Q. 3:99; 4:55, 160; 7:45; 8:47; 9:9; 11:19; 16:88; 22:25; 47:1, 34; 63:2

yeast of the Pharisees, which is hypocrisy. [2]But there is nothing covered up that will not be revealed [s], nor hidden that will not be known. [3]Therefore whatever you have said in the darkness will be heard in the light. What you have spoken in the ear in the inner rooms will be proclaimed on the housetops.[t]

[4]"I tell you, my friends, don't be afraid of those who kill the body, and after that have no more that they can do. [5]But I will warn you whom you should fear. Fear him who after he has killed, has power to cast into Gehenna.[u][*] Yes, I tell you, fear him.

[6]"Aren't five sparrows sold for two assaria coins[†]? Not one of them is forgotten by God. [7]But the very hairs of your head are all counted. Therefore don't be afraid. You are of more value than many sparrows.

[8]"I tell you, everyone who confesses me before men, the Son of Man will also confess before the angels of God; [9]but he who denies me in the presence of men will be denied in the presence of God's angels. [10]Everyone who speaks a word against the Son of Man will be forgiven, but those who blaspheme against the Holy Spirit will not be forgiven. [11]When they bring you before the synagogues, the rulers, and the authorities, don't be anxious how or what you will answer or what you will say; [12]for the Holy Spirit will teach you in that same hour what you must say."

[13]One of the multitude said to him, "Teacher, tell my brother to divide the inheritance with me." [14]But he said to him, "Man, who made me a judge or an arbitrator over you?" [15]He said to them, "Beware! Keep yourselves from covetousness, for a man's life doesn't consist of the abundance[v] of the things which he possesses." [16]He spoke a parable to them, saying, "The ground of a certain rich man

[s] Q. 64:8

[t] Q. 27:25; 69:18

[u] Q. 3:131

[v] Q. 89:20

---

[*] 12:5 or, Hell

[†] 12:6 An assarion was a small copper coin worth about an hour's wages for an agricultural laborer

w see footnote

x Q. 18:34

y Q. 18:36; 77:43

z Q. 18:36; 63:11

a Q. 7:34; 16:61

produced abundantly.ʷ* ¹⁷He reasoned within himself, saying, 'What will I do, because I don't have room to store my crops?' ¹⁸He said, 'This is what I will do. I will pull down my barns, build bigger ones, and there I will store all my grain and my goods.ˣ ¹⁹I will tell my soul, "Soul, you have many goods laid up for many years. Take your ease, eat, drink, and be merry."'ʸ ²⁰"But God said to him, 'You foolish one, tonight your soul is required of you.ᶻ The things which you have prepared—whose will they be?' ²¹So is he who lays up treasure for himself, and is not rich toward God."

²²He said to his disciples, "Therefore I tell you, don't be anxious for your life, what you will eat, nor yet for your body, what you will wear. ²³Life is more than food, and the body is more than clothing. ²⁴Consider the ravens: they don't sow, they don't reap, they have no warehouse or barn, and God feeds them. How much more valuable are you than birds! ²⁵Which of you by being anxious can add a cubit† to his height? ²⁶If then you aren't able to do even the least things, why are you anxious about the rest?ᵃ ²⁷Consider the lilies, how they grow. They don't toil, neither do they spin; yet I tell you, even Solomon in all his glory was not arrayed like one of these. ²⁸But if this is how God clothes the grass in the field, which today exists and tomorrow is cast into the oven, how much more will he clothe you, O you of little faith? ²⁹"Don't seek what you will eat or what you will drink; neither be anxious. ³⁰For the nations of the world seek after all of these things, but your Father knows that you need these things. ³¹But seek God's Kingdom, and all these things will be added to you. ³²"Don't be afraid, little flock, for it is your Father's good pleasure to give you the Kingdom. ³³Sell what you have and give gifts to the needy. Make for yourselves purses which don't grow old, a treasure in the heavens that doesn't fail, where no thief approaches and no

---

* ʷ Q. 3:91; 6:44; 18:33; 43:32; 102:1; 104:3

† 12:25 A cubit is the length from the tip of the middle finger to the elbow on a man's arm, or about 18 inches or 46 centimeters.

moth destroys. [34]For where your treasure is, there will your heart be also.

[35]"Let your waist be dressed and your lamps burning. [36]Be like men watching for their lord when he returns from the wedding feast, that when he comes and knocks, they may immediately open to him. [37]Blessed are those servants whom the lord will find watching when he comes. Most certainly I tell you that he will dress himself, make them recline, and will come and serve them. [38]They will be blessed if he comes in the second or third watch and finds them so. [39]But know this, that if the master of the house had known in what hour the thief was coming, he would have watched and not allowed his house to be broken into. [40]Therefore be ready also, for the Son of Man is coming in an hour that you don't expect him."

[41]Peter said to him, "Lord, are you telling this parable to us, or to everybody?" The Lord said, "Who then is the faithful and wise steward, whom his lord will set over his household, to give them their portion of food at the right times? [43]Blessed is that servant whom his lord will find doing so when he comes. [44]Truly I tell you that he will set him over all that he has. [45]But if that servant says in his heart, 'My lord delays his coming,' and begins to beat the menservants and the maidservants, and to eat and drink and to be drunken, [46]then the lord of that servant will come in a day when he isn't expecting him and in an hour that he doesn't know, and will cut him in two, and place his portion with the unfaithful.[b] [47]That servant who knew his lord's will, and didn't prepare nor do what he wanted, will be beaten with many stripes,[c] [48]but he who didn't know, and did things worthy of stripes, will be beaten with few stripes. To whomever much is given, of him will much be required; and to whom much was entrusted, of him more will be asked.[d]

[49]"I came to throw fire on the earth. I wish it were already kindled. [50]But I have a baptism to be baptized with, and how

[b] Q. 16:76

[c] Q. 24:11

[d] Q. 84:6

distressed I am until it is accomplished! ⁵¹Do you think that I have come to give peace in the earth? I tell you, no, but rather division. ⁵²For from now on, there will be five in one house divided, three against two, and two against three. ⁵³They will be divided, father against son, and son against father; mother against daughter, and daughter against her mother; mother-in-law against her daughter-in-law, and daughter-in-law against her mother-in-law."*

⁵⁴He said to the multitudes also, "When you see a cloud rising from the west, immediately you say, 'A shower is coming,' and so it happens. ⁵⁵When a south wind blows, you say, 'There will be a scorching heat,' and it happens. ⁵⁶You hypocrites! You know how to interpret the appearance of the earth and the sky, but how is it that you don't interpret this time?

⁵⁷"Why don't you judge for yourselves what is right? ⁵⁸For when you are going with your adversary before the magistrate, try diligently on the way to be released from him, lest perhaps he drag you to the judge, and the judge deliver you to the officer, and the officer throw you into prison. ⁵⁹I tell you, you will by no means get out of there until you have paid the very last penny.†"

13

¹Now there were some present at the same time who told him about the Galileans whose blood Pilate had mixed with their sacrifices. ²Jesus answered them, "Do you think that these Galileans were worse sinners than all the other Galileans, because they suffered such things? ³I tell you, no, but unless you repent, you will all perish in the same way. ⁴Or those eighteen on whom the tower in Siloam fell and killed

---

* 12:53 Micah 7:6

† 12:59 literally, lepton. A lepton is a very small brass Jewish coin worth half a Roman quadrans each, which is worth a quarter of the copper assarion. Lepta are worth less than 1% of an agricultural worker's daily wages

them—do you think that they were worse offenders than all the men who dwell in Jerusalem? [5]I tell you, no, but, unless you repent, you will all perish in the same way."

[6]He spoke this parable. "A certain man had a fig tree planted in his vineyard, and he came seeking fruit on it and found none. [7]He said to the vine dresser, 'Behold, these three years I have come looking for fruit on this fig tree, and found none. Cut it down! Why does it waste the soil?' [8]He answered, 'Lord, leave it alone this year also, until I dig around it and fertilize it. [9]If it bears fruit, fine; but if not, after that, you can cut it down.' "

[10]He was teaching in one of the synagogues on the Sabbath day. [11]Behold, there was a woman who had a spirit of infirmity eighteen years. She was bent over and could in no way straighten herself up. [12]When Jesus saw her, he called her and said to her, "Woman, you are freed from your infirmity."[e] [13]He laid his hands on her, and immediately she stood up straight and glorified God. [14]The ruler of the synagogue, being indignant because Jesus had healed on the Sabbath, said to the multitude, "There are six days in which men ought to work. Therefore come on those days and be healed, and not on the Sabbath day!" [15]Therefore the Lord answered him, "You hypocrites! Doesn't each one of you free his ox or his donkey from the stall on the Sabbath and lead him away to water? [16]Ought not this woman, being a daughter of Abraham whom Satan had bound eighteen long years, be freed from this bondage on the Sabbath day?" [17]As he said these things, all his adversaries were disappointed; and all the multitude rejoiced for all the glorious things that were done by him.

[18]He said, "What is God's Kingdom like? To what shall I compare it? [19]It is like a grain of mustard seed which a man took and put in his own garden. It grew and became a large tree, and the birds of the sky live in its branches."[f]

[20]Again he said, "To what shall I compare God's

[e] Q. 3:49

[f] Q. 14:24; 31:16

Kingdom? ²¹It is like yeast, which a woman took and hid in three measures[*] of flour, until it was all leavened."

²²He went on his way through cities and villages, teaching, and traveling on to Jerusalem. ²³One said to him, "Lord, are they few who are saved?"^g He said to them, ²⁴"Strive to enter in by the narrow door, for many, I tell you, will seek to enter in and will not be able. ²⁵When once the master of the house has risen up and has shut the door, and you begin to stand outside and to knock at the door, saying, 'Lord, Lord, open to us!' then he will answer and tell you, 'I don't know you or where you come from.' ²⁶Then you will begin to say, 'We ate and drank in your presence, and you taught in our streets.' ²⁷He will say, 'I tell you, I don't know where you come from. Depart from me, all you workers of iniquity.' ²⁸There will be weeping and gnashing of teeth when you see Abraham, Isaac, Jacob, and all the prophets in God's Kingdom, and yourselves being thrown outside.^{h†} ²⁹They will come from the east, west, north, and south,ⁱ and will sit down in God's Kingdom. ³⁰Behold, there are some who are last who will be first, and there are some who are first who will be last."

³¹On that same day, some Pharisees came, saying to him, "Get out of here and go away, for Herod wants to kill you." ³²He said to them, "Go and tell that fox, 'Behold, I cast out demons and perform cures today and tomorrow, and the third day I complete my mission. ³³Nevertheless I must go on my way today and tomorrow and the next day, for it can't be that a prophet would perish outside of Jerusalem.' ³⁴"Jerusalem, Jerusalem, you who kills the prophets and stones those who are sent to her! How often I wanted to gather your children together, like a hen gathers her own brood under her wings, and you refused!^j ³⁵Behold, your house is left to you desolate. I tell you, you

^g Q. 3:82

^h see footnote

ⁱ Q. 70:40

^j Q. 2:176

---

[*] 13:21 literally, three sata. 3 sata is about 39 liters or a bit more than a bushel.

^{† h} Q. 2:196; 3:11; 5:2; 8:13; 13:6; 40:3; 59:4

will not see me until you say, 'Blessed is he who comes in the name of the Lord!' "*

14[k]

[1]When he went into the house of one of the rulers of the Pharisees on a Sabbath to eat bread, they were watching him. [2]Behold, a certain man who had dropsy was in front of him. [3]Jesus, answering, spoke to the lawyers and Pharisees, saying, "Is it lawful to heal on the Sabbath?" [4]But they were silent. He took him, and healed[l] him, and let him go. [5]He answered them, "Which of you, if your son[†] or an ox fell into a well, wouldn't immediately pull him out on a Sabbath day?" [6]They couldn't him regarding these things.

[7]He spoke a parable to those who were invited, when he noticed how they chose the best seats, and said to them, [8]"When you are invited by anyone to a wedding feast, don't sit in the best seat, since perhaps someone more honorable than you might be invited by him, [9]and he who invited both of you would come and tell you, 'Make room for this person.' Then you would begin, with shame, to take the lowest place. [10]But when you are invited, go and sit in the lowest place, so that when he who invited you comes, he may tell you, 'Friend, move up higher.' Then you will be honored in the presence of all who sit at the table with you.[m] [11]For everyone who exalts himself will be humbled, and whoever humbles himself will be exalted."

[12]He also said to the one who had invited him, "When you make a dinner or a supper, don't call your friends, nor your brothers, nor your kinsmen, nor rich neighbors, or perhaps they might also return the favor, and pay you back. [13]But when you make a feast, ask the poor[n], the maimed,

[k] Q. 2:87, 253; 3:49; 5:110; 19:30

[l] Q. 3:49

[m] Q. 58:11

[n] Q. 69:34

---

* 13:35 Psalm 118:26
† 14:5 TR reads "donkey" instead of "son"

the lame, or the blind; [14]and you will be blessed, because they don't have the resources to repay you. For you will be repaid in the resurrection of the righteous.'"[o]

When one of those who sat at the table with him heard these things, he said to him, "Blessed is he who will feast in God's Kingdom!"

[15]But he said to him, "A certain man made a great supper, and he invited many people. [17]He sent out his servant at supper time to tell those who were invited, 'Come, for everything is ready now.' [18]They all as one began to make excuses. "The first said to him, 'I have bought a field, and I must go and see it. Please have me excused.' [19]"Another said, 'I have bought five yoke of oxen, and I must go try them out. Please have me excused.' [20]"Another said, 'I have married a wife, and therefore I can't come.' "That servant came, and told his lord these things.

Then the master of the house, being angry, said to his servant, 'Go out quickly into the streets and lanes of the city, and bring in the poor, maimed, blind, and lame.' [22]"The servant said, 'Lord, it is done as you commanded, and there is still room.' [23]"The lord said to the servant, 'Go out into the highways and hedges, and compel them to come in, that my house may be filled. [24]For I tell you that none of those men who were invited will taste of my supper.'"

[25]Now great multitudes were going with him. He turned and said to them, [26]"If anyone comes to me, and doesn't disregard[*] his own father, mother, wife, children, brothers, and sisters, yes, and his own life also, he can't be my disciple.[p] [27]Whoever doesn't bear his own cross and come after me, can't be my disciple. [28]For which of you, desiring to build a tower, doesn't first sit down and count the cost, to see if he has enough to complete it? [29]Or perhaps, when he has laid a foundation and isn't able to

[o] Q.
24:38;
36:27;
40:17;
53:39;
81:14

[p] Q.
9:24;
58:22;
64:15

---

[*] 14:26 or, hate

finish, everyone who sees begins to mock him, ³⁰saying, 'This man began to build and wasn't able to finish.' ³¹Or what king, as he goes to encounter another king in war, will not sit down first and consider whether he is able with ten thousand to meet him who comes against him with twenty thousand? ³²Or else, while the other is yet a great way off, he sends an envoy and asks for conditions of peace. ³³So therefore, whoever of you who doesn't renounce all that he has, he can't be my disciple.

³⁴"Salt is good, but if the salt becomes flat and tasteless, with what do you season it? ³⁵It is fit neither for the soil nor for the manure pile. It is thrown out. He who has ears to hear, let him hear."

15

¹Now all the tax collectors and sinners were coming close to him to hear him. ²The Pharisees and the scribes murmured, saying, "This man welcomes sinners, and eats with them."

³He told them this parable: ⁴"Which of you men, if you had one hundred sheep and lost one of them, wouldn't leave the ninety-nine in the wilderness and go after the one that was lost, until he found it?�q ⁵When he has found it, he carries it on his shoulders, rejoicing. ⁶When he comes home, he calls together his friends and his neighbors, saying to them, 'Rejoice with me, for I have found my sheep which was lost!' ⁷I tell you that even so there will be more joy in heaven over one sinner who repents, than over ninety-nine righteous people who need no repentance.

⁸"Or what woman, if she had ten drachma* coins, if she lost one drachma coin, wouldn't light a lamp, sweep the

q Q. 93:7

---

* 15:8 A drachma coin was worth about 2 days wages for an agricultural laborer

house, and seek diligently until she found it? ⁹When she has found it, she calls together her friends and neighbors, saying, 'Rejoice with me, for I have found the drachma which I had lost!' ¹⁰Even so, I tell you, there is joy in the presence of the angels of God over one sinner repenting."

¹¹He said, "A certain man had two sons. ¹²The younger of them said to his father, 'Father, give me my share of your property.' So he divided his livelihood between them. ¹³Not many days after, the younger son gathered all of this together and traveled into a far country. There he wasted his property with riotous living. ¹⁴When he had spent all of it, there arose a severe famine in that country, and he began to be in need. ¹⁵He went and joined himself to one of the citizens of that country, and he sent him into his fields to feed pigs. ¹⁶He wanted to fill his belly with the pods that the pigs ate, but no one gave him any.

¹⁷But when he came to himself, he said, 'How many hired servants of my father's have bread enough to spare, and I'm dying with hunger! ¹⁸I will get up and go to my father, and will tell him, "Father, I have sinned against heaven and in your sight. ¹⁹I am no more worthy to be called your son. Make me as one of your hired servants."' ²⁰"He arose and came to his father. But while he was still far off, his father saw him and was moved with compassion, and ran, fell on his neck, and kissed him. ²¹The son said to him, 'Father, I have sinned against heaven and in your sight. I am no longer worthy to be called your son.' ²²"But the father said to his servants, 'Bring out the best robe and put it on him. Put a ring on his hand and sandals on his feet. ²³Bring the fattened calf, kill it, and let's eat and celebrate; ²⁴for this, my son, was dead and is alive again. He was lost and is found.' Then they began to celebrate.

²⁵"Now his elder son was in the field. As he came near to the house, he heard music and dancing. ²⁶He called one of the servants to him and asked what was going on. ²⁷He said to him, 'Your brother has come, and your father has killed

the fattened calf, because he has received him back safe and healthy.' ²⁸But he was angry and would not go in. Therefore his father came out and begged him. ²⁹But he answered his father, 'Behold, these many years I have served you, and I never disobeyed a commandment of yours, but you never gave me a goat, that I might celebrate with my friends. ³⁰But when this your son came, who has devoured your living with prostitutes, you killed the fattened calf for him.' ³¹"He said to him, 'Son, you are always with me, and all that is mine is yours. ³²But it was appropriate to celebrate and be glad, for this, your brother, was dead, and is alive again. He was lost, and is found.' "

16

¹He also said to his disciples, "There was a certain rich man who had a manager. An accusation was made to him that this man was wasting his possessions. ²He called him, and said to him, 'What is this that I hear about you? Give an accounting of your management, for you can no longer be manager.' ³"The manager said within himself, 'What will I do, seeing that my lord is taking away the management position from me? I don't have strength to dig. I am ashamed to beg. ⁴I know what I will do, so that when I am removed from management, they may receive me into their houses.' ⁵Calling each one of his lord's debtors to him, he said to the first, 'How much do you owe to my lord?' ⁶He said, 'A hundred batos[*] of oil.' He said to him, 'Take your bill, and sit down quickly and write fifty.' ⁷Then he said to another, 'How much do you owe?' He said, 'A hundred cors[†] of wheat.' He said to him, 'Take your bill, and write eighty.' ⁸"His lord commended the dishonest manager because he had done wisely, for the children of

---

[*] 16:6 100 batos is about 395 liters or 104 U. S. gallons.
[†] 16:7 100 cors = about 2,110 liters or 600 bushels

this world are, in their own generation, wiser than the children of the light. ⁹I tell you, make for yourselves friends by means of unrighteous mammon, so that when you fail, they may receive you into the eternal tents.

¹⁰He who is faithful in a very little is faithful also in much. He who is dishonest in a very little is also dishonest in much.ʳ ¹¹If therefore you have not been faithful in the unrighteous mammon, who will commit to your trust the true riches? ¹²If you have not been faithful in that which is another's, who will give you that which is your own? ¹³No servant can serve two masters, for either he will hate the one and love the other; or else he will hold to one and despise the other. You aren't able to serve God and Mammon."*

¹⁴The Pharisees, who were lovers of money, also heard all these things, and they scoffed at him. ¹⁵He said to them, "You are those who justify yourselves in the sight of men, but God knows your hearts.ˢ† For that which is exalted among men is an abomination in the sight of God.

¹⁶"The law and the prophets were until John. From that time the Good News of God's Kingdom is preached, and everyone is forcing his way into it. ¹⁷But it is easier for heaven and earth to pass away than for one tiny stroke of a pen in the law to fall.

¹⁸"Everyone who divorcesᵗ his wife and marries another commits adultery. He who marries one who is divorced from a husband commits adultery.

¹⁹"Now there was a certain rich man, and he was clothed in purple and fine linen, living in luxury every day.ᵘ‡ ²⁰A certain beggar, named Lazarus, was taken to his gate, full of sores, ²¹and desiring to be fed with the crumbs that fell from the rich man's table.ᵛ Yes, even the dogs came

ʳ Q. 89:16

ˢ see footnote

ᵗ Q. 65:1

ᵘ see footnote

ᵛ Q. 2:254

---

* 16:13 "Mammon" refers to riches or a false god of wealth
† ˢ Q. 3:29; 5:7; 16:70; 17:25; 29:10; 31:23; 33:51; 35:38; 39:7; 42:24; 57:6; 64:4; 67:13
‡ ᵘ Q. 3:91; 17:83; 26:98; 56:45; 57:13; 92:11

and licked his sores. ²²The beggar died, and he was carried away by the angels to Abraham's bosom. The rich man also died and was buried. ²³In Hades,ʷ* he lifted up his eyes,ˣ being in torment, and saw Abraham far off, and Lazarus at his bosom. ²⁴He cried and said, 'Father Abraham, have mercy on me, and send Lazarus, that he may dip the tip of his finger in water and cool my tongue!ʸ For I am in anguish in this flame.' ²⁵"But Abraham said, 'Son, remember that you, in your lifetime, received your good things, and Lazarus, in the same way, bad things. But here he is now comforted and you are in anguish.ᶻ† ²⁶Besides all this,between us and you there is a great gulf fixed, that those who want to pass from here to you are not able, and that no one may cross over from there to us.'ᵃ²⁷"He said, 'I ask you therefore, father, that you would send him to my father's house— ²⁸for I have five brothers—that he may testify to them, so they won't also come into this place of torment.' ²⁹"But Abraham said to him, 'They have Moses and the prophets. Let them listen to them.' ³⁰"He said, 'No, father Abraham, but if one goes to them from the dead, they will repent.'ᵇ ³¹"He said to him, 'If they don't listen to Moses and the prophets,ᶜneither will they be persuaded if one rises from the dead.'"

17ᵈ

¹He said to the disciples, "It is impossible that no occasions of stumbling should come, but woe to him through whom they come! ²It would be better for him if a millstone were hung around his neck, and he were thrown

ʷ see footnote

ˣ Q. 2:7

ʸ Q. 39:58; 40:49; 78:24

ᶻ see footnote

ᵃ Q. 7:46; 23:100

ᵇ Q. 77:6

ᶜ Q. 2:177

ᵈ Q. 3:49; 5:110; 19:30

---

* ʷ Q. 3:4; 4:14; 5:18; 6:15; 7:38, 50; 8:14; 9:3; 10:4; 11:3; 12:107; 13:34; 14:2; 15:50; 16:63; 17:10; 18:55; 20:61; 22:2; 24:19; 25:19; 26:135; 27:5; 29:23; 30:16; 31:6; 32:14; 33:8; 34:5; 35:7; 37:9; 38:8; 39:13; 40:7; 41:16; 42:16; 43:39; 44:47-48; 45:8; 46:20; 48:6; 50:26; 51:37; 52:7; 57:20; 58:4; 59:3; 61:10; 64:5; 65:10; 67:5; 68:33; 70:1; 71:1; 72:17; 73:18; 76:31; 78:30; 84:24; 85:10; 88:24
† ᶻ Q. 3:24; 7:50; 34:35; 46:20

into the sea, rather than that he should cause one of these little ones to stumble. ³Be careful. If your brother sins against you, rebuke him. If he repents, forgive him. ⁴If he sins against you[e] seven times in the day, and seven times returns, saying, 'I repent,' you shall forgive him."

e Q.
43:39

⁵The apostles said to the Lord, "Increase our faith." ⁶The Lord said, "If you had faith like a grain of mustard seed, you would tell this sycamore tree, 'Be uprooted and be planted in the sea,' and it would obey you.

f Q.
31:16

⁷But who is there among you, having a servant plowing or keeping sheep, that will say when he comes in from the field, 'Come immediately and sit down at the table'? ⁸Wouldn't he rather tell him, 'Prepare my supper, clothe yourself properly, and serve me while I eat and drink. Afterward you shall eat and drink'? ⁹Does he thank that servant because he did the things that were commanded? I think not. ¹⁰Even so you also, when you have done all the things that are commanded you, say, 'We are unworthy servants. We have done our duty.' "

¹¹As he was on his way to Jerusalem, he was passing along the borders of Samaria and Galilee. ¹²As he entered into a certain village, ten men who were lepers[g] met him, who stood at a distance. ¹³They lifted up their voices, saying, "Jesus, Master, have mercy on us!" ¹⁴When he saw them, he said to them, "Go and show yourselves to the priests." As they went, they were cleansed. ¹⁵One of them, when he saw that he was healed, turned back, glorifying God with a loud voice. ¹⁶He fell on his face at Jesus' feet, giving him thanks; and he was a Samaritan. ¹⁷Jesus answered, "Weren't the ten cleansed? But where are the nine? ¹⁸Were there none found who returned to give glory to God, except this foreigner?" ¹⁹Then he said to him, "Get up, and go your way. Your faith has healed you."[h]

g Q.
5:110

h Q.
3:49

²⁰Being asked by the Pharisees when God's Kingdom would come, he answered them, "God's Kingdom doesn't come with observation; ²¹neither will they say, 'Look, here!'

or, 'Look, there!' for behold, God's Kingdom is within you."

²²He said to the disciples, "The days will come when you will desire to see one of the days of the Son of Man, and you will not see it. ²³They will tell you, 'Look, here!' or 'Look, there!' Don't go away or follow after them, ²⁴for as the lightning, when it flashes out of one part under the sky, shines to another part under the sky, so will the Son of Man be in his day. ²⁵But first, he must suffer many things and be rejected by this generation. ²⁶As it was in the days of Noah, even so it will also be in the days of the Son of Man. ²⁷They ate, they drank, they married, and they were given in marriage until the day that Noah entered into the ship,[i] and the flood came and destroyed them all. ²⁸Likewise, even as it was in the days of Lot: they ate, they drank, they bought, they sold, they planted, they built; ²⁹but in the day that Lot went out from Sodom, it rained fire and sulfur from the sky and destroyed them all.[j] ³⁰It will be the same way in the day that the Son of Man is revealed. ³¹In that day, he who will be on the housetop and his goods in the house, let him not go down to take them away. Let him who is in the field likewise not turn back. ³²Remember Lot's wife![k] ³³Whoever seeks to save his life loses it, but whoever loses his life preserves it. ³⁴I tell you, in that night there will be two people in one bed. One will be taken and the other will be left. ³⁵There will be two grinding grain together. One will be taken and the other will be left." ³⁷They, answering, asked him, "Where, Lord?" He said to them, "Where the body is, there the vultures will also be gathered together."

[i] Q. 53:32

[j] Q. 26:172

[k] Q. 26:171; 27:57; 66:10

18[1]

¹He also spoke a parable to them that they must always pray and not give up, ²saying, "There was a judge in a certain city who didn't fear God and didn't respect man. ³A widow was in that city, and she often came to him, saying, 'Defend me from my adversary!' ⁴He wouldn't for a while; but

[1] Q. 2:87, 253; 5:110; 19:30

afterward he said to himself, 'Though I neither fear God nor respect man, [5]yet because this widow bothers me, I will defend her, or else she will wear me out by her continual coming.' " [6]The Lord said, "Listen to what the unrighteous judge says. [7]Won't God avenge his chosen ones who are crying out to him day and night, and yet he exercises patience with them? [8]I tell you that he will avenge them quickly. Nevertheless, when the Son of Man comes, will he find faith on the earth?"

[9]He also spoke this parable to certain people who were convinced of their own righteousness, and who despised all others: [10]"Two men went up into the temple to pray; one was a Pharisee, and the other was a tax collector. [11]The Pharisee stood and prayed by himself like this: 'God, I thank you that I am not like the rest of men: extortionists, unrighteous, adulterers, or even like this tax collector. [12]I fast twice a week. I give tithes of all that I get.' [13]But the tax collector, standing far away, wouldn't even lift up his eyes to heaven, but beat his breast, saying, 'God, be merciful to me, a sinner!' [14]I tell you, this man went down to his house justified rather than the other; for everyone who exalts himself will be humbled, but he who humbles himself will be exalted."

[15]They were also bringing their babies to him, that he might touch them. But when the disciples saw it, they rebuked them. [16]Jesus summoned them, saying, "Allow the little children to come to me, and don't hinder them, for God's Kingdom belongs to such as these. [17]Most certainly, I tell you, whoever doesn't receive God's Kingdom like a little child, he will in no way enter into it."

[18]A certain ruler asked him, saying, "Good Teacher, what shall I do to inherit eternal life?" [19]Jesus asked him, "Why do you call me good? No one is good, except one: God. [20]You know the commandments: 'Don't commit adultery,' 'Don't murder,' 'Don't steal,' 'Don't give false testimony,' 'Honor

your father and your mother.' "* ²¹He said, "I have observed all these things from my youth up." ²²When Jesus heard these things, he said to him, "You still lack one thing. Sell all that you have and distribute it to the poor. Then you will have treasure in heaven; then come, follow me."ᵐ ²³But when he heard these things, he became very sad, he was very rich. ²⁴Jesus, seeing that he became very sad, said, "How hard it is for those who have riches to enter into God's Kingdom! ²⁵For it is easier for a camel to enter in through a needle's eye than for a rich man to enter into God's Kingdom."ⁿ ²⁶Those who heard it said, "Then who can be saved?" ²⁷But he said, "The things which are impossible with men are possible with God." ²⁸Peter said, "Look, we have left everything and followed you." ²⁹He said to them, "Most certainly I tell you, there is no one who has left house, or wife, or brothers, or parents, or children, for God's Kingdom's sake, ³⁰who will not receive many times more in this time, and in the world to come,º eternal life."ᵖ

³¹He took the twelve aside and said to them, "Behold, we are going up to Jerusalem, and all the things that are written through the prophets concerning the Son of Man will be completed. ³²For he will be delivered up to the Gentiles, will be mocked�q†, treated shamefully, and spit on. ³³They will scourge and kill him. On the third day, he will rise again."

³⁵They understood none of these things. This saying was hidden from them, and they didn't understand the things that were said. As he came near Jericho, a certain blind man sat by the road, begging. ³⁶Hearing a multitude going by, he asked what this meant. ³⁷They told him that Jesus of Nazareth was passing by. ³⁸He cried out, "Jesus, you son of David, have mercy on me!" ³⁹Those who led the way rebuked him, that he should be quiet; but he cried out all the more, "You son of David, have mercy on me!"

ᵐ Q. 30:38
ⁿ Q. 7:40; 28:84
º Q. 16:30, 41
ᵖ Q. 3:148
q see footnote

* 18:20 Exodus 20:12-16; Deuteronomy 5:16-20
† q Q. 6:10; 13:32; 15:11; 21:41; 36:30; 43:7

⁴⁰Standing still, Jesus commanded him to be brought to him. When he had come near, he asked him, ⁴¹"What do you want me to do?" He said, "Lord, that I may see again." ⁴²Jesus said to him, "Receive your sight. Your faith has healed you." ⁴³Immediately he received his sight and followed him, glorifying God. All the people, when they saw it, praised God.

19

¹He entered and was passing through Jericho. ²There was a man named Zacchaeus. He was a chief tax collector, and he was rich. ³He was trying to see who Jesus was, and couldn't because of the crowd, because he was short. ⁴He ran on ahead and climbed up into a sycamore tree to see him, for he was going to pass that way. ⁵When Jesus came to the place, he looked up and saw him, and said to him, "Zacchaeus, hurry and come down, for today I must stay at your house." ⁶He hurried, came down, and received him joyfully. ⁷When they saw it, they all murmured, saying, "He has gone in to lodge with a man who is a sinner." ⁸Zacchaeus stood and said to the Lord, "Behold, Lord, half of my goods I give to the poor.ʳ If I have wrongfully exacted anything of anyone, I restore four times as much." ⁹Jesus said to him, "Today, salvation has come to this house, because he also is a son of Abraham. ¹⁰For the Son of Man came to seek and to save that which was lost."ˢ*

¹¹As they heard these things, he went on and told a parable, because he was near Jerusalem, and they supposed that God's Kingdom would be revealed immediately. ¹²He said therefore, "A certain nobleman went into a far country to receive for himself a kingdom and to return. ¹³He called ten servants of his and gave them ten mina coins,† and told

ʳ Q.
2:177;
69:34

ˢ see
footnote

---

* ˢ Q. 10:44; 12:53; 14:34; 16:61; 17:67; 22:65; 29:21-22; 33:73; 42:52; 43:13; 80:3; 91:9; 103:3

† 19:13 10 minas was more than 3 years' wages for an agricultural laborer.

them, 'Conduct business until I come.' ¹⁴But his citizens hated him, and sent an envoy after him, saying, 'We don't want this man to reign over us.' ¹⁵"When he had come back again, having received the kingdom, he commanded these servants, to whom he had given the money, to be called to him, that he might know what they had gained by conducting business. ¹⁶The first came before him, saying, 'Lord, your mina has made ten more minas.' ¹⁷"He said to him, 'Well done, you good servant! Because you were found faithful with very little, you shall have authority over ten cities.'ᵗ ¹⁸"The second came, saying, 'Your mina, Lord, has made five minas. ¹⁹"So he said to him, 'And you are to be over five cities.' ²⁰Another came, saying, 'Lord, behold, your mina, which I kept laid away in a handkerchief, ²¹for I feared you, because you are an exacting man. You take up that which you didn't lay down, and reap that which you didn't sow.' ²²"He said to him, 'Out of your own mouth I will judge you, you wicked servant! You knew that I am an exacting man, taking up that which I didn't lay down and reaping that which I didn't sow. ²³Then why didn't you deposit my money in the bank, and at my coming, I might have earned interest on it?' ²⁴He said to those who stood by, 'Take the mina away from him and give it to him who has the ten minas.'ᵘ ²⁵"They said to him, 'Lord, he has ten minas!' ²⁶'For I tell you that to everyone who has, will more be given;ᵛ but from him who doesn't have, even that which he has will be taken away from him. ²⁷But bring those enemies of mine who didn't want me to reign over them here, and kill them before me.'"ʷ*

²⁸Having said these things, he went on ahead, going up to Jerusalem. ²⁹When he came near to Bethsphage† and Bethany, at the mountain that is called Olivet, he sent two of his disciples, ³⁰saying, "Go your way into the village on the other side, in which, as you enter, you will find a colt tied,

ᵗ Q. 24:55; 36:54

ᵘ Q. 34:21

ᵛ Q. 14:7

ʷ see footnote

---

* ʷ Q. 2:196; 3:11; 5:2; 8:13; 13:6; 59:4
† 19:29 TR, NU read "Bethpage" instead of "Bethsphage"

which no man has ever sat upon. Untie it and bring it. ³¹If anyone asks you, 'Why are you untying it?' say to him: 'The Lord needs it.'" ³²Those who were sent went away and found things just as he had told them. ³³As they were untying the colt, its owners said to them, "Why are you untying the colt?" ³⁴They said, "The Lord needs it." ³⁵Then they brought it to Jesus. They threw their cloaks on the colt and sat Jesus on them. ³⁶As he went, they spread their cloaks on the road. ³⁷As he was now getting near, at the descent of the Mount of Olives, the whole multitude of the disciples began to rejoice and praise God with a loud voice for all the mighty works which they had seen, ³⁸saying, "Blessed is the King who comes in the name of the Lord!* Peace in heaven, and glory in the highest!" ³⁹Some of the Pharisees from the multitude said to him, "Teacher, rebuke your disciples!" ⁴⁰He answered them, "I tell you that if these were silent, the stones would cry out."ˣ

ˣ Q.
2:74;
21:79;
40:3

⁴¹When he came near, he saw the city and wept over it, ⁴²saying, "If you, even you, had known today the things which belong to your peace! But now, they are hidden from your eyes. ⁴³For the days will come on you when your enemies will throw up a barricade against you, surround you, hem you in on every side, ⁴⁴and will dash you and your children within you to the ground. They will not leave in you one stone on another, because you didn't know the time of your visitation."

⁴⁵He entered into the temple and began to drive out those who bought and sold in it, ⁴⁶saying to them, "It is written, 'My house is a house of prayer,'† but you have made it a 'den of robbers'!"‡

⁴⁷He was teaching daily in the temple, but the chief priests, the scribes, and the leading men among the people sought to destroy him. ⁴⁸They couldn't find what they

---

* 19:38 Psalm 118:26

† 19:46 Isaiah 56:7

‡ 19:46 Jeremiah 7:11

might do, for all the people hung on to every word that he said.

20

¹On one of those days, as he was teaching the people in the temple and preaching the Good News, the* priests and scribes came to him with the elders. ²They asked him, "Tell us: by what authority do you do these things? Or who is giving you this authority?" ³He answered them, "I also will ask you one question. Tell me: ⁴the baptism of John, was it from heaven, or from men?" ⁵They reasoned with themselves, saying, "If we say, 'From heaven,' he will say, 'Why didn't you believe him?' ⁶But if we say, 'From men,' all the people will stone us, for they are persuaded that John was a prophet." ⁷They answered that they didn't know where it was from. ⁸Jesus said to them, "Neither will I tell you by what authority I do these things."

⁹He began to tell the people this parable: "A† man planted a vineyard and rented it out to some farmers, and went into another country for a long time. ¹⁰At the proper season, he sent a servant to the farmers to collect his share of the fruit of the vineyard. But the farmers beat him and sent him away empty. ¹¹He sent yet another servant, and they also beat him and treated him shamefully, and sent him away empty. ¹²He sent yet a third, and they also wounded him and threw him out. ¹³The lord of the vineyard said, 'What shall I do? I will send my beloved son. It may be that seeing him, they will respect him.' ¹⁴"But when the farmers saw him, they reasoned among themselves, saying, 'This is the heir. Come, let's kill him, that the inheritance may be ours.' ¹⁵Then they threw him out of the vineyard and killed him. What therefore will the lord of the vineyard do to them?

---

* 20:1 TR adds "chief"

† 20:9 NU (in brackets) and TR add "certain"

176

He will come and destroy these farmers, and will give the vineyard to others."ʸ When they heard that, they said, "May that never be!" ¹⁷But he looked at them and said, "Then what is this that is written,

'The stone which the builders rejected
was made the chief cornerstone?'*

¹⁸Everyone who falls on that stone will be broken to pieces, but it will crush whomever it falls on to dust."

¹⁹The chief priests and the scribes sought to lay hands on him that very hour, but they feared the people — for they knew he had spoken this parable against them. ²⁰They watched him and sent out spies, who pretended to be righteous, that they might trap him in something he said, so as to deliver him up to the power and authority of the governor. ²¹They asked him, "Teacher, we know that you say and teach what is right, and aren't partial to anyone, but truly teach the way of God. ²²Is it lawful for us to pay taxes to Caesar, or not?" ²³But he perceived their craftiness, and said to them, "Why do you test me? ²⁴Show me a denarius. Whose image and inscription are on it?" They answered, "Caesar's." He said to them, "Then give to Caesar the things that are Caesar's, and to God the things that are God's." They weren't able to trap him in his words before the people. They marveled at his answer and were silent.

²⁷Some of the Sadducees came to him, those who deny that there is a resurrection. ²⁸They asked him, "Teacher, Moses wrote to us that if a man's brother dies having a wife, and he is childless, his brother should take the wife and raise up children for his brother. ²⁹There were therefore seven brothers. The first took a wife, and died childless. ³⁰The second took her as wife, and he died childless. ³¹The third took her, and likewise the seven all left no children, and died. ³²Afterward the woman also died.

---

* 20:17 Psalm 118:22

³³Therefore in the resurrection whose wife of them will she be? For the seven had her as a wife."

³⁴Jesus said to them, "The children of this age marry and are given in marriage. ³⁵But those who are considered worthy to attain to that age and the resurrection from the dead neither marry nor are given in marriage. ³⁶For they can't die any more, for they are like the angels and are children of God, being children of the resurrection. ³⁷But that the dead are raised, even Moses showed at the bush, when he called the Lord 'The God of Abraham, the God of Isaac, and the God of Jacob.'* ³⁸Now he is not the God of the dead, but of the living, for all are alive to him." ³⁹Some of the scribes answered, "Teacher, you speak well." ⁴⁰They didn't dare to ask him any more questions.

⁴¹He said to them, "Why do they say that the Christ is David's son? ⁴²David himself says in the book of Psalms,

'The Lord said to my Lord, "Sit at my right hand,

⁴³until I make your enemies the footstool of your feet."'†

⁴⁴"David therefore calls him Lord, so how is he his son?"

⁴⁵In the hearing of all the people, he said to his disciples, ⁴⁶"Beware of those scribes who like to walk in long robes, and love greetings in the marketplaces, the best seats in the synagogues, and the best places at feasts; ⁴⁷who devour widows' houses, and for a pretense make long prayers. These will receive greater condemnation."

21

¹He looked up and saw the rich people who were putting their gifts into the treasury. ²He saw a certain poor

---

* 20:37 Exodus 3:6
† 20:43 Psalm 110:1

widow casting in two small brass coins.[*] ³He said, "Truly I tell you, this poor widow put in more than all of them, ⁴for all these put in gifts for God from their abundance, but she, out of her poverty, put in all that she had to live on."

⁵As some were talking about the temple and how it was decorated with beautiful stones and gifts, he said, ⁶"As for these things which you see, the days will come in which there will not be left here one stone on another that will not be thrown down." ⁷They asked him, "Teacher, so when will these things be? What is the sign that these things are about to happen?" ⁸He said, "Watch out that you don't get led astray, for many will come in my name, saying, 'I am he[†],' and, 'The time is at hand.' Therefore don't follow them. ⁹When you hear of wars and disturbances, don't be terrified, for these things must happen first, but the end won't come immediately."

¹⁰Then he said to them, "Nation will rise against nation, and kingdom against kingdom. ¹¹There will be great earthquakes, famines, and plagues in various places. There will be terrors and great signs from heaven. ¹²But before all these things, they will lay their hands on you and will persecute you, delivering you up to synagogues and prisons, bringing you before kings and governors for my name's sake. ¹³It will turn out as a testimony for you. ¹⁴Settle it therefore in your hearts not to meditate beforehand how to answer, ¹⁵for I will give you a mouth and wisdom which all your adversaries will not be able to withstand or to contradict. ¹⁶You will be handed over even by parents, brothers, relatives, and friends. They will cause some of you to be put to death.^z ¹⁷You will be hated by all men for my name's sake. ¹⁸And not a hair of your head will perish. ¹⁹"By your endurance you will win your

---

[*] 21:2 literally, "two lepta." 2 lepta was about 1% of a day's wages for an agricultural laborer.
[†] 21:8 or, I AM

lives.

20"But when you see Jerusalem surrounded by armies, then know that its desolation is at hand.[a] 21Then let those who are in Judea flee to the mountains. Let those who are in the middle of her depart. Let those who are in the country not enter therein. 22For these are days of vengeance, that all things which are written may be fulfilled. 23Woe to those who are pregnant and to those who nurse infants in those days! For there will be great distress in the land and wrath to this people. 24They will fall by the edge of the sword, and will be led captive into all the nations. Jerusalem will be trampled down by the Gentiles until the times of the Gentiles are fulfilled.

25"There will be signs in the sun, moon, and stars; and on the earth anxiety of nations, in perplexity for the roaring of the sea[b] and the waves; 26men fainting for fear and for expectation of the things which are coming on the world, for the powers of the heavens will be shaken. 27Then they will see the Son of Man coming in a cloud with power and great glory. 28But when these things begin to happen, look up and lift up your heads, because your redemption is near."[c]

29He told them a parable. "See the fig tree and all the trees. 30When they are already budding, you see it and know by your own selves that the summer is already near. 31Even so you also, when you see these things happening, know that God's Kingdom is near. 32Most certainly I tell you, this generation will not pass away until all things are accomplished. 33Heaven and earth will pass away, but my words will by no means pass away.

34"So be careful, or your hearts will be loaded down with carousing, drunkenness, and cares of this life, and that day will come on you suddenly.[d] 35For it will come like a snare on all those who dwell on the surface of all the earth. 36Therefore be watchful all the time, praying that you may be counted worthy to escape all these things that

[a] Q. 17:7

[b] Q. 81:6

[c] Q. 39:68; 43:61

[d] Q. 2:219; 22:55; 74:46

will happen, and to stand before the Son of Man." ³⁷Every day Jesus was teaching in the temple, and every night he would go out and spend the night on the mountain that is called Olivet. ³⁸All the people came early in the morning to him in the temple to hear him.

22ᵉ*

ᵉ see footnote

¹Now the feast of unleavened bread, which is called the Passover, was approaching. ²The chief priests and the scribes sought how they might put him to death, for they feared the people.

³Satan entered into Judas, who was also called Iscariot, who was counted with the twelve. ⁴He went away and talked with the chief priests and captains about how he might deliver him to them. ⁵They were glad, and agreed to give him money. ⁶He consented and sought an opportunity to deliver him to them in the absence of the multitude.

⁷The day of unleavened bread came, on which the Passover must be sacrificed. ⁸Jesus sent Peter and John, saying, "Go and prepare the Passover for us, that we may eat." They said to him, ⁹"Where do you want us to prepare?" ¹⁰He said to them, "Behold, when you have entered into the city, a man carrying a pitcher of water will meet you. Follow him into the house which he enters. ¹¹Tell the master of the house, 'The Teacher says to you, "Where is the guest room, where I may eat the Passover with my disciples?"'¹²He will show you a large, furnished upper room. Make preparations there." ¹³They went, found things as Jesus had told them, and they prepared the Passover.

¹⁴When the hour had come, he sat down with the twelve apostles. ¹⁵He said to them, "I have earnestly desired to eat this Passover with you before I suffer, ¹⁶for I tell you, I will

---

* ᵉ Q. 2:87, 253; 3:49, 52; 5:110, 112; 19:30; 43:63

no longer by any means eat of it until it is fulfilled in God's Kingdom." [17]He received a cup, and when he had given thanks, he said, "Take this and share it among yourselves, [18]for I tell you, I will not drink at all again from the fruit of the vine, until God's Kingdom comes." [19]He took bread, and when he had given thanks, he broke and gave it to them, saying, "This is my body which is given for you. Do this in memory of me." [20]Likewise, he took the cup after supper, saying, "This cup is the new covenant in my blood, which is poured out for you. [21]But behold, the hand of him who betrays me is with me on the table. [22]The Son of Man indeed goes as it has been determined, but woe to that man through whom he is betrayed!" [23]They began to question among themselves which of them it was who would do this thing.

[24]A dispute also arose among them, which of them was considered to be greatest. [25]He said to them, "The kings of the nations lord it over them, and those who have authority over them are called 'benefactors.' [26]But not so with you. Rather, the one who is greater among you, let him become as the younger, and one who is governing, as one who serves. [27]For who is greater, one who sits at the table, or one who serves? Isn't it he who sits at the table? But I am among you as one who serves.

[28]"But you are those who have continued with me in my trials. [29]I confer on you a kingdom, even as my Father conferred on me, [30]that you may eat[f] and drink at my table in my Kingdom. You will sit on thrones, judging the twelve tribes of Israel."

[f] Q. 52:22

[31]The Lord said, "Simon, Simon, behold, Satan asked to have all of you, that he might sift you as wheat, [32]but I prayed for you, that your faith wouldn't fail. You, when once you have turned again, establish your brothers."[*]

[33]He said to him, "Lord, I am ready to go with you both to

[*] 22:32 The word for "brothers" here may be also correctly translated "brothers and sisters" or "siblings."

prison and to death!" ³⁴He said, "I tell you, Peter, the rooster will by no means crow today until you deny that you know me three times."

³⁵He said to them, "When I sent you out without purse, bag, and sandals, did you lack anything?" They said, "Nothing." ³⁶Then he said to them, "But now, whoever has a purse, let him take it, and likewise a bag. Whoever has none, let him sell his cloak, and buy a sword. ³⁷For I tell you that this which is written must still be fulfilled in me: 'He was counted with transgressors.'* For that which concerns me is being fulfilled." ³⁸They said, "Lord, behold, here are two swords." He said to them, "That is enough."

³⁹He came out and went, as his custom was, to the Mount of Olives. His disciples also followed him. ⁴⁰When he was at the place, he said to them, "Pray that you don't enter into temptation." ⁴¹He was withdrawn from them about a stone's throw, and he knelt down and prayed, ⁴²saying, "Father, if you are willing, remove this cup from me. Nevertheless, not my will, but yours, be done." ⁴³An angel from heaven appeared to him, strengthening him. ⁴⁴Being in agony, he prayed more earnestly. His sweat became like great drops of blood falling down on the ground. ⁴⁵When he rose up from his prayer, he came to the disciples and found them sleeping because of grief, ⁴⁶and said to them, "Why do you sleep? Rise and pray that you may not enter into temptation."

⁴⁷While he was still speaking, a crowd appeared. He who was called Judas, one of the twelve, was leading them. He came near to Jesus to kiss him. ⁴⁸But Jesus said to him, "Judas, do you betray the Son of Man with a kiss?" ⁴⁹When those who were around him saw what was about to happen, they said to him, "Lord, shall we strike with the sword?" ⁵⁰A certain one of them struck the servant of the high priest, and cut off his right ear. ⁵¹But Jesus answered, "Let me at least

---

* 22:37 Isaiah 53:12

do this"—and he touched his ear and healed him. ⁵²Jesus said to the chief priests, captains of the temple, and elders, who had come against him, "Have you come out as against a robber, with swords and clubs? ⁵³When I was with you in the temple daily, you didn't stretch out your hands against me. But this is your hour, and the power of darkness."

⁵⁴They seized him and led him away, and brought him into the high priest's house. But Peter followed from a distance. ⁵⁵When they had kindled a fire in the middle of the courtyard and had sat down together, Peter sat among them. ⁵⁶A certain servant girl saw him as he sat in the light, and looking intently at him, said, "This man also was with him." ⁵⁷He denied Jesus, saying, "Woman, I don't know him." ⁵⁸After a little while someone else saw him and said, "You also are one of them!" But Peter answered, "Man, I am not!" ⁵⁹After about one hour passed, another confidently affirmed, saying, "Truly this man also was with him, for he is a Galilean!" ⁶⁰But Peter said, "Man, I don't know what you are talking about!" Immediately, while he was still speaking, a rooster crowed. ⁶¹The Lord turned and looked at Peter. Then Peter remembered the Lord's word, how he said to him, "Before the rooster crows you will deny me three times." ⁶²He went out, and wept bitterly.

⁶³The men who held Jesus mocked[g] him and beat him. ⁶⁴Having blindfolded him, they struck him on the face and asked him, "Prophesy! Who is the one who struck you?" ⁶⁵They spoke many other things against him, insulting him.

⁶⁶As soon as it was day, the assembly of the elders of the people were gathered together, both chief priests and scribes, and they led him away into their council, saying, ⁶⁷"If you are the Christ, tell us." But he said to them, "If I tell you, you won't believe, ⁶⁸and if I ask, you will in no way answer me or let me go. ⁶⁹From now on, the Son of Man will be seated at the right hand of the power of God." ⁷⁰They all said, "Are you then the Son of God?" He said to them, "You say it, because I am." ⁷¹They said, "Why do we need any more

[g] Q. 6:10; 13:32; 15:11; 36:30

witness? For we ourselves have heard from his own mouth!"

23

¹The whole company of them rose up and brought him before Pilate. ²They began to accuse him, saying, "We found this man perverting the nation, forbidding paying taxes to Caesar, and saying that he himself is Christ, a king." ³Pilate asked him, "Are you the King of the Jews?" He answered him, "So you say." ⁴Pilate said to the chief priests and the multitudes, "I find no basis for a charge against this man." ⁵But they insisted, saying, "He stirs up the people, teaching throughout all Judea, beginning from Galilee even to this place."

⁶But when Pilate heard Galilee mentioned, he asked if the man was a Galilean. ⁷When he found out that he was in Herod's jurisdiction, he sent him to Herod, who was also in Jerusalem during those days. ⁸Now when Herod saw Jesus, he was exceedingly glad, for he had wanted to see him for a long time, because he had heard many things about him. He hoped to see some miracle done by him. ⁹He questioned him with many words, but he gave no answers. ¹⁰The chief priests and the scribes stood, vehemently accusing him. ¹¹Herod with his soldiers humiliated him and mocked[h] him. Dressing him in luxurious clothing, they sent him back to Pilate. ¹²Herod and Pilate became friends with each other that very day, for before that they were enemies with each other.

¹³Pilate called together the chief priests, the rulers, and the people, ¹⁴and said to them, "You brought this man to me as one that perverts the people, and behold, having examined him before you, I found no basis for a charge against this man concerning those things of which you accuse him. ¹⁵Neither has Herod, for I sent you to him, and see, nothing worthy of death has been done by him. ¹⁶I will therefore chastise him and release him." ¹⁷Now he

[h] Q. 6:10; 13:32; 15:11; 21:41; 36:30; 43:7

had to release one prisoner to them at the feast.* ¹⁸But they all cried out together, saying, "Away with this man! Release to us Barabbas!"— ¹⁹one who was thrown into prison for a certain revolt in the city, and for murder. ²⁰Then Pilate spoke to them again, wanting to release Jesus, ²¹but they shouted, saying, "Crucify! Crucify him!" ²²He said to them the third time, "Why? What evil has this man done? I have found no capital crime in him. I will therefore chastise him and release him." ²³But they were urgent with loud voices, asking that he might be crucified. Their voices and the voices of the chief priests prevailed. ²⁴Pilate decreed that what they asked for should be done. ²⁵He released him who had been thrown into prison for insurrection and murder, for whom they asked, but he delivered Jesus up to their will.

²⁶When they led him away, they grabbed one Simon of Cyrene, coming from the country, and laid the cross on him to carry it after Jesus. ²⁷A great multitude of the people followed him, including women who also mourned and lamented him. ²⁸But Jesus, turning to them, said, "Daughters of Jerusalem, don't weep for me, but weep for yourselves and for your children. ²⁹For behold, the days are coming in which they will say, 'Blessed are the barren, the wombs that never bore, and the breasts that never nursed.' ³⁰Then they will begin to tell the mountains, 'Fall on us!' and tell the hills, 'Cover us.'† ³¹For if they do these things in the green tree,ⁱ what will be done in the dry?"

ⁱ Q. 36:80

³²There were also others, two criminals, led with him to be put to death. ³³When they came to the place that is called "The Skull", they crucified him there with the criminals, one on the right and the other on the left. ³⁴Jesus said, "Father, forgive them,ʲ for they don't know what they are doing." Dividing his garments among them,

ʲ Q. 3:159

* 23:17 NU omits verse 17
† 23:30 Hosea 10:8

they cast lots. ³⁵The people stood watching. The rulers with them also scoffed at him, saying, "He saved others. ˢLet him save himself, if this is the Christ of God, his chosen one!" ³⁶The soldiers also mocked[k] him, coming to him and offering him vinegar, ³⁷and saying, "If you are the King of the Jews, save yourself!" ³⁸An inscription was also written over him in letters of Greek, Latin, and Hebrew: "THIS IS THE KING OF THE JEWS."

³⁹One of the criminals who was hanged insulted him, saying, "If you are the Christ, save yourself and us!" ⁴⁰But the other answered, and rebuking him said, "Don't you even fear God, seeing you are under the same condemnation? ⁴¹And we indeed justly, for we receive the due reward for our deeds, but this man has done nothing wrong." ⁴²He said to Jesus, "Lord, remember me when you come into your Kingdom." ⁴³Jesus said to him, "Assuredly I tell you, today you will be with me in Paradise."[l]

⁴⁴It was now about the sixth hour,* and darkness came over the whole land until the ninth hour.† ⁴⁵The sun was darkened, and the veil of the temple was torn in two. ⁴⁶Jesus, crying with a loud voice, said, "Father, into your hands I commit my spirit!"[m] Having said this, he breathed his last. ⁴⁷When the centurion saw what was done, he glorified God, saying, "Certainly this was a righteous man." ⁴⁸All the multitudes that came together to see this, when they saw the things that were done, returned home beating their breasts. ⁴⁹All his acquaintances and the women who followed with him from Galilee stood at a distance, watching these things.

⁵⁰Behold, there was a man named Joseph, who was a member of the council, a good and righteous man ⁵¹(he had not consented to their counsel and deed), from Arimathaea, a city of the Jews, who was also waiting for God's Kingdom. ⁵²This man went to Pilate, and asked for Jesus' body. ⁵³He

[k] Q. 6:10; 13:32; 15:11; 21:41; 36:30; 43:7

[l] Q. 18:107

[m] Q. 2:156; 39:42

---

* 23:44 Time was counted from sunrise, so the sixth hour was about noon
† 23:44 3:00 p.m

took it down and wrapped it in a linen cloth, and laid him in a tomb that was cut in stone, where no one had ever been laid. [54]It was the day of the Preparation, and the Sabbath was drawing near. [55]The women who had come with him out of Galilee followed after, and saw the tomb and how his body was laid. [56]They returned and prepared spices and ointments.

On the Sabbath they rested according to the commandment.[n]*

[n] see footnote

24

[1]But on the first day of the week, at early dawn, they and some others came to the tomb, bringing the spices which they had prepared. [2]They found the stone rolled away from the tomb. [3]They entered in, and didn't find the Lord Jesus' body.[o] [4]While they were greatly perplexed about this, behold, two men stood by them in dazzling clothing. [5]Becoming terrified, they bowed their faces down to the earth. The men said to them, "Why do you seek the living among the dead? [6]He isn't here, but is risen.[p] Remember what he told you when he was still in Galilee, [7]saying that the Son of Man must be delivered up into the hands of sinful men and be crucified, and the third day rise again?" [8]They remembered his words, [9]returned from the tomb, and told all these things to the eleven and to all the rest. [10]Now they were Mary Magdalene, Joanna, and Mary the mother of James. The other women with them told these things to the apostles. [11]These words seemed to them to be nonsense, and they didn't believe them. [12]But Peter got up and ran to the tomb. Stooping and looking in, he saw the strips of linen lying by themselves, and he departed to his home, wondering what had happened.

[13]Behold, two of them were going that very day to a

[o] Q. 19:33

[p] Q. 6:95

---

* [n] Q. 2:65; 4:47, 154; 7:163; 16:124

village named Emmaus, which was sixty stadia* from Jerusalem. [14]They talked with each other about all of these things which had happened. [15]While they talked and questioned together, Jesus himself came near, and went with them. [16]But their eyes were kept from recognizing him. [17]He said to them, "What are you talking about as you walk, and are sad?" [18]One of them, named Cleopas, answered him, "Are you the only stranger in Jerusalem who doesn't know the things which have happened there in these days?" [19]He said to them, "What things?" They said to him, "The things concerning Jesus the Nazarene, who was a prophet mighty in deed and word before God and all the people; [20]and how the chief priests and our rulers delivered him up to be condemned to death, and crucified him. [21]But we were hoping that it was he who would redeem Israel. Yes, and besides all this, it is now the third day since these things happened. [22]Also, certain women of our company amazed us, having arrived early at the tomb; [23]and when they didn't find his body, they came saying that they had also seen a vision of angels, who said that he was alive. [24]Some of us went to the tomb and found it just like the women had said, but they didn't see him." [25]He said to them, "Foolish people, and slow of heart to believe in all that the prophets have spoken![q] [26]Didn't the Christ have to suffer these things and to enter into his glory?" [27]Beginning from Moses and from all the prophets,[r] he explained to them in all the Scriptures the things concerning himself.

[q] Q.
2:177

[r] Q.
2:177

[28]They came near to the village where they were going, and he acted like he would go further. [29]They urged him, saying, "Stay with us, for it is almost evening, and the day is almost over." went in to stay with them. [30]When he had sat down at the table with them, he took the bread and gave thanks. Breaking it, he gave it to them. [31]Their eyes were

---

* 24:13 60 stadia = about 11 kilometers or about 7 miles

opened and they recognized him; then he vanished out of their sight. ³²They said to one another, "Weren't our hearts burning within us while he spoke to us along the way, and while he opened the Scriptures to us?" ³³They rose up that very hour, returned to Jerusalem, and found the eleven gathered together, and those who were with them, ³⁴saying, "The Lord is risen indeed, and has appeared to Simon!" ³⁵They related the things that happened along the way, and how he was recognized by them in the breaking of the bread.

³⁶As they said these things, Jesus himself stood among them, and said to them, "Peace be to you." ³⁷But they were terrified and filled with fear, and supposed that they had seen a spirit. ³⁸He said to them, "Why are you troubled? Why do doubts arise in your hearts? ³⁹See my hands and my feet, that it is truly me. Touch me and see, for a spirit doesn't have flesh and bones, as you see that I have." ⁴⁰When he had said this, he showed them his hands and his feet. ⁴¹While they still didn't believe for joy, and wondered, he said to them, "Do you have anything here to eat?" ⁴²They gave him a piece of a broiled fish and some honeycomb. ⁴³He took them, and ate^s in front of them.

⁴⁴He said to them, "This is what I told you while I was still with you, that all things which are written^t in the law of Moses, the prophets, and the psalms concerning me must be fulfilled." ⁴⁵Then he opened their minds, that they might understand the Scriptures. ⁴⁶He said to them, "Thus it is written, and thus it was necessary for the Christ to suffer and to rise from the dead the third day, ⁴⁷and that repentance and remission of sins should be preached in his name to all the nations, beginning at Jerusalem. ⁴⁸You are witnesses of these things. ⁴⁹Behold, I send out the promise of my Father on you. But wait in the city of Jerusalem until you are clothed with power from on high."

⁵⁰He led them out as far as Bethany, and he lifted up his hands and blessed them. ⁵¹While he blessed them, he

^s Q. 5:75

^t Q. 3:48

withdrew from them and was carried up into heaven. [52]They worshiped him and returned to Jerusalem with great joy, [53]and were continually in the temple, praising and blessing God. Amen.

The Good News According to John

1

[a] Q.
3:39,
45;
4:171

[b] Q.
3:49

[c] Q.
4:174;
5:16;
9:32

[d] Q.
19:7;
21:90

[e] Q.
24:40

[f] Q.
3:49;
9:33

[1]In the beginning was the Word, and the Word was with God,[a] and the Word was God. [2]The same was in the beginning with God. [3]All things were made through him. Without him, nothing was made that has been made.[b] [4]In him was life, and the life was the light of men. [5]The light[c] shines in the darkness, and the darkness hasn't overcome[*] it.

[6]There came a man sent from God, whose name was John.[d] [7]The same came as a witness, that he might testify about the light, that all might believe through him. [8]He was not the light, but was sent that he might testify about the light.

[9]The true light[e] that enlightens everyone was coming into the world. [10]He was in the world, and the world was made through him,[f] and the world didn't recognize him. [11]He came to his own, and those who were his own didn't receive him. [12]But as many as received him, to them he gave the right to become God's children, to those who believe in his name: [13]who were born, not of blood, nor of the will of the flesh, nor of the will of man, but of God.

[*] 1:5The word translated "overcome" (κατέλαβεν) can also be translated "comprehended." It refers to getting a grip on an enemy to defeat him.

¹⁴The Word^g became flesh and lived among us. We saw his glory, such glory as of the only born[*] Son of the Father, full of grace and truth. ¹⁵John testified about him. He cried out, saying, "This was he of whom I said, 'He who comes after me has surpassed me, for he was before me.'" ¹⁶From his fullness we all received grace upon grace. ¹⁷For the law was given through Moses. Grace and truth were realized through Jesus Christ.[†] ¹⁸No one has seen God at any time. The only born§[‡] Son,[§] who is in the bosom of the Father, has declared him.

^g Q. 3:39, 45

¹⁹This is John's testimony, when the Jews sent priests and Levites from Jerusalem to ask him, "Who are you?" ²⁰He declared, and didn't deny, but he declared, "I am not the Christ." ²¹They asked him, "What then? Are you Elijah?" He said, "I am not." "Are you the prophet?" He answered, "No." ²²They said therefore to him, "Who are you? Give us an answer to take back to those who sent us. What do you say about yourself?" ²³He said, "I am the voice of one crying in the wilderness, 'Make straight the way of the Lord,' as Isaiah the prophet said."^h

^h Q. 3:39

²⁴The ones who had been sent were from the Pharisees. They asked²⁵ him, "Why then do you baptize if you are not the Christ, nor Elijah, nor the prophet?" ²⁶John answered them, "I baptize in water, but among you stands one whom you don't know. ²⁷He is the one who comes after me, who is preferred before me, whose sandal strap I'm not worthy to loosen." ²⁸These things were done in Bethany beyond the Jordan, where John was baptizing.

²⁹The next day, he saw Jesus coming to him, and said,

---

[*] 1:14The phrase "only born" is from the Greek word "μονογενους", which is sometimes translated "only begotten" or "one and only".
[†] 1:17"Christ" means "Anointed One".
[‡] 1:18The phrase "only born" is from the Greek word "μονογενη", which is sometimes translated "only begotten" or "one and only".
[§] 1:18NU reads "God" 1:23Isaiah 40:3

"Behold,[*] the Lamb of God, who takes away the sin of the world! [30]This is he of whom I said, 'After me comes a man who is preferred before me, for he was before me.' [31]I didn't know him, but for this reason I came baptizing in water, that he would be revealed to Israel." [32]John testified, saying, "I have seen the Spirit descending like a dove out of heaven, and it remained on him. [33]I didn't recognize him, but he who sent me to baptize in water said to me, 'On whomever you will see the Spirit descending and remaining on him is he who baptizes in the Holy Spirit.' [34]I have seen and have testified that this is the Son of God."[i]

[i] Q. 3:39

[35]Again, the next day, John was standing with two of his disciples, [36]and he looked at Jesus as he walked, and said, "Behold, the Lamb of God!" [37]The two disciples heard him speak, and they followed Jesus. [38]Jesus turned and saw them following, and said to them, "What are you looking for?" They said to him, "Rabbi" (which is to say, being interpreted, Teacher), "where are you staying?" [39]He said to them, "Come and see." They came and saw where he was staying, and they stayed with him that day. It was about the tenth hour.[†] [40]One of the two who heard John and followed him was Andrew, Simon Peter's brother. [41]He first found his own brother, Simon, and said to him, "We have found the Messiah!" (which is, being interpreted, Christ[‡]). [42]He brought him to Jesus. Jesus looked at him and said, "You are Simon the son of Jonah. You shall be called Cephas" (which is by interpretation, Peter).

[43]On the next day, he was determined to go out into Galilee, and he found Philip. Jesus said to him, "Follow me." [44]Now Philip was from Bethsaida, the city of Andrew and Peter. [45]Philip found Nathanael, and said to him, "We

---

[*] 1:29"Behold", from "ἰδού", means look at, take notice, observe, see, or gaze at. It is often used as an interjection.
[†] 1:394:00p.m
[‡] 1:41"Messiah" (Hebrew) and "Christ" (Greek) both mean "Anointed One".

have found him of whom Moses in the law and also the prophets, wrote: Jesus of Nazareth, the son of Joseph." ⁴⁶Nathanael said to him, "Can any good thing come out of Nazareth?" Philip said to him, "Come and see." ⁴⁷Jesus saw Nathanael coming to him, and said about him, "Behold, an Israelite indeed, in whom is no deceit!" ⁴⁸Nathanael said to him, "How do you know me?" Jesus answered him, "Before Philip called you, when you were under the fig tree, I saw you." ⁴⁹Nathanael answered him, "Rabbi, you are the Son of God! You are King of Israel!" ⁵⁰Jesus answered him, "Because I told you, 'I saw you underneath the fig tree,' do you believe? You will see greater things than these!" ⁵¹He said to him, "Most certainly, I tell you all, hereafter you will see heaven opened, and the angels of God ascendingʲ and descending on the Son of Man."

ʲ Q. 70:4

2ᵏ*

ᵏ see footnote

¹The third day, there was a wedding in Cana of Galilee. Jesus' mother was there. ²Jesus also was invited, with his disciples, to the wedding. ³When the wine ran out, Jesus' mother said to him, "They have no wine." ⁴Jesus said to her, "Woman, what does that have to do with you and me? My hour has not yet come." ⁵His mother said to the servants, "Whatever he says to you, do it."

⁶Now there were six water pots of stone set there after the Jews' way of purifying, containing two or three metretes† apiece. ⁷Jesus said to them, "Fill the water pots with water." So they filled them up to the brim. ⁸He said to them, "Now draw some out, and take it to the ruler of the feast." So they took it. ⁹When the ruler of the feast tasted the water now become wine, and didn't know where it came

---

* ᵏ Q. 2:87, 253; 3:49, 52; 5:110, 112; 19:30; 43:63
† 2:6 2 to 3 metretes is about 20 to 30 U. S. Gallons, or 75 to 115 liters.

from (but the servants who had drawn the water knew), the ruler of the feast called the bridegroom ¹⁰and said to him, "Everyone serves the good wine first, and when the guests have drunk freely, then that which is worse. You have kept the good wine until now!" ¹¹This beginning of his signs Jesus did in Cana of Galilee, and revealed his glory; and his disciples believed in him.

¹²After this, he went down to Capernaum, he, and his mother, his brothers, and his disciples; and they stayed there a few days.

¹³The Passover of the Jews was at hand, and Jesus went up to Jerusalem. ¹⁴He found in the temple those who sold oxen, sheep, and doves, and the changers of money sitting. ¹⁵He made a whip of cords and drove all out of the temple, both the sheep and the oxen; and he poured out the changers' money and overthrew their tables. ¹⁶To those who sold the doves, he said, "Take these things out of here! Don't make my Father's house a marketplace!" ¹⁷His disciples remembered that it was written, "Zeal for your house will eat me up." *

¹⁸The Jews therefore answered him, "What sign do you show us, seeing that you do these things?" ¹⁹Jesus answered them, "Destroy this temple, and in three days I will raise it up." ²⁰The Jews therefore said, "It took forty-six years to build this temple! Will you raise it up in three days?" ²¹But he spoke of the temple of his body. ²²When therefore he was raised from the dead, his disciples remembered that he said this, and they believed the Scripture and the word which Jesus had said.

²³Now when he was in Jerusalem at the Passover, during the feast, many believed in his name, observing his signs which he did. ²⁴But Jesus didn't entrust himself to them, because he knew everyone, ²⁵and because he didn't need for anyone to testify concerning man; for he himself

---

* 2:17Psalm 69:9

3

[1]Now there was a man of the Pharisees named Nicodemus, a ruler of the Jews. [2]He came to Jesus by night and said to him, "Rabbi, we know that you are a teacher come from God, for no one can do these signs that you do, unless God is with him." [3]Jesus answered him, "Most certainly I tell you, unless one is born anew,[m] * he can't see God's Kingdom." [4]Nicodemus said to him, "How can a man be born when he is old? Can he enter a second time into his mother's womb and be born?" [5]Jesus answered, "Most certainly I tell you, unless one is born of water and Spirit, he can't enter into God's Kingdom. [6]That which is born of the flesh is flesh. That which is born of the Spirit is spirit. [7]Don't marvel that I said to you, 'You must be born anew.' [8]The wind[n] blows where it wants to, and you hear its sound, but don't know where it comes from and where it is going. So is everyone who is born of the Spirit."

[9]Nicodemus answered him, "How can these things be?" [10]Jesus answered him, "Are you the teacher of Israel, and don't understand these things? [11]Most certainly I tell you, we speak that which we know and testify of that which we have seen, and you don't receive our witness. [12]If I told you earthly things and you don't believe, how will you believe if I tell you heavenly things? [13]No one has ascended into heaven but he who descended out of heaven, the Son of Man, who is in heaven. [14]As Moses lifted up the serpent in the wilderness, even so must the Son of Man be lifted up, [15]that whoever believes in him should not perish, but have eternal life.

[1] Q. 3:49; 29:10

[m] Q. 40:11

[n] Q. 30:46

---

* 3:3 The word translated "anew" here and in John 3:7 (ἄνωθεν) also means "again" and "from above".

¹⁶For God so loved the world, that he gave his only born[*] Son, that whoever believes in him should not perish, but have eternal life. ¹⁷For God didn't send his Son into the world to judge the world, but that the world should be saved through him. ¹⁸He who believes in him is not judged. He who doesn't believe has been judged already, because he has not believed in the name of the only born Son of God. ¹⁹This is the judgment, that the light has come into the world, and men loved the darkness rather than the light, for their works were evil. ²⁰For everyone who does evil hates the light and doesn't come to the light, lest his works would be exposed. ²¹But he who does the truth comes to the light, that his works may be revealed, that they have been done in God."

²²After these things, Jesus came with his disciples into the land of Judea. He stayed there with them and baptized. ²³John also was baptizing in Enon near Salim, because there was much water there. They came and were baptized; ²⁴for John was not yet thrown into prison.

²⁵Therefore a dispute arose on the part of John's disciples with some Jews about purification. ²⁶They came to John^o and said to him, "Rabbi, he who was with you beyond the Jordan, to whom you have testified, behold, he baptizes, and everyone is coming to him." ²⁷John answered, "A man can receive nothing unless it has been given him from heaven. ²⁸You yourselves testify that I said, 'I am not the Christ,' but, 'I have been sent before him.' ²⁹He who has the bride is the bridegroom; but the friend of the bridegroom, who stands and hears him, rejoices greatly because of the bridegroom's voice. Therefore my joy is made full. ³⁰He must increase, but I must decrease.

³¹"He who comes from above is above all. He who is from the earth belongs to the earth and speaks of the earth.

o Q. 19:7; 21:90

---

[*] 3:16The phrase "only born" is from the Greek word "μονογενη", which is sometimes translated "only begotten" or "one and only".

He who comes from heaven is above all. [32]What he has seen and heard, of that he testifies; and no one receives his witness. [33]He who has received his witness has set his seal to this, that God is true. [34]For he whom God has sent speaks the words of God; for God gives the Spirit without measure. [35]The Father loves the Son, and has given all things into his hand. [36]One who believes in the Son has eternal life,[p] but one who disobeys the Son won't see life, but the wrath of God remains on him."[q]

4[r]*

[1]Therefore when the Lord knew that the Pharisees had heard that Jesus was making and baptizing more disciples than John [2](although Jesus himself didn't baptize, but his disciples), [3]he left Judea and departed into Galilee. [4]He needed to pass through Samaria. [5]So he came to a city of Samaria called Sychar, near the parcel of ground that Jacob gave to his son Joseph. [6]Jacob's well was there. Jesus therefore, being tired from his journey, sat down by the well. It was about the sixth hour. [†]

[7]A woman of Samaria came to draw water. Jesus said to her, "Give me a drink." [8]For his disciples had gone away into the city to buy food. [9]The Samaritan woman therefore said to him, "How is it that you, being a Jew, ask for a drink from me, a Samaritan woman?" (For Jews have no dealings with Samaritans.) [10]Jesus answered her, "If you knew the gift of God, and who it is who says to you, 'Give me a drink,' you would have asked him, and he would have given you living water." [11]The woman said to him, "Sir, you have nothing to draw with, and the well is deep. So where do you get that living water? [12]Are you greater than

[p] Q. 93:4

[q] Q. 3:112; 42:16

[r] see footnote

---

* [r] Q. 2:87, 253; 3:49, 52; 5:110, 112; 19:30; 43:63
[†] 4:6 noon

our father Jacob, who gave us the well and drank from it himself, as did his children and his livestock?" ¹³Jesus answered her, "Everyone who drinks of this water will thirst again, ¹⁴but whoever drinks of the water that I will give him will never thirst again; but the water that I will give him will become in him a well of water springing up to eternal life."ˢ ¹⁵The woman said to him, "Sir, give me this water, so that I don't get thirsty, neither come all the way here to draw."

¹⁶Jesus said to her, "Go, call your husband, and come here." ¹⁷The woman answered, "I have no husband." Jesus said to her, "You said well, 'I have no husband,' ¹⁸for you have had five husbands; and he whom you now have is not your husband. This you have said truly." ¹⁹The woman said to him, "Sir, I perceive that you are a prophet. ²⁰Our fathers worshiped in this mountain, and you Jews say that in Jerusalem is the place where people ought to worship." ²¹Jesus said to her, "Woman, believe me, the hour is coming when neither in this mountain nor in Jerusalem will you worship the Father.ᵗ ²²You worship that which you don't know. We worship that which we know;ᵘ* for salvation is from the Jews. ²³But the hour comes, and now is, when the true worshipers will worship the Father in spirit and truth, for the Father seeks such to be his worshipers. ²⁴God is spirit, and those who worship him must worship in spirit and truth." ²⁵The woman said to him, "I know that Messiah is coming, he who is called Christ. When he has come, he will declare to us all things." ²⁶Jesus said to her, "I am he, the one who speaks to you."

²⁷Just then, his disciples came. They marveled that he was speaking with a woman; yet no one said, "What are you looking for?" or, "Why do you speak with her?" ²⁸So the woman left her water pot, went away into the city, and said to the people, ²⁹"Come, see a man who told me

ˢ Q. 31:9

ᵗ Q. 3:79

ᵘ see footnote

---

* ᵘ Q. 2:144; 8:34; 9:7; 17:1; 22:25; 48:26

everything that I have done. Can this be the Christ?" ³⁰They went out of the city, and were coming to him.

³¹In the meanwhile, the disciples urged him, saying, "Rabbi, eat." ³²But he said to them, "I have food to eat that you don't know about." ³³The disciples therefore said to one another, "Has any one brought him something to eat?" ³⁴Jesus said to them, "My food is to do the will of him who sent me and to accomplish his work. ³⁵Don't you say, 'There are yet four months until the harvest?' Behold, I tell you, lift up your eyes and look at the fields, that they are white for harvest already. ³⁶He who reaps receives wages and gathers fruit to eternal life, that both he who sows and he who reaps may rejoice together. ³⁷For in this the saying is true, 'One sows, and another reaps.' ³⁸I sent you to reap that for which you haven't labored. Others have labored, and you have entered into their labor."

³⁹From that city many of the Samaritans believed in him because of the word of the woman, who testified, "He told me everything that I have done." ⁴⁰So when the Samaritans came to him, they begged him to stay with them. He stayed there two days. ⁴¹Many more believed because of his word. ⁴²They said to the woman, "Now we believe, not because of your speaking; for we have heard for ourselves, and know that this is indeed the Christ, the Savior of the world."

⁴³After the two days he went out from there and went into Galilee. ⁴⁴For Jesus himself testified that a prophet has no honor in his own country. ⁴⁵So when he came into Galilee, the Galileans received him, having seen all the things that he did in Jerusalem at the feast, for they also went to the feast.

⁴⁶Jesus came therefore again to Cana of Galilee, where he made the water into wine. There was a certain nobleman whose son was sick at Capernaum. ⁴⁷When he heard that Jesus had come out of Judea into Galilee, he went to him and begged him that he would come down and heal[v] his son, for he was at the point of death. ⁴⁸Jesus therefore said to

ᵛ Q. 3:49

him, "Unless you see signs and wonders, you will in no way believe."[w] [49]The nobleman said to him, "Sir, come down before my child dies." [50]Jesus said to him, "Go your way. Your son lives." The man believed the word that Jesus spoke to him, and he went his way. [51]As he was going down, his servants met him and reported, saying "Your child lives!" [52]So he inquired of them the hour when he began to get better. They said therefore to him, "Yesterday at the seventh hour, the fever left him." [53]So the father knew that it was at that hour in which Jesus said to him, "Your son lives." He believed, as did his whole house. [54]This is again the second sign that Jesus did, having come out of Judea into Galilee.

[w] Q. 2:118

[x] see footnote

5[x]*

[1]After these things, there was a feast of the Jews, and Jesus went up to Jerusalem.

[2]Now in Jerusalem by the sheep gate, there is a pool, which is called in Hebrew, "Bethesda", having five porches. [3]In these lay a great multitude of those who were sick, blind, lame, or paralyzed, waiting for the moving of the water; [4]for an angel went down at certain times into the pool and stirred up the water. Whoever stepped in first after the stirring of the water was healed of whatever disease he had. [5]A certain man was there who had been sick for thirty-eight years. [6]When Jesus saw him lying there, and knew that he had been sick for a long time, he asked him, "Do you want to be made well?" [7]The sick man answered him, "Sir, I have no one to put me into the pool when the water is stirred up, but while I'm coming, another steps down before me." [8]Jesus said to him, "Arise, take up your mat, and walk." [9]Immediately, the man was made well,[y] and took up his mat and walked. Now that day was a Sabbath. [10]So the Jews said to him who was cured, "It is the Sabbath. It is not lawful for you to carry the

[y] Q. 3:49

---

* [x] Q. 2:87, 253; 3:49, 52; 5:110, 112; 19:30; 43:63

mat." ¹¹He answered them, "He who made me well said to me, 'Take up your mat and walk.'" ¹²Then they asked him, "Who is the man who said to you, 'Take up your mat and walk'?" ¹³But he who was healed didn't know who it was, for Jesus had withdrawn, a crowd being in the place. ¹⁴Afterward Jesus found him in the temple and said to him, "Behold, you are made well. Sin no more, so that nothing worse happens to you." ¹⁵The man went away, and told the Jews that it was Jesus who had made him well. ¹⁶For this cause the Jews persecuted Jesus and sought to kill him, because he did these things on the Sabbath. ¹⁷But Jesus answered them, "My Father is still working, so I am working, too."

¹⁸For this cause therefore the Jews sought all the more to kill him, because he not only broke the Sabbath, but also called God his own Father, making himself equal with God.

¹⁹Jesus therefore answered them, "Most certainly, I tell you, the Son can do nothing of himself, but what he sees the Father doing. For whatever things he does, these the Son also does likewise. ²⁰For the Father has affection for the Son, and shows him all things that he himself does. He will show him greater works than these, that you may marvel. ²¹For as the Father raises the dead and gives them life, even so the Son also gives life to whom he desires.ᶻ ²²For the Father judges no one, but he has given all judgment to the Son, ²³that all may honor the Son, even as they honor the Father. He who doesn't honor the Son doesn't honor the Father who sent him. ²⁴"Most certainly I tell you, he who hears my word and believes him who sent me has eternal life,ᵃ and doesn't come into judgment, but has passed out of death into life.

²⁵Most certainly I tell you, the hour comes,ᵇ and now is, when the dead will hear the Son of God's voice; and those who hear will live.ᶜ ²⁶For as the Father has life in himself,

ᶻ Q. 5:18; 7:29; 41:39

ᵃ see footnote

ᵇ Q. 15:85; 22:7; 40:59; 41:50

ᶜ Q. 6:36

---

* ᵃ Q. 2:4; 6:72; 27:3; 31:4; 38:84; 43:63; 75:18

even so he gave to the Son also to have life in himself. [27]He also gave him authority to execute judgment, because he is a son of man. [28]Don't marvel at this, for the hour comes in which all who are in the tombs will hear his voice [29]and will come out;[d*] those who have done good, to the resurrection of life; and those who have done evil, to the resurrection of judgment.[e]

[30]I can of myself do nothing. As I hear, I judge; and my judgment is righteous, because I don't seek my own will, but the will of my Father who sent me.[31]"If I testify about myself, my witness is not valid. [32]It is another who testifies about me. I know that the testimony which he testifies about me is true. [33]You have sent to John, and he has testified to the truth. [34]But the testimony which I receive is not from man. However, I say these things that you may be saved. [35]He was the burning and shining lamp,[f] and you were willing to rejoice for a while in his light. [36]But the testimony which I have is greater than that of John;[g] for the works which the Father gave me to accomplish, the very works that I do, testify about me, that the Father has sent me. [37]The Father himself, who sent me, has testified about me. You have neither heard his voice at any time, nor seen his form. [38]You don't have his word living in you, because you don't believe him whom he sent. [39]"You search the Scriptures, because you think that in them you have eternal life;[h†] and these are they which testify about me.[i] [40]Yet you will not come to me, that you may have life. [41]I don't receive glory from men. [42]But I know you, that you don't have God's love in yourselves. [43]I have come in my Father's name, and you don't receive me. If another comes in his own name, you will receive him. [44]How can you believe, who receive glory from one another, and you don't seek the glory that comes from the only God? [45]"Don't think that I will accuse you to the Father. There is one who accuses you, even Moses, on

[d] see footnote

[e] Q. 3:49; 30:44; 42:22; 64:7; 99:8

[f] Q. 33:46

[g] Q. 19:7; 21:90

[h] see footnote

[i] Q. 2:256

[* d] Q. 2:212; 18:21; 30:12; 54:7; 58:18; 70:43
[† h] Q. 3:107, 136; 5:43; 7:169

whom you have set your hope. ⁴⁶For if you believed Moses, you would believe me; for he wrote about me. ⁴⁷But if you don't believe his writings, how will you believe my words?"ʲ

ʲ Q. 5:43

6ᵏ*

ᵏ see footnote

¹After these things, Jesus went away to the other side of the sea of Galilee, which is also called the Sea of Tiberias. ²A great multitude followed him, because they saw his signs which he did on those who were sick. ³Jesus went up into the mountain, and he sat there with his disciples. ⁴Now the Passover, the feast of the Jews, was at hand. ⁵Jesus therefore, lifting up his eyes and seeing that a great multitude was coming to him, said to Philip, "Where are we to buy bread, that these may eat?" ⁶He said this to test him, for he himself knew what he would do. ⁷Philip answered him, "Two hundred denarii worth of bread is not sufficient for them, that every one of them may receive a little." ⁸One of his disciples, Andrew, Simon Peter's brother, said to him, ⁹"There is a boy here who has five barley loaves and two fish, but what are these among so many?"ˡ ¹⁰Jesus said, "Have the people sit down." Now there was much grass in that place. So the men sat down, in number about five thousand. ¹¹Jesus took the loaves, and having given thanks, he distributed to the disciples, and the disciples to those who were sitting down, likewise also of the fish as much as they desired. ¹²When they were filled, he said to his disciples, "Gather up the broken pieces which are left over, that nothing be lost." ¹³So they gathered them up, and filled twelve baskets with broken pieces from the five barley loaves, which were left over by those who had eaten. ¹⁴When therefore the people saw the sign which Jesus did, they said, "This is truly the prophet who comes into the world." ¹⁵Jesus therefore,

ˡ Q. 5:112

---

* ᵏ Q. 2:87, 253; 3:49, 52; 5:110, 112; 19:30; 43:63

perceiving that they were about to come and take him by force to make him king, withdrew again to the mountain by himself.

[16]When evening came, his disciples went down to the sea. [17]They entered into the boat, and were going over the sea to Capernaum. It was now dark, and Jesus had not come to them. [18]The sea was tossed by a great wind blowing. [19]When therefore they had rowed about twenty-five or thirty stadia,[*] they saw Jesus walking on the sea and drawing near to the boat; and they were afraid.[†] [20]But he said to them, "It is I.[‡] Don't be afraid." [21]They were willing therefore to receive him into the boat. Immediately the boat was at the land where they were going.

[22]On the next day, the multitude that stood on the other side of the sea saw that there was no other boat there, except the one in which his disciples had embarked, and that Jesus hadn't entered with his disciples into the boat, but his disciples had gone away alone. [23]However, boats from Tiberias came near to the place where they ate the bread after the Lord had given thanks. [24]When the multitude therefore saw that Jesus wasn't there, nor his disciples, they themselves got into the boats and came to Capernaum, seeking Jesus.

[25]When they found him on the other side of the sea, they asked him, "Rabbi, when did you come here?" [26]Jesus answered them, "Most certainly I tell you, you seek me, not because you saw signs, but because you ate of the loaves and were filled. [27]Don't work for the food which perishes, but for the food which remains to eternal life, which the Son of Man will give to you. For God the Father has sealed him." [28]They said therefore to him, "What must we do, that we may work the works of God?" [29]Jesus

---

[*] 6:19 25 to 30 stadia is about 5 to 6 kilometers or about 3 to 4miles

[†] 6:19 See Job 9:8

[‡] 6:20or, I AM

answered them, "This is the work of God, that you believe in him whom he has sent." ³⁰They said therefore to him, "What then do you do for a sign, that we may see and believe you? What work do you do? ³¹Our fathers ate the manna in the wilderness. As it is written, 'He gave them bread out of heaven§* to eat.'" ³²Jesus therefore said to them, "Most certainly, I tell you, it wasn't Moses who gave you the bread out of heaven, but my Father gives you the true bread out out of heaven.³³For the bread of God is he who comes down from heaven and gives life to the world." ³⁴They said therefore to him, "Lord, always give us this bread."

³⁵Jesus said to them, "I am the bread of life. Whoever comes to me will not be hungry, and whoever believes in me will never be thirsty. ³⁶But I told you that you have seen me, and yet you don't believe. ³⁷All those whom the Father gives me will come to me. He who comes to me I will in no way throw out. ³⁸For I have come down from heaven, not to do my own will, but the will of him who sent me. ³⁹This is the will of my Father who sent me, that of all he has given to me I should lose nothing, but should raise him up at the last day. ⁴⁰This is the will of the one who sent me, that everyone who sees the Son and believes in him should have eternal life; and I will raise him up at the last day."

⁴¹The Jews therefore murmured concerning him, because he said, "I am the bread which came down out of heaven." ⁴²They said, "Isn't this Jesus, the son of Joseph, whose father and mother we know? How then does he say, 'I have come down out of heaven?'" ⁴³Therefore Jesus answered them, "Don't murmur among yourselves. ⁴⁴No one can come to me unless the Father who sent me draws him; and I will raise him up in the last day. ⁴⁵It is written in

---

* 6:31Greek and Hebrew use the same word for "heaven", "the heavens", "the sky", and "the air". 6:31Exodus 16:4; Nehemiah 9:15; Psalm 78:24-25

the prophets, 'They will all be taught by God.'* Therefore everyone who hears from the Father and has learned, comes to me. ⁴⁶Not that anyone has seen the Father, except he who is from God. He has seen the Father. ⁴⁷Most certainly, I tell you, he who believes in me has eternal life. ⁴⁸I am the bread of life. ⁴⁹Your fathers ate the manna in the wilderness and they died. ⁵⁰This is the bread which comes down out of heaven, that anyone may eat of it and not die. ⁵¹I am the living bread which came down out of heaven. If anyone eats of this bread, he will live forever. Yes, the bread which I will give for the life of the world is my flesh."

⁵²The Jews therefore contended with one another, saying, "How can this man give us his flesh to eat?" ⁵³Jesus therefore said to them, "Most certainly I tell you, unless you eat the flesh of the Son of Man and drink his blood, you don't have life in yourselves. ⁵⁴He who eats my flesh and drinks my blood has eternal life, and I will raise him up at the last day. ⁵⁵For my flesh is food indeed, and my blood is drink indeed. ⁵⁶He who eats my flesh and drinks my blood lives in me, and I in him. ⁵⁷As the living Father sent me, and I live because of the Father, so he who feeds on me will also live because of me. ⁵⁸This is the bread which came down out of heaven —not as our fathers ate the manna and died. He who eats this bread will live forever." ⁵⁹He said these things in the synagogue, as he taught in Capernaum.

⁶⁰Therefore many of his disciples, when they heard this, said, "This is a hard saying! Who can listen to it?" ⁶¹But Jesus knowing in himself that his disciples murmured at this, said to them, "Does this cause you to stumble? ⁶²Then what if you would see the Son of Man ascending to where he was before? ⁶³It is the spirit who gives life. The flesh profits nothing. The words that I speak to you are spirit, and are life. ⁶⁴But there are some of you who don't believe." For Jesus knew from the beginning

---

* 6:45 Isaiah 54:13

who they were who didn't believe,^m and who it was who would betray him. ⁶⁵He said, "For this cause I have said to you that no one can come to me, unless it is given to him by my Father."

⁶⁶At this, many of his disciples went back and walked no more with him. ⁶⁷Jesus said therefore to the twelve, "You don't also want to go away, do you?" ⁶⁸Simon Peter answered him, "Lord, to whom would we go? You have the words of eternal life. ⁶⁹We have come to believe and know that you are the Christ, the Son of the living God." ⁷⁰Jesus answered them, "Didn't I choose you, the twelve, and one of you is a devil?"ⁿ ⁷¹Now he spoke of Judas, the son of Simon Iscariot, for it was he who would betray him, being one of the twelve.

n Q. 61:14

7

¹After these things, Jesus was walking in Galilee, for he wouldn't walk in Judea, because the Jews sought to kill him. ²Now the feast of the Jews, the Feast of Booths, was at hand. ³His brothers therefore said to him, "Depart from here and go into Judea, that your disciples also may see your works which you do. ⁴For no one does anything in secret while he seeks to be known openly. If you do these things, reveal yourself to the world." ⁵For even his brothers didn't believe in him. ⁶Jesus therefore said to them, "My time has not yet come, but your time is always ready. ⁷The world can't hate you, but it hates me, because I testify about it, that its works are evil. ⁸You go up to the feast. I am not yet going up to this feast, because my time is not yet fulfilled." ⁹Having said these things to them, he stayed in Galilee.

¹⁰But when his brothers had gone up to the feast, then he also went up, not publicly, but as it were in secret. ¹¹The Jews therefore sought him at the feast, and said, "Where is he?" ¹²There was much murmuring among the multitudes concerning him. Some said, "He is a good

man." Others said, "Not so, but he leads the multitude astray." [13]Yet no one spoke openly of him for fear of the Jews.

[14]But when it was now the middle of the feast, Jesus went up into the temple and taught. [15]The Jews therefore marveled, saying, "How does this man know letters, having never been educated?" [16]Jesus therefore answered them, "My teaching is not mine, but his who sent me. [17]If anyone desires to do his will, he will know about the teaching, whether it is from God or if I am speaking from myself. [18]He who speaks from himself seeks his own glory, but he who seeks the glory of him who sent him is true, and no unrighteousness is in him. [19]Didn't Moses give you the law, and yet none of you keeps the law? Why do you seek to kill me?" [20]The multitude answered, "You have a demon! Who seeks to kill you?" [21]Jesus answered them, "I did one work and you all marvel because of it. [22]Moses has given you circumcision (not that it is of Moses, but of the fathers), and on the Sabbath you circumcise a boy. [23]If a boy receives circumcision on the Sabbath, that the law of Moses may not be broken, are you angry with me because I made a man completely healthy on the Sabbath? [24]Don't judge according to appearance, but judge righteous judgment."

[25]Therefore some of them of Jerusalem said, "Isn't this he whom they seek to kill? [26]Behold, he speaks openly, and they say nothing to him. Can it be that the rulers indeed know that this is truly the Christ? [27]However, we know where this man comes from, but when the Christ comes, no one will know where he comes from." [28]Jesus therefore cried out in the temple, teaching and saying, "You both know me, and know where I am from. I have not come of myself, but he who sent me is true, whom you don't know. [29]I know him, because I am from him, and he sent me." [30]They sought therefore to take him; but no one laid a hand on him, because his hour had not yet come. [31]But of

the multitude, many believed in him. They said, "When the Christ comes, he won't do more signs than those which this man has done, will he?"[o]

[32]The Pharisees heard the multitude murmuring these things concerning him, and the chief priests and the Pharisees sent officers to arrest him. [33]Then Jesus said, "I will be with you a little while longer, then I go to him who sent me. [34]You will seek me and won't find me. You can't come where I am." [35]The Jews therefore said among themselves, "Where will this man go that we won't find him? Will he go to the Dispersion among the Greeks and teach the Greeks? [36]What is this word that he said, 'You will seek me, and won't find me;' and 'Where I am, you can't come'?"

[37]Now on the last and greatest day of the feast, Jesus stood and cried out, "If anyone is thirsty, let him come to me and drink! [38]He who believes in me, as the Scripture has said, from within him will flow rivers of living water." [39]But he said this about the Spirit, which those believing in him were to receive. For the Holy Spirit was not yet given, because Jesus wasn't yet glorified.

[40]Many of the multitude therefore, when they heard these words, said, "This is truly the prophet." [41]Others said, "This is the Christ." But some said, "What, does the Christ come out of Galilee? [42]Hasn't the Scripture said that the Christ comes of the offspring[*] of David, and from Bethlehem, the village where David was?" [43]So a division arose in the multitude because of him. [44]Some of them would have arrested him, but no one laid hands on him.

[45]The officers therefore came to the chief priests and Pharisees; and they said to them, "Why didn't you bring him?" [46]The officers answered, "No man ever spoke like this man!" [47]The Pharisees therefore answered them, "You aren't also led astray, are you? [48]Have any of the rulers or

---

[*] 7:42or, seed 7:422Samuel 7:127:42Micah 5:2

any of the Pharisees believed in him? ⁴⁹But this multitude that doesn't know the law is cursed." ⁵⁰Nicodemus (he who came to him by night, being one of them) said to them, ⁵¹"Does our law judge a man unless it first hears from him personally and knows what he does?" ⁵²They answered him, "Are you also from Galilee? Search and see that no prophet has arisen out of Galilee." *⁵³Everyone went to his own house,

8

¹but Jesus went to the Mount of Olives. ²Now very early in the morning, he came again into the temple, and all the people came to him. He sat down and taught them. ³The scribes and the Pharisees brought a woman taken in adultery. Having set her in the middle, ⁴they told him, "Teacher, we found this woman in adultery, in the very act. ⁵Now in our law, Moses commanded us to stone such women. What then do you say about her?" ⁶They said this testing him, that they might have something to accuse him of. But Jesus stooped down and wrote on the ground with his finger. ⁷But when they continued asking him, he looked up and said to them, "He who is without sin among you, let him throw the first stone at her." ⁸Again he stooped down and wrote on the ground with his finger. ⁹They, when they heard it, being convicted by their conscience, went out one by one, beginning from the oldest, even to the last. Jesus was left alone with the woman where she was, in the middle. ¹⁰Jesus, standing up, saw her and said, "Woman, where are your accusers? Did no one condemn you?" ¹¹She said, "No one, Lord." Jesus said, "Neither do I condemn you. Go your way. From now on, sin no more."†

---

* 7:52 See Isaiah 9:1; Matthew 4:13-168:5 Leviticus 20:10; Deuteronomy 22:22
† 8:11 NU includes John 7:53–John 8:11, but puts brackets around it to

¹²Again, therefore, Jesus spoke to them, saying, "I am the light of the world. He who follows me will not walk in the darkness, but will have the light* of life."ᵖ ¹³The Pharisees therefore said to him, "You testify about yourself. Your testimony is not valid." Jesus answered them, "Even if I testify about myself, my testimony is true, for I know where I came from, and where I am going; but you don't know where I came from, or where I am going. ¹⁵You judge according to the flesh. I judge no one. ¹⁶Even if I do judge, my judgment is true, for I am not alone, but I am with the Father who sent me.¹⁷ It's also written in your law that the testimony of two people is valid. † ¹⁸I am one who testifies about myself, and the Father who sent me testifies about me." ¹⁹They said therefore to him, "Where is your Father?" Jesus answered, "You know neither me nor my Father. If you knew me, you would know my Father also." ²⁰Jesus spoke these words in the treasury, as he taught in the temple. Yet no one arrested him, because his hour had not yet come.�q

²¹Jesus said therefore again to them, "I am going away, and you will seek me, and you will die in your sins. Where I go, you can't come." ²²The Jews therefore said, "Will he kill himself, because he says, 'Where I am going, you can't come'?" ²³He said to them, "You are from beneath. I am from above. You are of this world. I am not of this world. ²⁴I said therefore to you that you will die in your sins; for unless you believe that I am‡ he, you will die in your sins." ²⁵They said therefore to him, "Who are you?" Jesus said to them, "Just what I have been saying to you from the beginning. ²⁶I have many things to speak and to judge concerning you. However, he who sent me is true; and the things which I heard from him, these I say to the world." ²⁷They didn't

ᵖ Q.
2:257;
14:5;
24:35;
57:9;
61:8

q Q.
5:110

---

indicate that the textual critics had less confidence that this was original
* 8:12 Isaiah 60:1
† 8:17 Deuteronomy 17:6; 19:15
‡ 8:24 or, I AM

understand that he spoke to them about the Father. [28]Jesus therefore said to them, "When you have lifted up the Son of Man, then you will know that I am he, and I do nothing of myself, but as my Father taught me, I say these things. [29]He who sent me is with me. The Father hasn't left me alone, for I always do the things that are pleasing to him." [30]As he spoke these things, many believed in him.

[31]Jesus therefore said to those Jews who had believed him, "If you remain in my word, then you are truly my disciples. [32]You will know the truth,[r] and the truth will make you free." [*] [33]They answered him, "We are Abraham's offspring,[s] and have never been in bondage to anyone. How do you say, 'You will be made free'?"

[34]Jesus answered them, "Most certainly I tell you, everyone who commits sin is the bondservant of sin. [35]A bondservant doesn't live in the house forever. A son remains forever. [36]If therefore the Son makes you free, you will be free indeed. [37]I know that you are Abraham's offspring, yet you seek to kill me, because my word finds no place in you. [38]I say the things which I have seen with my Father; and you also do the things which you have seen with your father."

[39]They answered him, "Our father is Abraham." Jesus said to them, "If you were Abraham's children, you would do the works of Abraham. [40]But now you seek to kill me, a man who has told you the truth which I heard from God. Abraham didn't do this. [41]You do the works of your father." They said to him, "We were not born of sexual immorality. We have one Father, God." [42]Therefore Jesus said to them, "If God were your father, you would love me, for I came out and have come from God. For I haven't come of myself, but he sent me. [43]Why don't you understand my speech? Because you can't hear my word. [44]You are of your father the devil, and you want to do the desires of your father. He was a murderer from the beginning, and doesn't stand

[r] Q. 43:78; 103:3

[s] Q. 3:68

---

[*] 8:32 Psalm 119:45

in the truth, because there is no truth in him.[t] When he speaks a lie, he speaks on his own; for he is a liar, and the father of lies. [45]But because I tell the truth, you don't believe me. [46]Which of you convicts me of sin? If I tell the truth, why do you not believe me? [47]He who is of God hears the words of God. For this cause you don't hear, because you are not of God."

[48]Then the Jews answered him, "Don't we say well that you are a Samaritan, and have a demon?" Jesus answered, "I don't have a demon, but I honor my Father and you dishonor me. [50]But I don't seek my own glory. There is one who seeks and judges. [51]Most certainly, I tell you, if a person keeps my word, he will never see death." [52]Then the Jews said to him, "Now we know that you have a demon. Abraham died, as did the prophets; and you say, 'If a man keeps my word, he will never taste of death.' [53]Are you greater than our father Abraham, who died? The prophets died. Who do you make yourself out to be?" [54]Jesus answered, "If I glorify myself, my glory is nothing. It is my Father who glorifies me, of whom you say that he is our God. [55]You have not known him, but I know him. If I said, 'I don't know him,' I would be like you, a liar. But I know him and keep his word. [56]Your father Abraham[u] rejoiced to see my day. He saw it and was glad." [57]The Jews therefore said to him, "You are not yet fifty years old! Have you seen Abraham?" Jesus said to them, "Most certainly, I tell you, before Abraham came into existence, I AM." Therefore they took up stones to throw at him, but Jesus was hid himself and went out of the temple, having gone through the middle of them, and so passed by.

[t] Q. 14:22; 72:4

[u] Q. 37:108

ᵛ see
footnote

9ᵛ*

¹As he passed by, he saw a man blind from birth. ²His disciples asked him, "Rabbi, who sinned, this man or his parents, that he was born blind?" ³Jesus answered, "This man didn't sin, nor did his parents, but that the works of God might be revealed in him. ⁴I must work the works of him who sent me while it is day. The night is coming, when no one can work. ⁵While I am in the world, I am the light of the world." ⁶When he had said this, he spat on the ground, made mud with the saliva, anointed the blind man's eyes with the mud, ⁷and said to him, "Go, wash in the pool of Siloam" (which means "Sent"). So he went away, washed, and came back seeing.ʷ

ʷ Q.
3:49;
5:110

⁸Therefore the neighbors and those who saw that he was blind before said, "Isn't this he who sat and begged?" ⁹Others were saying, "It is he." Still others were saying, "He looks like him." He said, "I am he." ¹⁰They therefore were asking him, "How were your eyes opened?" ¹¹He answered, "A man called Jesus made mud, anointed my eyes, and said to me, 'Go to the pool of Siloam and wash.' So I went away and washed, and I received sight." ¹²Then they asked him, "Where is he?" He said, "I don't know."

¹³They brought him who had been blind to the Pharisees. ¹⁴It was a Sabbath when Jesus made the mud and opened his eyes. ¹⁵Again therefore the Pharisees also asked him how he received his sight. He said to them, "He put mud on my eyes, I washed, and I see." ¹⁶Some therefore of the Pharisees said, "This man is not from God, because he doesn't keep the Sabbath." Others said, "How can a man who is a sinner do such signs?" So there was division among them. ¹⁷Therefore they asked the blind man again, "What do you say about him, because he opened your eyes?" He said, "He is a prophet."

¹⁸The Jews therefore didn't believe concerning him,

---

* ᵛ Q. 2:87, 253; 3:49, 52; 5:110, 112; 19:30; 43:63

that he had been blind and had received his sight, until they called the parents of him who had received his sight, and asked them, "Is this your son, whom you say was born blind? How then does he now see?" 20His parents answered them, "We know that this is our son, and that he was born blind; 21but how he now sees, we don't know; or who opened his eyes, we don't know. He is of age. Ask him. He will speak for himself." 22His parents said these things because they feared the Jews; for the Jews had already agreed that if any man would confess him as Christ, he would be put out of the synagogue. 23Therefore his parents said, "He is of age. Ask him."

24So they called the man who was blind a second time, and said to him, "Give glory to God. We know that this man is a sinner." 25 therefore he answered, "I don't know if he is a sinner. One thing I do know: that though I was blind, now I see." 26They said to him again, "What did he do to you? How did he open your eyes?" 27He answered them, "I told you already, and you didn't listen. Why do you want to hear it again? You don't also want to become his disciples, do you?" 28They insulted him and said, "You are his disciple, but we are disciples of Moses. 29We know that God has spoken to Moses. But as for this man, we don't know where he comes from." 30The man answered them, "How amazing! You don't know where he comes from, yet he opened my eyes. 31We know that God doesn't listen to sinners, but if anyone is a worshiper of God and does his will, he listens to him. * 32Since the world began it has never been heard of that anyone opened the eyes of someone born blind. 33If this man were not from God, he could do nothing." 34They answered him, "You were altogether born in sins, and do you teach us?" Then they threw him out.

35Jesus heard that they had thrown him out, and finding him, he said, "Do you believe in the Son of God?" 36He

---

* 9:31 Psalm 66:18; Proverbs 15:29; 28:9

answered, "Who is he, Lord, that I may believe in him?" [37]Jesus said to him, "You have both seen him, and it is he who speaks with you." [38]He said, "Lord, I believe!" and he worshiped him. [39]Jesus said, "I came into this world for judgment, that those who don't see may see; and that those who see may become blind."[x] [40]Those of the Pharisees who were with him heard these things, and said to him, "Are we also blind?" [41]Jesus said to them, "If you were blind, you would have no sin; but now you say, 'We see.' Therefore your sin remains.

[x] Q. 5:71

10

[1]"Most certainly, I tell you, one who doesn't enter by the door into the sheep fold, but climbs up some other way, is a thief and a robber. [2]But one who enters in by the door is the shepherd of the sheep.[y] [3]The gatekeeper opens the gate for him, and the sheep listen to his voice. He calls his own sheep by name and leads them out. [4]Whenever he brings out his own sheep, he goes before them; and the sheep follow him, for they know his voice. [5]They will by no means follow a stranger, but will flee from him; for they don't know the voice of strangers." [6]Jesus spoke this parable to them, but they didn't understand what he was telling them.

[y] Q. 2:189

[7]Jesus therefore said to them again, "Most certainly, I tell you, I am the sheep's door. [8]All who came before me are thieves and robbers, but the sheep didn't listen to them. [9]I am the door. If anyone enters in by me, he will be saved, and will go in and go out and will find pasture. [10]The thief only comes to steal, kill, and destroy. I came that they may have life, and may have it abundantly. [11]"I am the good shepherd. The good shepherd lays down his life for the sheep. *[12]He who is a hired hand, and not a shepherd, who

---

* 10:11 Isaiah 40:11; Ezekiel 34:11-12,15,22

doesn't own the sheep, sees the wolf coming, leaves the sheep, and flees. The wolf snatches the sheep and scatters them. ¹³The hired hand flees because he is a hired hand and doesn't care for the sheep. ¹⁴I am the good shepherd. I know my own, and I'm known by my own; ¹⁵even as the Father knows me, and I know the Father. I lay down my life for the sheep.^z ¹⁶I have other sheep which are not of this fold. I must bring them also, and they will hear my voice. They will become one flock with one shepherd. [*] ¹⁷Therefore the Father loves me, because I lay down my life, that I may take it again. ^{†18}No one takes it away from me, but I lay it down by myself. I have power to lay it down, and I have power to take it again. I received this commandment from my Father."

^z Q. 4:157

¹⁹Therefore a division arose again among the Jews because of these words. ²⁰Many of them said, "He has a demon and is insane! Why do you listen to him?" ²¹Others said, "These are not the sayings of one possessed by a demon. It isn't possible for a demon to open the eyes of the blind, is it?" [‡]

²²It was the Feast of the Dedication[§] at Jerusalem. ²³It was winter, and Jesus was walking in the temple, in Solomon's porch. ²⁴The Jews therefore came around him and said to him, "How long will you hold us in suspense? If you are the Christ, tell us plainly." ²⁵Jesus answered them, "I told you, and you don't believe. The works that I do in my Father's name, these testify about me. ²⁶But you don't believe, because you are not of my sheep, as I told you. ²⁷My sheep hear my voice, and I know them, and they follow me. ²⁸I give eternal life to them. They will never perish, and no one will snatch them out of my hand. ²⁹My Father who has

---

[*] 10:16 Isaiah 56:8
[†] 10:17 Isaiah 53:7-8
[‡] 10:21 Exodus 4:11
[§] 10:22 The "Feast of the Dedication" is the Greek name for "Hanukkah", a celebration of the rededication of the Temple.

given them to me is greater than all. No one is able to snatch them out of my Father's hand. [30]I and the Father are one."

[31]Therefore the Jews took up stones again to stone him. [32]Jesus answered them, "I have shown you many good works from my Father. For which of those works do you stone me?" [33]The Jews answered him, "We don't stone you for good work, but for blasphemy, because you, being a man, make yourself God." [34]Jesus answered them, "Isn't it written in your law, 'I said, you are gods?' [*][35]If he called them gods, to whom the word of God came (and the Scripture can't be broken), [36]do you say of him whom the Father sanctified and sent into the world, 'You blaspheme,' because I said, 'I am the Son of God?' [37]If I don't do the works of my Father, don't believe me. [38]But if I do them, though you don't believe me, believe the works, that you may know and believe that the Father is in me, and I in the Father." [39]They sought again to seize him, and he went out of their hand.

[40]He went away again beyond the Jordan into the place where John was baptizing at first, and he stayed there. [41]Many came to him. They said, "John[a] indeed did no sign, but everything that John said about this man is true." [42]Many believed in him there.

11[b][†]

[1]Now a certain man was sick, Lazarus from Bethany, of the village of Mary and her sister, Martha. [2]It was that Mary who had anointed the Lord with ointment and wiped his feet with her hair, whose brother Lazarus, was sick. [3]The sisters therefore sent to him, saying, "Lord, behold, he for whom you have great affection is sick." [4]But when Jesus heard it, he said, "This sickness is not to death, but for

[a] Q. 19:7; 21:90

[b] see footnote

---

[*] 10:34 Psalm 82:6
[†] [b] Q. 2:87, 253; 3:49, 52; 5:110, 112; 19:30; 43:63

2

the glory of God, that God's Son may be glorified by it."

⁵Now Jesus loved Martha, and her sister, and Lazarus. ⁶When therefore he heard that he was sick, he stayed two days in the place where he was. ⁷Then after this he said to the disciples, "Let's go into Judea again." ⁸The disciples asked him, "Rabbi, the Jews were just trying to stone you. Are you going there again?" ⁹Jesus answered, "Aren't there twelve hours of day- light? If a man walks in the day, he doesn't stumble, because he sees the light of this world. ¹⁰But if a man walks in the night, he stumbles, because the light isn't in him." ¹¹He said these things, and after that, he said to them, "Our friend Lazarus has fallen asleep, but I am going so that I may awake him out of sleep." ¹²The disciples therefore said, "Lord, if he has fallen asleep, he will recover." ¹³Now Jesus had spoken of his death, but they thought that he spoke of taking rest in sleep. ¹⁴So Jesus said to them plainly then, "Lazarus is dead.ᶜ ¹⁵I am glad for your sakes that I was not there, so that you may believe. Nevertheless, let's go to him." ¹⁶Thomas therefore, who is called Didymus,* said to his fellow disciples, "Let's also go, that we may die with him."

ᶜ Q. 5:110

¹⁷So when Jesus came, he found that he had been in the tomb four days already. ¹⁸Now Bethany was near Jerusalem, about fifteen stadia† away. ¹⁹Many of the Jews had joined the women around Martha and Mary, to console them concerning their brother. ²⁰Then when Martha heard that Jesus was coming, she went and met him, but Mary stayed in the house. ²¹Therefore Martha said to Jesus, "Lord, if you would have been here, my brother wouldn't have died. ²²Even now I know that whatever you ask of God, God will give you."ᵈ ²³Jesus said to her, "Your brother will rise again." ²⁴Martha said to him, "I know that he will rise again in the resurrection at the last

ᵈ Q. 14:34; 40:60

---

* 11:16 "Didymus" means "Twin".
† 11:18 15 stadia is about 2.8 kilometers or 1.7 miles

^e Q.
23:16

day."^e ²⁵Jesus said to her, "I am the resurrection and the life. He who believes in me will still live, even if he dies. ²⁶Whoever lives and believes in me will never die. Do you believe this?" ²⁷She said to him, "Yes, Lord. I have come to believe that you are the Christ, God's Son, he who comes into the world."

²⁸When she had said this, she went away and called Mary, her sister, secretly, saying, "The Teacher is here and is calling you." ²⁹When she heard this, she arose quickly and went to him. ³⁰Now Jesus had not yet come into the village, but was in the place where Martha met him. ³¹Then the Jews who were with her in the house and were consoling her, when they saw Mary, that she rose up quickly and went out, followed her, saying, "She is going to the tomb to weep there." ³²Therefore when Mary came to where Jesus was and saw him, she fell down at his feet, saying to him, "Lord, if you would have been here, my brother wouldn't have died." ³³When Jesus therefore saw her weeping, and the Jews weeping who came with her, he groaned in the spirit and was troubled, ³⁴and said, "Where have you laid him?" They told him, "Lord, come and see." ³⁵Jesus wept. ³⁶The Jews therefore said, "See how much affection he had for him!" ³⁷Some of them said, "Couldn't this man, who opened the eyes of him who was blind, have also kept this man from dying?"

³⁸Jesus therefore, again groaning in himself, came to the tomb. Now it was a cave, and a stone lay against it. ³⁹Jesus said, "Take away the stone." Martha, the sister of him who was dead, said to him, "Lord, by this time there is a stench, for he has been dead four days." ⁴⁰Jesus said to her, "Didn't I tell you that if you believed, you would see God's glory?" ⁴¹So they took away the stone from the place where the dead man was lying.[*] Jesus lifted up his eyes and said, "Father, I thank you that you listened to me. ⁴²I

---

[*] 11:41 NU omits "from the place where the dead man was lying."

know that you always listen to me, but because of the multitude standing around I said this, that they may believe that you sent me." ⁴³When he had said this, he cried with a loud voice, "Lazarus, come out!" ⁴⁴He who was dead came out,ᶠ bound hand and foot with wrappings, and his face was wrapped around with a cloth. Jesus said to them, "Free him, and let him go."

ᶠ Q. 3:49; 5:32

⁴⁵Therefore many of the Jews who came to Mary and saw what Jesus did believed in him. ⁴⁶But some of them went away to the Pharisees and told them the things which Jesus had done. ⁴⁷The chief priests therefore and the Pharisees gathered a council, and said, "What are we doing? For this man does many signs. ⁴⁸If we leave him alone like this, everyone will believe in him, and the Romans will come and take away both our place and our nation." ⁴⁹But a certain one of them, Caiaphas, being high priest that year, said to them, "You know nothing at all, ⁵⁰nor do you consider that it is advantageous for us that one man should die for the people, and that the whole nation not perish." ⁵¹Now he didn't say this of himself, but being high priest that year, he prophesied that Jesus would die for the nation, ⁵²and not for the nation only, but that he might also gather together into one the children of God who are scattered abroad. ⁵³So from that day forward they took counsel that they might put him to death. ⁵⁴Jesus therefore walked no more openly among the Jews, but departed from there into the country near the wilderness, to a city called Ephraim. He stayed there with his disciples.

⁵⁵Now the Passover of the Jews was at hand. Many went up from the country to Jerusalem before the Passover, to purify themselves. ⁵⁶Then they sought for Jesus and spoke with one another as they stood in the temple, "What do you think —that he isn't coming to the feast at all?" ⁵⁷Now the chief priests and the Pharisees had commanded that if anyone knew where he was, he should report it, that they might seize him.

12

¹Then, six days before the Passover, Jesus came to Bethany, where Lazarus was, who had been dead, whom he raised from the dead. ²So they made him a supper there. Martha served, but Lazarus was one of those who sat at the table with him. ³Therefore Mary took a pound* of ointment of pure nard, very precious, and anointed Jesus's feet and wiped his feet with her hair. The house was filled with the fragrance of the ointment.⁴Then Judas Iscariot, Simon's son, one of his disciples, who would betray him, said, ⁵"Why wasn't this ointment sold for three hundred denarii† and given to the poor?" ⁶Now he said this, not because he cared for the poor, but because he was a thief, and having the money box, used to steal what was put into it. ⁷But Jesus said, "Leave her alone. She has kept this for the day of my burial. ⁸For you always have the poor with you, but you don't always have me."

⁹A large crowd therefore of the Jews learned that he was there; and they came, not for Jesus' sake only, but that they might see Lazarus also, whom he had raised from the dead. ¹⁰But the chief priests conspired to put Lazarus to death also, ¹¹because on account of him many of the Jews went away and believed in Jesus.

¹²On the next day a great multitude had come to the feast. When they heard that Jesus was coming to Jerusalem, ¹³they took the branches of the palm trees and went out to meet him, and cried out, "Hosanna!‡ Blessed is he who comes in the name of the Lord, the King of Israel!"§ ¹⁴Jesus, having found a young donkey, sat on it. As it is written,

¹⁵"Don't be afraid, daughter of Zion.

Behold, your King comes,

---

* 12:3a Roman pound of 12 ounces, or about 340 grams
† 12:5 300 denarii was about a year's wages for an agricultural laborer
‡ 12:13 "Hosanna" means "save us" or "help us, we pray".
§ 12:13 Psalm 118:25-2612:15 Zechariah 9:9

sitting on a donkey's colt."

[16]His disciples didn't understand these things at first, but when Jesus was glorified, then they remembered that these things were written about him, and that they had done these things to him. [17]The multitude therefore that was with him when he called Lazarus out of the tomb and raised him from the dead was testifying about it. [18]For this cause also the multitude went and met him, because they heard that he had done this sign. [19]The Pharisees therefore said among themselves, "See how you accomplish nothing. Behold, the world has gone after him."

[20]Now there were certain Greeks among those who went up to worship at the feast. [21]Therefore, these came to Philip, who was from Bethsaida of Galilee, and asked him, saying, "Sir, we want to see Jesus." [22]Philip came and told Andrew, and in turn, Andrew came with Philip, and they told Jesus. [23]Jesus answered them, "The time has come for the Son of Man to be glorified. [24]Most certainly I tell you, unless a grain of wheat falls into the earth and dies, it remains by itself alone. But if it dies, it bears much fruit. [25]He who loves his life will lose it. He who hates his life in this world will keep it to eternal life. [26]If anyone serves me, let him follow me. Where I am, there my servant will also be. If anyone serves me, the Father will honor him.[g]

[g] Q. 36:27

[27]"Now my soul is troubled. What shall I say? 'Father, save me from this time?' But I came to this time for this cause. [28]Father, glorify your name!" Then a voice came out of the sky, saying, "I have both glorified it and will glorify it again." [29]Therefore the multitude who stood by and heard it said that it had thundered. Others said, "An angel has spoken to him." [30]Jesus answered, "This voice hasn't come for my sake, but for your sakes. [31]Now is the judgment of this world. Now the prince of this world will be cast out. [32]And I, if I am lifted up from the earth, will draw all people to myself." [33]But he said this, signifying by what kind of death he should die. [34]The multitude answered him, "We

have heard out of the law that the Christ remains forever. How do you say, 'The Son of Man must be lifted up?' Who is this Son of Man?"[*] [35]Jesus therefore said to them, "Yet a little while the light is with you. Walk while you have the light, that darkness doesn't overtake you. He who walks in the darkness doesn't know where he is going. [36]While you have the light, believe in the light, that you may become children of light."

Jesus said these things, and he departed and hid himself from them. [37]But though he had done so many signs before them, yet they didn't believe in him, [38]that the word of Isaiah the prophet might be fulfilled, which he spoke:

"Lord, who has believed our report?

To whom has the arm of the

Lord been revealed?" [†]

[39]For this cause they couldn't believe, for Isaiah said again:

[40]"He has blinded their eyes and he hardened their heart, lest they should see with their eyes,

and perceive with their heart, and would turn,

and I would heal them."[‡]

[41]Isaiah said these things when he saw his glory, and spoke of him.[§] [42]Nevertheless, even many of the rulers believed in him, but because of the Pharisees they didn't confess it, so that they wouldn't be put out of the synagogue, [43]for they loved men's praise more than God's praise.[h]

[h] Q. 4:77

[44]Jesus cried out and said, "Whoever believes in me, believes not in me, but in him who sent me. [45]He who sees me sees him who sent me. [46]I have come as a light[i] into the world, that whoever believes in me may not remain in the darkness. [47]If anyone listens to my sayings and doesn't

[i] Q. 24:35

---

[*] 12:34 Isaiah 9:7; Daniel 2:44; See Isaiah 53:8

[†] 12:38 Isaiah 53:1

[‡] 12:40 Isaiah 6

[§] 10 12:41 Isaiah 6:1

believe, I don't judge him. For I came not to judge the world, but to save the world. ⁴⁸He who rejects me, and doesn't receive my sayings, has one who judges him. The word that I spoke will judge him in the last day. ⁴⁹For I spoke not from myself, but the Father who sent me gave me a commandment, what I should say and what I should speak. ⁵⁰I know that his commandment is eternal life. The things therefore which I speak, even as the Father has said to me, so I speak."

13

¹Now before the feast of the Passover, Jesus, knowing that his time had come that he would depart from this world to the Father, having loved his own who were in the world, he loved them to the end. ²During supper, the devil having already put into the heart of Judas Iscariot, Simon's son, to betray him, ³Jesus, knowing that the Father had given all things into his hands, and that he came from God and was going to God, ⁴arose from supper, and laid aside his outer garments. He took a towel and wrapped a towel around his waist. ⁵Then he poured water into the basin, and began to wash the disciples' feet and to wipe them with the towel that was wrapped around him. ⁶Then he came to Simon Peter. He said to him, "Lord, do you wash my feet?" ⁷Jesus answered him, "You don't know what I am doing now, but you will understand later." ⁸Peter said to him, "You will never wash my feet!" Jesus answered him, "If I don't wash you, you have no part with me." ⁹Simon Peter said to him, "Lord, not my feet only, but also my hands and my head!" ¹⁰Jesus said to him, "Someone who has bathed only needs to have his feet washed, but is completely clean. You are clean, but not all of you." ¹¹For he knew him who would betray him; therefore he said, "You are not all clean."

¹²So when he had washed their feet, put his outer

garment back on, and sat down again, he said to them, "Do you know what I have done to you? [13]You call me, 'Teacher' and 'Lord.' You say so correctly, for so I am. [14]If I then, the Lord and the Teacher, have washed your feet, you also ought to wash one another's feet. [15]For I have given you an example, that you should also do as I have done to you. [16]Most certainly I tell you, a servant is not greater than his lord, neither is one who is sent greater than he who sent him. [17]If you know these things, blessed are you if you do them. [18]I don't speak concerning all of you. I know whom I have chosen; but that the Scripture may be fulfilled, 'He who eats bread with me has lifted up his heel against me.'[*] [19]From now on, I tell you before it happens, that when it happens, you may believe that I am he. [20]Most certainly I tell you, he who receives whomever I send, receives me; and he who receives me, receives him who sent me."

[21]When Jesus had said this, he was troubled in spirit, and testified, "Most certainly I tell you that one of you will betray me." [22]The disciples looked at one another, perplexed about whom he spoke. [23]One of his disciples, whom Jesus loved, was at the table, leaning against Jesus' breast. [24]Simon Peter therefore beckoned to him, and said to him, "Tell us who it is of whom he speaks." [25]He, leaning back, as he was, on Jesus' breast, asked him, "Lord, who is it?" [26]Jesus therefore answered, "It is he to whom I will give this piece of bread when I have dipped it." So when he had dipped the piece of bread, he gave it to Judas, the son of Simon Iscariot. [27]After the piece of bread, then Satan entered into him. Then Jesus said to him, "What you do, do quickly." [28]Now nobody at the table knew why he said this to him. [29]For some thought, because Judas had the money box, that Jesus said to him, "Buy what things we need for the feast," or that he should give something to the poor. [30]Therefore

---

[*] 13:18 Psalm 41:9

having received that morsel, he went out immediately. It was night.

[31]When he had gone out, Jesus said, "Now the Son of Man has been glorified, and God has been glorified in him. [32]If God has been glorified in him, God will also glorify him in himself, and he will glorify him immediately. [33]Little children, I will be with you a little while longer. You will seek me, and as I said to the Jews, 'Where I am going, you can't come,' so now I tell you. [34]A new commandment I give to you, that you love one another. Just as I have loved you, you also love one another. [35]By this everyone will know that you are my disciples, if you have love for one another."

[36]Simon Peter said to him, "Lord, where are you going?" Jesus answered, "Where I am going, you can't follow now, but you will follow afterwards." [37]Peter said to him, "Lord, why can't I follow you now? I will lay down my life for you." [38]Jesus answered him, "Will you lay down your life for me? Most certainly I tell you, the rooster won't crow until you have denied me three times.

14

[1]"Don't let your heart be troubled. Believe in God. Believe also in me. [2]In my Father's house are many homes. If it weren't so, I would have told you. I am going to prepare a place for you.[j]* [3]If I go and prepare a place for you, I will come again and will receive you to myself; that where I am, you may be there also. [4]You know where I go, and you know the way." [5]Thomas said to him, "Lord, we don't know where you are going. How can we know the way?" [6]Jesus said to him, "I am the way, the truth,[k] and the life. No one comes to the Father, except through me. [7]If you had known me, you would have known my Father also. From now on, you know him and have seen him."

[j] see footnote

[k] Q. 6:66; 31:30

* [j] Q. 6:127; 18:88; 21:103; 25:75; 32:19; 34:37; 39:20; 52:17; 54:55; 88:16

⁸Philip said to him, "Lord, show us the Father, and that will be enough for us." ⁹Jesus said to him, "Have I been with you such a long time, and do you not know me, Philip? He who has seen me has seen the Father. How do you say, 'Show us the Father?' ¹⁰Don't you believe that I am in the Father, and the Father in me? The words that I tell you, I speak not from myself; but the Father who lives in me does his works. ¹¹Believe me that I am in the Father, and the Father in me; or else believe me for the very works' sake.

¹²Most certainly I tell you, he who believes in me, the works that I do, he will do also; and he will do greater works than these, because I am going to my Father. ¹³Whatever you will ask in my name, I will do it, that the Father may be glorified in the Son. ¹⁴If you will ask anything in my name, I will do it. ¹⁵If you love me, keep my commandments. ¹⁶I will pray to the Father, and he will give you another Counselor,¹* that he may be with you forever: ¹⁷the Spirit of truth, whom the world can't receive, for it doesn't see him and doesn't know him. You know him, for he lives with you and will be in you. ¹⁸I will not leave you orphans. I will come to you. ¹⁹Yet a little while, and the world will see me no more; but you will see me. Because I live, you will live also. ²⁰In that day you will know that I am in my Father, and you in me, and I in you. ²¹One who has my commandments and keeps them, that person is one who loves me. One who loves me will be loved by my Father, and I will love him, and will reveal myself to him."

²²Judas (not Iscariot) said to him, "Lord, what has happened that you are about to reveal yourself to us, and not to the world?" ²³Jesus answered him, "If a man loves me, he will keep my word. My Father will love him,ᵐ and we will come to him and make our home with him. ²⁴He who doesn't love me doesn't keep my words. The word which you hear isn't mine, but the Father's who sent me.

¹ Q. 61:6

ᵐ Q. 3:159

---

* 14:16 Greek παρακλητον: Counselor, Helper, Intercessor, Advocate, and Comforter

²⁵"I have said these things to you while still living with you. ²⁶But the Counselor, the Holy Spirit,ⁿ whom the Father will send in my name, will teach you all things, and will remind you of all that I said to you. ²⁷Peace I leave with you. My peace I give to you; not as the world gives, I give to you. Don't let your heart be troubled,^o neither let it be fearful. ²⁸You heard how I told you, 'I am going away, and I will come back to you.' If you loved me, you would have rejoiced because I said 'I am going to my Father;' for the Father is greater than I. ²⁹Now I have told you before it happens so that when it happens, you may believe. ³⁰I will no more speak much with you, for the prince of the world comes, and he has nothing in me.^p ³¹But that the world may know that I love the Father, and as the Father commanded me, even so I do. Arise, let's go from here.

ⁿ Q. 17:85; 97:4

^o Q. 3:126; 6:127

^p Q. 15:42; 16:99; 17:65; 34:21

15

¹"I am the true vine, and my Father is the farmer. ²Every branch in me that doesn't bear fruit, he takes away. Every branch that bears fruit, he prunes, that it may bear more fruit. ³You are already pruned clean because of the word which I have spoken to you. ⁴Remain in me, and I in you. As the branch can't bear fruit by itself unless it remains in the vine, so neither can you, unless you remain in me. ⁵I am the vine. You are the branches. He who remains in me and I in him bears much fruit, for apart from me you can do nothing. ⁶If a man doesn't remain in me, he is thrown out as a branch and is withered; and they gather them, throw them into the fire, and they are burned.[*] ⁷If you remain in me, and my words remain in you, you will ask whatever you desire, and it will be done for you. ⁸"In this my Father is glorified, that you bear much fruit; and so you will be my

---

[*] Q. 2:203; 3:9, 158; 4:87; 5:96; 6:12; 8:24; 10:28; 11:103; 15:25; 17:97; 18:99; 19:68; 20:102; 23:79; 25:17; 27:83; 34:40; 37:22; 41:19; 42:7; 45:26; 46:6; 56:50; 58:9; 64:9; 67:15; 77:38

disciples. ⁹Even as the Father has loved me, I also have loved you. Remain in my love. ¹⁰If you keep my commandments, you will remain in my love, even as I have kept my Father's commandments and remain in his love. ¹¹I have spoken these things to you, that my joy may remain in you, and that your joy may be made full.

¹²"This is my commandment, that you love one another, even as I have loved you. ¹³Greater love has no one than this, that someone lay down his life for his friends. ¹⁴You are my friends if you do whatever I command you. ¹⁵No longer do I call you servants, for the servant doesn't know what his lord does. But I have called you friends, for everything that I heard from my Father, I have made known to you. ¹⁶You didn't choose me, but I chose you and appointed you, that you should go and bear fruit, and that your fruit should remain; that whatever you will ask of the Father in my name, he may give it to you. ¹⁷"I command these things to you, that you may love one another.

¹⁸If the world hates you, you know that it has hated me before it hated you. ¹⁹If you were of the world, the world would love its own. But because you are not of the world, since I chose you out of the world, therefore the world hates you. ²⁰Remember the word that I said to you: 'A servant is not greater than his lord.' If they persecuted me, they will also persecute you. If they kept my word, they will also keep yours. *²¹But they will do all these things to you for my name's sake, because they don't know him who sent me. ²²If I had not come and spoken to them, they would not have had sin; but now they have no excuse for their sin. ²³He who hates me, hates my Father also. ²⁴If I hadn't done among them the works which no one else did, they wouldn't have had sin. But now they have seen and also hated both me and my Father. ²⁵But this happened so that the word may be fulfilled which was written in their law,

---

* 15:20 John 13:16

'They hated me without a cause.'*

²⁶"When the Counselor[†] has come, whom I will send to you from the Father, the Spirit of truth, who proceeds from the Father, he will testify about me. ²⁷You will also testify, because you have been with me from the beginning.

16

¹"I have said these things to you so that you wouldn't be caused to stumble. ²They will put you out of the synagogues. Yes, the time is coming that whoever kills you will think that he offers service to God. ³They will do these things[‡] because they have not known the Father nor me. ⁴But I have told you these things so that when the time comes, you may remember that I told you about them.

I didn't tell you these things from the beginning, because I was with you. ⁵But now I am going to him who sent me, and none of you asks me, 'Where are you going?' ⁶But because I have told you these things, sorrow has filled your heart. ⁷Nevertheless I tell you the truth: It is to your advantage that I go away; for if I don't go away, the Counselor won't come to you. But if I go, I will send him to you.^q ⁸When he has come, he will convict the world about sin, about righteousness, and about judgment; ⁹about sin, because they don't believe in me; ¹⁰about righteousness, because I am going to my Father, and you won't see me any more; ¹¹about judgment, because the prince of this world has been judged.

^q Q. 40:15

¹²"I still have many things to tell you, but you can't bear them now. ¹³However, when he, the Spirit of truth, has come, he will guide you into all truth, for he will not speak from himself; but whatever he hears, he will speak. He will

---

* 15:25 Psalm 35:19; 69:4
† 15:26 Greek Parakletos: Counselor, Helper, Advocate, Intercessor, and Comforter.
‡ 16:3 TR adds "to you"

declare to you things that are coming. ¹⁴He will glorify me, for he will take from what is mine and will declare it to you. ¹⁵All things that the Father has are mine; therefore I said that he takes* of mine and will declare it to you.

¹⁶"A little while, and you will not see me. Again a little while, and you will see me." ¹⁷Some of his disciples therefore said to one another, "What is this that he says to us, 'A little while, and you won't see me, and again a little while, and you will see me;' and, 'Because I go to the Father'?" ¹⁸They said therefore, "What is this that he says, 'A little while'? We don't know what he is saying." ¹⁹Therefore Jesus perceived that they wanted to ask him, and he said to them, "Do you inquire among yourselves concerning this, that I said, 'A little while, and you won't see me, and again a little while, and you will see me?' ²⁰Most certainly I tell you that you will weep and lament, but the world will rejoice. You will be sorrowful, but your sorrow will be turned into joy. ²¹A woman, when she gives birth, has sorrow because her time has come. But when she has delivered the child, she doesn't remember the anguish any more, for the joy that a human being is born into the world. ²²Therefore you now have sorrow, but I will see you again, and your heart will rejoice, and no one will take your joy away from you. ²³"In that day you will ask me no questions. Most certainly I tell you, whatever you may ask of the Father in my name, he will give it to you. ²⁴Until now, you have asked nothing in my name. Ask, and you will receive, that your joy may be made full.

²⁵"I have spoken these things to you in figures of speech. But the time is coming when I will no more speak to you in figures of speech, but will tell you plainly about the Father. ²⁶In that day you will ask in my name; and I don't say to you that I will pray to the Father for you, ²⁷for the Father himself loves you, because you have loved me, and have believed

---

* 16:15 TR reads "will take" instead of "takes"

that I came from God. ²⁸I came from the Father and have come into the world. Again, I leave the world and go to the Father."

²⁹His disciples said to him, "Behold, now you are speaking plainly, and using no figures of speech. ³⁰Now we know that you know all things,[r] and don't need for anyone to question you. By this we believe that you came from God." ³¹Jesus answered them, "Do you now believe? ³²Behold, the time is coming, yes, and has now come, that you will be scattered, everyone to his own place, and you will leave me alone. Yet I am not alone, because the Father is with me. ³³I have told you these things, that in me you may have peace. In the world you have trouble; but cheer up! I have overcome the world."

[r] Q. 42:12

17

¹Jesus said these things, then lifting up his eyes to heaven, he said, "Father, the time has come. Glorify your Son, that your Son may also glorify you; ²even as you gave him authority over all flesh, so he will give eternal life to all whom you have given him. ³This is eternal life, that they should know you, the only true God,[s] and him whom you sent, Jesus Christ. ⁴I glorified you on the earth. I have accomplished the work which you have given me to do. ⁵Now, Father, glorify me with your own self with the glory which I had with you before the world existed.

[s] Q. 31:30

⁶"I revealed your name to the people whom you have given me out of the world. They were yours, and you have given them to me. They have kept your word. ⁷Now they have known that all things whatever you have given me are from you, ⁸for the words which you have given me I have given to them; and they received them, and knew for sure that I came from you. They have believed that you sent me. ⁹I pray for them. I don't pray for the world, but for those whom you have given me, for they are yours.

[10]All things that are mine are yours, and yours are mine, and I am glorified in them. [11]I am no more in the world, but these are in the world, and I am coming to you. Holy Father, keep them through your name which you have given me, that they may be one, even as we are. [12]While I was with them in the world, I kept them in your name. I have kept those whom you have given me. None of them is lost except the son of destruction, that the Scripture might be fulfilled. [13]But now I come to you, and I say these things in the world, that they may have my joy made full in themselves. [14]I have given them your word. The world hated them because they are not of the world, even as I am not of the world. [15]I pray not that you would take them from the world, but that you would keep them from the evil one. [16]They are not of the world, even as I am not of the world. [17]Sanctify them in your truth. Your word is truth.[*] [18]As you sent me into the world, even so I have sent them into the world. [19]For their sakes I sanctify myself, that they themselves also may be sanctified in truth.

[20]"Not for these only do I pray, but for those also who will believe in me through their word, [21]that they may all be one[t]; even as you, Father, are in me, and I in you, that they also may be one in us; that the world may believe that you sent me. [22]The glory which you have given me, I have given to them, that they may be one, even as we are one, [23]I in them, and you in me, that they may be perfected into one, that the world may know that you sent me and loved them, even as you loved me. [24]Father, I desire that they also whom you have given me be with me where I am, that they may see my glory which you have given me, for you loved me before the foundation of the world. [25]Righteous Father, the world hasn't known you, but I knew you; and these knew that you sent me. [26]I made known to them your

[t] Q. 8:63; 42:13

---

[*] 17:17 Psalm 119:142

name, and will make it known; that the love with which you loved me may be in them, and I in them."

18

¹When Jesus had spoken these words, he went out with his disciples over the brook Kidron, where there was a garden, into which he and his disciples entered. ²Now Judas, who betrayed him, also knew the place, for Jesus often met there with his disciples. ³Judas then, having taken a detachment of soldiers and officers from the chief priests and the Pharisees, came there with lanterns, torches, and weapons. ⁴Jesus therefore, knowing all the things that were happening to him, went out and said to them, "Who are you looking for?" ⁵They answered him, "Jesus of Nazareth." Jesus said to them, "I am he." Judas also, who betrayed him, was standing with them. ⁶When therefore he said to them, "I am he," they went backward and fell to the ground. ⁷Again therefore he asked them, "Who are you looking for?" They said, "Jesus of Nazareth." ⁸Jesus answered, "I told you that I am he. If therefore you seek me, let these go their way," ⁹that the word might be fulfilled which he spoke, "Of those whom you have given me, I have lost none."* ¹⁰Simon Peter therefore, having a sword, drew it, struck the high priest's servant, and cut off his right ear. The servant's name was Malchus. ¹¹Jesus therefore said to Peter, "Put the sword into its sheath. The cup which the Father has given me, shall I not surely drink it?"

¹²So the detachment, the commanding officer, and the officers of the Jews seized Jesus and bound him, ¹³and led him to Annas first, for he was father-in-law to Caiaphas, who was high priest that year. ¹⁴Now it was Caiaphas who advised the Jews that it was expedient that one man should perish for the people.

---

* 18:9 John 6:39

[15]Simon Peter followed Jesus, as did another disciple. Now that disciple was known to the high priest, and entered in with Jesus into the court of the high priest; [16]but Peter was standing at the door outside. So the other disciple, who was known to the high priest, went out and spoke to her who kept the door, and brought in Peter. [17]Then the maid who kept the door said to Peter, "Are you also one of this man's disciples?" He said, "I am not." [18]Now the servants and the officers were standing there, having made a fire of coals, for it was cold. They were warming themselves. Peter was with them, standing and warming himself.

[19]The high priest therefore asked Jesus about his disciples and about his teaching. [20]Jesus answered him, "I spoke openly to the world. I always taught in synagogues and in the temple, where the Jews always meet. I said nothing in secret. [21]Why do you ask me? Ask those who have heard me what I said to them. Behold, they know the things which I said." [22]When he had said this, one of the officers standing by slapped Jesus with his hand, saying, "Do you answer the high priest like that?" [23]Jesus answered him, "If I have spoken evil, testify of the evil; but if well, why do you beat me?" [24]Annas sent him bound to Caiaphas, the high priest.

[25]Now Simon Peter was standing and warming himself. They said therefore to him, "You aren't also one of his disciples, are you?" He denied it and said, "I am not." [26]One of the servants of the high priest, being a relative of him whose ear Peter had cut off, said, "Didn't I see you in the garden with him?" [27]Peter therefore denied it again, and immediately the rooster crowed.

[28]They led Jesus therefore from Caiaphas into the Praetorium. It was early, and they themselves didn't enter into the Praetorium, that they might not be defiled, but might eat the Passover. [29]Pilate therefore went out to them and said, "What accusation do you bring against this man?" [30]They answered him, "If this man weren't an evildoer, we wouldn't have delivered him up to you."

³¹Pilate therefore said to them, "Take him yourselves, and judge him according to your law." Therefore the Jews said to him, "It is illegal for us to put anyone to death," ³²that the word of Jesus might be fulfilled, which he spoke, signifying by what kind of death he should die.

³³Pilate therefore entered again into the Praetorium, called Jesus, and said to him, "Are you the King of the Jews?" ³⁴Jesus answered him, "Do you say this by yourself, or did others tell you about me?" ³⁵Pilate answered, "I'm not a Jew, am I? Your own nation and the chief priests delivered you to me. What have you done?" ³⁶Jesus answered, "My Kingdom is not of this world.[u] If my Kingdom were of this world, then my servants would fight, that I wouldn't be delivered to the Jews. But now my Kingdom is not from here." ³⁷Pilate therefore said to him, "Are you a king then?" Jesus answered, "You say that I am a king. For this reason I have been born, and for this reason I have come into the world, that I should testify to the truth. Everyone who is of the truth listens to my voice." ³⁸Pilate said to him, "What is truth?"

When he had said this, he went out again to the Jews, and said to them, "I find no basis for a charge against him. ³⁹But you have a custom that I should release someone to you at the Passover. Therefore, do you want me to release to you the King of the Jews?" ⁴⁰Then they all shouted again, saying, "Not this man, but Barabbas!" Now Barabbas was a robber.

[u] Q. 43:85

19

¹So Pilate then took Jesus and flogged him. ²The soldiers twisted thorns into a crown and put it on his head, and dressed him in a purple garment. ³They kept saying, "Hail, King of the Jews!" and they kept slapping him. ⁴Then Pilate went out again, and said to them, "Behold, I bring him out to you, that you may know that I find no

basis for a charge against him." ⁵Jesus therefore came out, wearing the crown of thorns and the purple garment. Pilate said to them, "Behold, the man!" ⁶When therefore the chief priests and the officers saw him, they shouted, saying, "Crucify! Crucify!" Pilate said to them, "Take him yourselves and crucify him, for I find no basis for a charge against him." ⁷The Jews answered him, "We have a law, and by our law he ought to die, because he made himself the Son of God." ⁸When therefore Pilate heard this saying, he was more afraid. ⁹He entered into the Praetorium again, and said to Jesus, "Where are you from?" But Jesus gave him no answer. ¹⁰Pilate therefore said to him, "Aren't you speaking to me? Don't you know that I have power to release you and have power to crucify you?" ¹¹Jesus answered, "You would have no power at all against me,ᵛ unless it were given to you from above. Therefore he who delivered me to you has greater sin."

ᵛ Q.
14:22
15:42;
16:99;
17:65;
34:21

¹²At this, Pilate was seeking to release him, but the Jews cried out, saying, "If you release this man, you aren't Caesar's friend! Everyone who makes himself a king speaks against Caesar!" ¹³When Pilate therefore heard these words, he brought Jesus out and sat down on the judgment seat at a place called "The Pavement", but in Hebrew, "Gabbatha." ¹⁴Now it was the Preparation Day of the Passover, at about the sixth hour.* He said to the Jews, "Behold, your King!" ¹⁵They cried out, "Away with him! Away with him! Crucify him!" Pilate said to them, "Shall I crucify your King?" The chief priests answered, "We have no king but Caesar!" ¹⁶So then he delivered him to them to be crucified.

So they took Jesus and led him away. ¹⁷He went out, bearing his cross, to the place called "The Place of a Skull", which is called in Hebrew, "Golgotha", ¹⁸where they crucified him, and with him two others, on either side one,

---

* 19:14 "the sixth hour" would have been 6:00a.m. according to the Roman time keeping system, or noon for the Jewish time keeping system in use, then.

and Jesus in the middle. ¹⁹Pilate wrote a title also, and put it on the cross. There was written, "JESUS OF NAZARETH, THE KING OF THE JEWS." ²⁰Therefore many of the Jews read this title, for the place where Jesus was crucified was near the city; and it was written in Hebrew, in Latin, and in Greek. ²¹The chief priests of the Jews therefore said to Pilate, "Don't write, 'The King of the Jews,' but, 'he said, "I am King of the Jews."'" ²²Pilate answered, "What I have written, I have written."

²³Then the soldiers, when they had crucified Jesus, took his garments and made four parts, to every soldier a part; and also the tunic. Now the tunic was without seam, woven from the top throughout. ²⁴Then they said to one another, "Let's not tear it, but cast lots for it to decide whose it will be," that the Scripture might be fulfilled, which says,

"They parted my garments among them.
They cast lots for my clothing."

Therefore the soldiers did these things.* ²⁵But standing by Jesus' cross were his mother, his mother's sister, Mary the wife of Clopas, and Mary Magdalene. ²⁶Therefore when Jesus saw his mother, and the disciple whom he loved standing there, he said to his mother, "Woman, behold, your son!" ²⁷Then he said to the disciple, "Behold, your mother!" From that hour, the disciple took her to his own home.

²⁸After this, Jesus, seeing† that all things were now finished, that the Scripture might be fulfilled, said, "I am thirsty!" ²⁹Now a vessel full of vinegar was set there; so they put a sponge full of the vinegar on hyssop, and held it at his mouth. ³⁰When Jesus therefore had received the vinegar, he said, "It is finished!" Then he bowed his head and gave up his spirit.

³¹Therefore the Jews, because it was the Preparation

* 19:24 Psalm 22:18
† 19:28 NU, TR read "knowing" instead of "seeing"

Day, so that the bodies wouldn't remain on the cross on the Sabbath (for that Sabbath was a special one), asked of Pilate that their legs might be broken and that they might be taken away. ³²Therefore the soldiers came and broke the legs of the first and of the other who was crucified with him; ³³but when they came to Jesus and saw that he was already dead, they didn't break his legs. ³⁴However, one of the soldiers pierced his side with a spear, and immediately blood and water came out. ³⁵He who has seen has testified, and his testimony is true. He knows that he tells the truth, that you may believe. ³⁶For these things happened that the Scripture might be fulfilled, "A bone of him will not be broken."* ³⁷Again another Scripture says, "They will look on him whom they pierced."

³⁸After these things, Joseph of Arimathaea, being a disciple of Jesus, but secretly for fear of the Jews,^w asked of Pilate that he might take away Jesus' body. Pilate gave him permission. He came therefore and took away his body. ³⁹Nicodemus, who at first came to Jesus by night, also came bringing a mixture of myrrh and aloes, about a hundred Roman pounds.[†] ⁴⁰So they took Jesus' body, and bound it in linen cloths with the spices, as the custom of the Jews is to bury. ⁴¹Now in the place where he was crucified there was a garden. In the garden was a new tomb in which no man had ever yet been laid. ⁴²Then, because of the Jews' Preparation Day (for the tomb was near at hand), they laid Jesus there.

^w Q.
40:28

20

¹Now on the first day of the week, Mary Magdalene went early, while it was still dark, to the tomb, and saw that the stone had been taken away from the tomb. ²Therefore she

---

* 19:36 Exodus 12:46; Numbers 9:12; Psalm 34:2019:37 Zechariah 12:10
† 19:39 100 Roman pounds of 12ounces each, or about 72pounds, or 33Kilograms.

ran and came to Simon Peter and to the other disciple whom Jesus loved, and said to them, "They have taken away the Lord out of the tomb, and we don't know where they have laid him!" ³Therefore Peter and the other disciple went out, and they went toward the tomb. ⁴They both ran together. The other disciple outran Peter and came to the tomb first. ⁵Stooping and looking in, he saw the linen cloths lying there; yet he didn't enter in. ⁶Then Simon Peter came, following him, and entered into the tomb. He saw the linen cloths lying, ⁷and the cloth that had been on his head, not lying with the linen cloths, but rolled up in a place by itself. ⁸So then the other disciple who came first to the tomb also entered in, and he saw and believed. ⁹For as yet they didn't know the Scripture, that he must rise from the dead. ¹⁰So the disciples went away again to their own homes.

¹¹But Mary was standing outside at the tomb weeping. So as she wept, she stooped and looked into the tomb, ¹²and she saw two angels in white sitting, one at the head and one at the feet, where the body of Jesus had lain. ¹³They asked her, "Woman, why are you weeping?" She said to them, "Because they have taken away my Lord, and I don't know where they have laid him." ¹⁴When she had said this, she turned around and saw Jesus standing, and didn't know that it was Jesus. ¹⁵Jesus said to her, "Woman, why are you weeping? Who are you looking for?" She, supposing him to be the gardener, said to him, "Sir, if you have carried him away, tell me where you have laid him, and I will take him away." ¹⁶Jesus said to her, "Mary." She turned and said to him, "Rabboni!"* which is to say, "Teacher!"† ¹⁷Jesus said to her, "Don't hold me, for I haven't yet ascended to my Father; but go to my brothers and tell them, 'I am ascending to my Father and your Father, to my God and

---

* 20:16 Rabboni is a transliteration of the Hebrew word for "great teacher."
† 20:16 or, Master

x Q.
3:51;
5:72,
117;
19:36;
43:64

your God.'"x 18Mary Magdalene came and told the disciples that she had seen the Lord, and that he had said these things to her.

19When therefore it was evening on that day, the first day of the week, and when the doors were locked where the disciples were assembled, for fear of the Jews, Jesus came and stood in the middle and said to them, "Peace be to you." 20When he had said this, he showed them his hands and his side. The disciples therefore were glad when they saw the Lord. 21Jesus therefore said to them again, "Peace be to you. As the Father has sent me, even so I send you." 22When he had said this, he breathed on them, and said to them, "Receive the Holy Spirit! 23If you forgive anyone's sins, they have been forgiven them. If you retain anyone's sins, they have been retained."

24But Thomas, one of the twelve, called Didymus,* wasn't with them when Jesus came. 25The other disciples therefore said to him, "We have seen the Lord!" But he said to them, "Unless I see in his hands the print of the nails, put my finger into the print of the nails, and put my hand into his side, I will not believe."

26After eight days, again his disciples were inside and Thomas was with them. Jesus came, the doors being locked, and stood in the middle, and said, "Peace be to you." 27Then he said to Thomas, "Reach here your finger, and see my hands. Reach here your hand, and put it into my side. Don't be unbelieving, but believing." 28Thomas answered him, "My Lord and my God!" 29Jesus said to him, "Because you have seen me,† you have believed. Blessed are those who have not seen and have believed."

30Therefore Jesus did many other signs in the presence of his disciples, which are not written in this book; 31but these are written that you may believe that Jesus is the

---

* 20:24 or, Twin
† 20:29 TR adds "Thomas,"

Christ, the Son of God, and that believing you may have life in his name.

21

[1]After these things, Jesus revealed himself again to the disciples at the sea of Tiberias. He revealed himself this way. [2]Simon Peter, Thomas called Didymus,[*] Nathanael of Cana in Galilee, and the sons of Zebedee, and two others of his disciples were together. [3]Simon Peter said to them, "I'm going fishing." They told him, "We are also coming with you." They immediately went out and entered into the boat. That night, they caught nothing.

[4]But when day had already come, Jesus stood on the beach; yet the disciples didn't know that it was Jesus. [5]Jesus therefore said to them, "Children, have you anything to eat?" They answered him, "No." [6]He said to them, "Cast the net on the right side of the boat, and you will find some." They cast it therefore, and now they weren't able to draw it in for the multitude of fish. [7]That disciple therefore whom Jesus loved said to Peter, "It's the Lord!" So when Simon Peter heard that it was the Lord, he wrapped his coat around himself (for he was naked), and threw himself into the sea. [8]But the other disciples came in the little boat (for they were not far from the land, but about two hundred cubits[†] away), dragging the net full of fish.

[9]So when they got out on the land, they saw a fire of coals there, with fish and bread laid on it. [10]Jesus said to them, "Bring some of the fish which you have just caught." [11]Simon Peter went up, and drew the net to land, full of one hundred fifty-three great fish. Even though there were so many, the net wasn't torn. [12]Jesus said to them, "Come and eat breakfast!" None of the disciples dared inquire of

---

[*] 21:2 or, Twin

[†] 21:8 200 cubits is about 100 yards or about 91 meters

him, "Who are you?" knowing that it was the Lord. Then Jesus came and took the bread, gave it to them, and the fish likewise. [14]This is now the third time that Jesus was revealed to his disciples after he had risen from the dead.

[15]So when they had eaten their breakfast, Jesus said to Simon Peter, "Simon, son of Jonah, do you love me more than these?" He said to him, "Yes, Lord; you know that I have affection for you." He said to him, "Feed my lambs." [16]He said to him again a second time, "Simon, son of Jonah, do you love me?" He said to him, "Yes, Lord; you know that I have affection for you." He said to him, "Tend my sheep." [17]He said to him the third time, "Simon, son of Jonah, do you have affection for me?" Peter was grieved because he asked him the third time, "Do you have affection for me?" He said to him, "Lord, you know everything. You know that I have affection for you." Jesus said to him, "Feed my sheep. [18]Most certainly I tell you, when you were young, you dressed yourself and walked where you wanted to. But when you are old, you will stretch out your hands, and another will dress you and carry you where you don't want to go." Now he said this, signifying by what kind of death he would glorify God. When he had said this, he said to him, "Follow me."

[20]Then Peter, turning around, saw a disciple following. This was the disciple whom Jesus loved, the one who had also leaned on Jesus' breast at the supper and asked, "Lord, who is going to betray you?" [21]Peter, seeing him, said to Jesus, "Lord, what about this man?" [22]Jesus said to him, "If I desire that he stay until I come, what is that to you? You follow me." [23]This saying therefore went out among the brothers[*] that this disciple wouldn't die. Yet Jesus didn't say to him that he wouldn't die, but, "If I desire that he stay until I come, what is that to you?"

[24]This is the disciple who testifies about these things,

---

[*] 21:23 The word for "brothers" here may be also correctly translated "brothers and sisters" or "siblings."

and wrote these things. We know that his witness is true.

25There are also many other things which Jesus did, which if they would all be written, I suppose that even the world itself wouldn't have room for the books that would be written.[y]

[y] Q. 3:49; 18:109; 31:27

You may obtain this, and many other fine resources made available by Proclaim Publishers by contacting us:

Web:

proclaimpublishers.com

Email:

info@proclaimpublishers.com

Postal Mail:

1317 Edgewater Drive, Suite 4774

Orlando, FL, 32804

SOLIDEOGLORIA

www.ingramcontent.com/pod-product-compliance
Lightning Source LLC
Chambersburg PA
CBHW061724270326
41928CB00011B/2099